PRAISE FOR

K. Charles Cannon's *The Ultimate Guide to Your Legal Career*

"This should be required reading for all law students, young lawyers, and those considering a career in the law. Cannon's book is chock full of practical advice and insider knowledge."

—Theodore N. Stern, vice president and general counsel, ePals, Inc.

"Cannon's book reads like sound advice from a trusted older sibling. While *The Ultimate Guide to Your Legal Career* offers specific advice for the short term, it also asks young lawyers and law students to consider where they want to be further down the road. The book is more than just a primer on how to get a job; Cannon provides insight into how young lawyers can lay the foundation today for a happy and successful career many years from now. Most importantly, Cannon describes what to do and what *not* to do in detail, rather than leaving the reader with the typical recitation of bromides and generalities."

—Timothy P. Peterson, Debevoise & Plimpton LLP,
former SEC Senior Counsel

"I wish I had access to a book such as this when I was going through law school. Kimble's truly unusual breadth of experience across different legal functions and practice areas gives him an extraordinary vantage point from which to comment on the profession. His book is replete with astute observations and practical advice."

—Eric John Finseth, Mayer, Brown, Rowe & Maw LLP

ABOUT THE AUTHOR

K. CHARLES CANNON GRADUATED from Columbia Law School as a Harlan Fiske Stone Scholar. After spending two years clerking for a federal judge and teaching corporate law at the University of Miami School of Law, he went to work for leading Washington, D.C. law firm Wilmer, Cutler & Pickering. Two years later, he joined New York-based firm Cleary, Gottlieb, Steen & Hamilton. The author cofounded a Washington and Shanghai-based software company and, after selling it, joined the United States Securities and Exchange Commission, serving first in the Division of Enforcement as a senior counsel and then as personal counsel to one of the five commissioners appointed by the president to lead the agency. The author also holds an MBA from The Wharton School at the University of Pennsylvania. He currently divides his time between Los Angeles and New York. To learn more, please visit www.legalcareerguide.com

THE ULTIMATE GUIDE

TO YOUR

LEGAL CAREER

THE ULTIMATE GUIDE

TO YOUR LEGAL CAREER

What Every Young Lawyer Must Know to Avoid the
Mistakes and Maximize the Value of a Career in the Law

K. Charles Cannon

MARLOWE & COMPANY
NEW YORK

THE ULTIMATE GUIDE TO YOUR LEGAL CAREER:
*What Every Young Lawyer Must Know to
Avoid the Mistakes and Maximize the Value of a Career in the Law*

Copyright © 2007 by K. Charles Cannon

Published by
Marlowe and Company
An imprint of Avalon Publishing Group, Incorporated
245 West 17th Street • 11th Floor
New York, NY 10011-5300

AVALON
publishing group incorporated

Library of Congress Cataloging-in-Publication Data is available

ISBN-10: 1-60094-005-6
ISBN-13: 978-1-60094-005-7

9 8 7 6 5 4 3 2 1

Interior Design by *Maria E. Torres*
Printed in the United States of America

CONTENTS

PREFACE

The sources of good advice ▪ xv

INTRODUCTION

Why did you write this book, and why should I read it? xxv ▪ *Being Street Smart about Your Legal Career* xxvi ▪ *The Need for Strategies* xxx ▪ *Speaking to Law Students* xxxii ▪ *Why do I need a long-term strategy?* xxxiv ▪ *Making Decisions* xxxvii

1. DECIDING ON A LEGAL CAREER

Are large numbers of lawyers really unhappy with their careers? 1 ▪ *Why are large numbers of lawyers apparently dissatisfied with their careers?* 3 ▪ *Are some kinds of lawyers more generally dissatisfied with their careers than are others?* 5 ▪ *Are lawyers predestined to be unhappy because of their personalities?* 7 ▪ *If lawyers are unhappy, why don't they just change careers?* 8 ▪ *What are some complaints voiced by associates working in large law firms?* 9 ▪ *Are law firm partners happier with their careers than young associates?* 11 ▪ *Can law schools and college career counselors take some of the blame for career dissatisfaction among lawyers?* 14 ▪ *Since so many lawyers are unhappy, why should I even consider law school?* 15 ▪ *What makes law firm jobs seem attractive during economic slowdowns and less attractive during periods of great (or at least perceived) economic expansion?* 16 ▪ *What am I giving up by choosing to go to law school?* 20 ▪ *What prevents law firms from firing large numbers of associates when they find they don't have enough business to keep everyone working profitably?* 22

2. BEFORE YOU GO TO LAW SCHOOL

Do I really need to plan my legal career before I even go to law school? 27
■ *Early Planning: What impact will the college I went to have on my legal career in the short and long term?* 29 ■ *One more time: Should I go to law school?* 30 ■ *What undergraduate classes should I take to prepare for my legal career?* 32 ■ *How can I apply option valuation techniques to my choice of majors in college?* 34 ■ *How do law schools admissions officers view grades versus the classes in which they were earned?* 35 ■ *Are there strategies I can use to improve my chances of earning a high GPA, and will pursuing them improve my chances of getting into law school?* 37 ■ *Should I get another graduate degree before I go to law school?* 39 ■ *When should I go to law school?* 40 ■ *What are the general arguments for and against going directly to law school after college?* 44 ■ *Are there jobs I should not take before going to law school?* 45 ■ *When am I too old to go to law school?* 46 ■ *Is there a way to earn a law degree in less than three years?* 49 ■ *What are some other unconventional law school degrees?* 57

3. DECIDING ON A LAW SCHOOL

Which law school should I go to? 55 ■ *What about going to Yale?* 57 ■ *Is it worth going to law school if I can't get into a really top law school?* 59 ■ *Do I need to go to an ABA-accredited law school?* 59 ■ *What are the general categories of law schools I can attend in California?* 62 ■ *What is the future of the unaccredited law schools?* 64 ■ *Can I practice law without ever having gone to law school?* 66

4. SOME SOCIAL ISSUES TO CONSIDER

I am a woman. What should I take into consideration based on my gender? 69 ■ *Is government service an attractive option for women?* 71 ■ *Do women do better in large firms than in smaller firms?* 72 ■ *What impact does having a child have on a woman's legal career?* 74 ■ *Are law firms really interested in creating an ethnically diverse workforce?* 75 ■

Are there particular types of employers or fields of practice that offer better opportunities for minority lawyers? 76 ▪ *I am gay. What impact will that have on my legal career?* 79

5. IMPROVING YOUR CHANCES OF LAW SCHOOL ADMISSION

How can I improve my chances of getting into law school? 81 ▪ *What impact can college internships have on my chance of gaining admission to law school?* 82 ▪ *How important are grades when applying to law school?* 83 ▪ *What is the LSAT?* 86 ▪ *How important is my LSAT score?* 87 ▪ *How can I perform better on the LSAT?* 89 ▪ *How important are law school application essays, and what should I write about?* 90 ▪ *Are there any unconventional routes to law school that I should consider?* 91

6. WHAT TO DO IN LAW SCHOOL

How important are good grades in law school? 93 ▪ *How can I get good grades in law school?* 94 ▪ *How important are study groups in law school?* 95 ▪ *How critical are good outlines and how do I make one?* 95 ▪ *How important is it to make law review?* 96 ▪ *Are the other journals good substitutes for law review?* 97 ▪ *What are clinics and should I do one?* 98 ▪ *What should I do during my first-year summer?* 99 ▪ *What should I do during my second-year summer clerkship?* 102 ▪ *What if I can't get a law firm job for the summer?* 103 ▪ *How important is it to get a permanent job offer from my summer clerkship?* 106 ▪ *What do I do if I don't get a job offer from my summer employer?* 107 ▪ *How do I write a memo?* 109 ▪ *What if I already know I want to be a banker after I graduate?* 110

7. JUDICIAL CLERKSHIPS

What is a judicial clerkship? 113 ▪ *What do federal law clerks do?* 114 ▪ *What is the difference between clerking for a judge on a U.S. Court of Appeals and clerking for a U.S. District Court judge?* 116 ▪ *Should I* clerk for a federal judge after graduation? 117 ▪ When should I clerk for a judge? 118 ▪ What about clerking for a state court judge? 119 ▪ How do I get a judicial clerkship? 120 ▪ How can I improve my chances of getting a clerkship? 121 ▪ What are some tactics that backfire in seeking clerkships? 122

8. THE BAR EXAMINATION

Which state bar examination or examinations should I sit for? 125 ▪ Should I sit for the bar in more than one state? 125 ▪ Should I prepare my essays on a computer or write them out by hand? 126 ▪ Can I belong to too many state bars? 126 ▪ How can I improve my chances of passing the bar exam? 127

9. PURSUING OTHER DEGREES

Should I get an MBA at the same time that I am getting my JD? 129 ▪ Should I consider getting an LL.M? 133 ▪ Why are there so many foreign LL.M students? 134 ▪ I am a foreign lawyer interested in getting an LL.M degree in the United States. What should I know? 136

10. BUILDING A LEGAL CAREER

The Big Lie (Part I) 139 ▪ The Big Lie (Part II) 140 ▪ What should I do after law school? 141 ▪ How much would I get paid as a law firm associate? 145 ▪ What are some common interviewing mistakes? 146 ▪ How can I guarantee that I won't get a job offer? 149 ▪ Are there shortcuts to getting a job at a leading law firm? 150 ▪ Any advice on how to write a résumé or how to prepare for interviews? 151 ▪ How should I dress for an interview? 153

11. WORKING FOR LAW FIRMS

Should I work for a law firm? 157 ▪ *Which law firm should I work for?* 159 ▪ *What are the best law firms in the country?* 161 ▪ *Are big law firms really that different from each other?* 163 ▪ *How can I expect a law firm to treat me in the long run?* 163 ▪ *What practice area should I work in?* 166 ▪ *What should I know about starting salaries at law firms?* 168 ▪ *What should I know about bonuses?* 169 ▪ *How have law firm salaries changed over time?* 171 ▪ *Competition on bonuses among firms* 174 ▪ *What city should I work in?* 176 ▪ *Should I avoid joining a satellite office of a national firm?* 176 ▪ *Should I go work for my firm's foreign office?* 177 ▪ *What is a "white shoe" law firm?* 178 ▪ *I have some family money. Should I try to hide this fact from people at my firm?* 179

12. THE POLITICS AND PITFALLS OF LAW FIRM LIFE

What can I do to be considered a successful first-year associate? 181 ▪ *How important are billable hours?* 182 ▪ *How many billable hours should I aim for?* 182 ▪ *What is the "four-legged, two-headed partner"?* 184 ▪ *Do associates use flirting as a means of career advancement?* 185 ▪ *What are some of the big mistakes associates make at law firms?* 186 ▪ *Will being active on the Associates' Committee get me noticed by partners as being partnership material?* 187 ▪ *Should I teach as an adjunct law professor?* 189 ▪ *Should I publish scholarly work?* 190 ▪ *What should I do if a partner asks me to write a law review piece and name him as the author?* 193

13. MAKING PARTNER

How do law firm partners decide whom to name as new partners? 195 ▪ *How can I increase my chances of making partner?* 197 ▪ *What kinds*

*of people make partner; can they be classified into different groups? 199
■ As part of my partnership strategy, should I really try to work with a
range of different partners or just do great work for one partner? 201 ■
How important is it to find a mentor at a law firm and how can I do this?
201 ■ Do I really want to make partner? 202 ■ It's hard to make
partner. Is there another way to achieve great power and wealth? 203 ■
What is the emotional effect on lawyers and their spouses of not making
partner? 205 ■ What is the secret of law firm partners who have had a
particularly successful legal career? 206*

14. ALTERNATIVES TO LAW FIRM LIFE

*Should I work for the government, and what are some disadvantages of
doing so? 209 ■ What federal agencies can I work for and what should
be my five-year plan if I do? 210 ■ What is it like to work at a prestigious federal agency like the United States Securities and Exchange Commission? 211 ■ Are some people better suited to working in the
government than others? 213 ■ How competitive is it to get a job with
a federal government agency like the Securities and Exchange Commission? 214 ■ What can I do to increase my chances of getting a job with
the SEC? 215 ■ How important is which law school I went to if I want
to work for the SEC? 217 ■ Can going to a top law school ever hurt your
employment chances? 218 ■ What are the disadvantages to practicing
law in a government agency? 219 ■ Should I work for Congress, the president, or either the Democratic or Republican party? 220 ■ How can I
position myself for an easy transition from government back into the
private sector? 223*

15. CHANGING JOBS

*What is a lateral? 227 ■ Should I change law firms? 228 ■ Is it pos-
sible to bypass the headhunters? 232 ■ What do senior attorneys look
for when choosing a new law firm? 233 ■ What should I ask for when*

negotiating a lateral move? 234 ■ *How are laterals viewed at the law firms they join?* 235 ■ *What about "going in-house"?* 236 ■ *Should I do something crazy like accept that offer to become the attorney general of Yap?* 240

16. ESCAPING FROM YOUR LEGAL CAREER

What type of job can a lawyer have other than practicing law? 243 ■ *Can I leave the law for a career in investment banking?* 244 ■ *Can I become a business consultant?* 247 ■ *Should I get an MBA?* 248 ■ *What about an executive MBA?* 251 ■ *What about law firm sabbaticals?* 254 · *When can I write my own ticket?* 255 ■ *Other Careers* 255

CONCLUSION—*On the value of relationships* ■ 259

Appendix A: *Unaccredited Law School Bar Exam Pass Rate* ■ 261

Appendix B: *Example of a NALP Form* ■ 262

Appendix C: *One Possible Format for a Law Student Résumé* ■ 263

Appendix D: *Associate Bonus Eligibility 1996–2001* ■ 265

Appendix E: *Median Starting Salaries for First-Year Associates by Firm Size, 1996–2001* ■ 266

Appendix F: *Median Starting Salaries for First-Year Associates in Firms of 251 or More—Chicago, Los Angeles, New York and Washington, D.C.* ■ 267

Appendix G: *Employment of Women 1975–2002* ■ 268

Appendix H: *Employment by Race/Ethnicity 1975–2002* ■ 269

Notes ■ 271
Index ■ 285

PREFACE

THE SOURCES OF GOOD ADVICE

ADVICE IS GENERALLY only as good as the source from which it comes. Therefore, if you are going to take my advice, you had better know something about my education, professional experience, successes and failures. If you understand my background, you will gain insight into what areas I am most likely to be knowledgeable about as well as in what ways my advice may be biased. All advice, even the best intentioned, contains some bias. Knowing my history should let you take my recommendations, carefully weigh them, add them to what you already know and only then make educated decisions that are right for you. In fact, I recommend this approach with all the varied and often conflicting advice you are likely to receive as you move down the road toward your successful legal career.

I graduated from Duke University with a BA, cum laude, in political science and received my law degree from Columbia Law School, where I was a Harlan Fiske Stone Scholar. At age twenty-six I became the youngest adjunct law professor ever to teach at the University of Miami School of Law. I have published articles on topics involving corporate and securities law in journals including the Columbia Business Law

Review and the Securities Regulation Law Journal. Citations to my published work have appeared in many leading law reviews, including the Stanford Law Review, Yale Law Journal, University of Pennsylvania Law Review, and Duke Law Journal. I clerked for two federal judges, the first in the United States District Court for the Southern District of New York (Manhattan) during the summer following my first year of law school and the second for the chief judge of the United States District Court for the Southern District of Florida (Miami) for two years following my graduation from law school.

I have practiced law with three of the leading law firms based in Washington D.C., New York, and Boston. In those firms—Cleary, Gottlieb, Steen & Hamilton; Wilmer, Cutler & Pickering; and Hale & Dorr—I practiced in fields as diverse as corporate transactions, securities litigation and bankruptcy. In addition, for nearly two years I served as general counsel and then as chief executive officer of a software company operating mainly in Shanghai, China. I also worked for three years at the United States Securities and Exchange Commission, first as a staff attorney, then as senior counsel in the Division of Enforcement, and finally as personal counsel to one of the five SEC commissioners appointed by the president of the United States.

During the course of my legal career, I have accumulated a unique insider's view of the legal profession. In addition, I have interviewed numerous aspiring and practicing lawyers at all levels, including college students seeking admission to law school, law students pursuing employment with my law firms, as well as senior lawyers with whom I have worked both in government and the private sector. I also hold an MBA, concentrating in finance, from The Wharton School at the University of Pennsylvania.

MY OWN—IMPERFECT—CAREER

I FIRST BEGAN CONSIDERING my own career options when I was a junior at Duke University. During my first two and a half years of college I had known, somewhere in the back of my mind, that I would someday need to find a way to pay the rent. But this reality had not played a significant roll in my decision-making up to that point. Unlike the then-popular song, "My Future's So Bright I Gotta Wear Shades," I had not studied nuclear science, nor had I focused on any other subject that would give me career-specific skills. I was neither an economist, an accountant, nor a scientist of any sort. Far from it; I was a political science major from a liberal arts college who had taken a few advanced English literature classes. In short, I had good reason to be concerned about my future fiscal security.

The job market was particularly soft when I graduated from college. There were few jobs, and even fewer jobs for liberal arts majors. Had I been a math or economics major, I might have found a job on Wall Street as an analyst. (Becoming an I-banking analyst would, incidentally, have pushed my career in an entirely different direction, the magnitude of which difference I only came to realize a decade after I graduated from law school.) Had I been a biology major, I might have gone to medical school or perhaps joined a biotech company. But none of these were to be. Thus, I, like nearly a third of my graduating college class, eventually succumbed to the inevitability of going directly to law school. Applying to law schools was easy at Duke in those days because the school employed an assistant dean whose primary job appears to have been to help graduating undergrads get into law school.

Although my course grades during my first two years of college had been middling (about a 3.0), I managed to pull nearly perfect grades during my junior year (nearly a 4.0). I therefore thought, at the start of my senior year, that I had a decent chance of getting into law school, and maybe even a good one. But in my first (and last) counseling session with the assistant dean-of-getting-unemployable-graduating-seniors-into-law-school, he was not quite as optimistic as I had hoped. He did not think that I would get into a top law school. He thought I had a decent chance of getting into some law school, but he advised that the competition (particularly with the economy being so bad and so many undergraduates seeking to avoid the real world) was intense. The dean thought that if I kept my grades up and did well on the LSAT, I might have a shot at getting into UVA or maybe staying at Duke for law school, but that even these would be a long shot given the number of students applying. With that sobering news, I went off to take the LSAT. Three months later I found out that I had done well, missing only two questions and getting a score one point shy of perfect. With that score and another semester of top grades, I felt I had a shot at getting into a top-five law school. In those days, as today, that meant Yale, Harvard, Stanford, Columbia, or Chicago.

I applied early decision to Columbia as well as to Harvard, Penn and Yale, with Georgetown as a backup. By November, Columbia had accepted me. Because I had signed an agreement with Columbia to withdraw my other applications upon acceptance, I wrote letters to Yale, Penn, Harvard, and Georgetown asking that they no longer consider my applications. Their responses ran the gamut. Georgetown and Penn accepted me anyway, Harvard's dean sent me a personal letter thanking me for being forthright and honest, and Yale failed to respond but then rejected me three months later anyway! With the admissions process completed, I was going to New York to attend Columbia Law.

After one last summer spent working as a lifeguard on the New Jersey shore, in late August I showed up in Manhattan fit and ready to face the rigors of life as a One L. My fitness and fine health would not last long. An initial week of misleading school-sponsored carousal became, by mid-October, long hours spent studying in the law library, with nutrition supplied mainly by cheap Chinese food (which Chinese restaurants, the closest of which was just two blocks down Amsterdam Avenue from the law school—you Columbia alums know what I am talking about— served even cheaper, "all you can drink" wine!). The competition for grades, a position on the Law Review, and eventually jobs with the best New York and Washington law firms defined the experience. Although I was in perhaps the greatest city on earth, my world came to revolve around the cold call of the Socratic method and long hours sequestered in the cavernous Butler Library reading rooms.

Somehow, I survived that first year, earned an editorial post on a law school journal, and got a job working for a United States District Court judge during my first summer. Although unpaid, the position was at least in the legal field. Many of my classmates had failed to get even unpaid legal positions, although a lucky few actually got paying positions as summer associate in law firms. I spent that first summer living in the West Village and making the short commute to the federal court-house at Foley Square in Manhattan. Although the judge's expectations of his interns were low, I gained a good introduction to the world of federal litigation and saw firsthand such personalities as the former junk bond king Michael Milken and a politically ambitious U.S. Attorney named Rudolph Giuliani.

After another two years and a summer spent clerking for a small corporate firm in Wilmington, Delaware, I graduated from Columbia as a Harlan Fiske Stone Scholar—which means I got pretty good grades—and went to clerk for a United States District judge in the Southern District of Florida. If I were going to clerk, I reasoned, I might as well do it in Miami. At the same time, I applied for various teaching jobs with the idea of teaching night classes after my responsibilities to the court had ended. Within a year of graduation I had published my first professional law review article in the *Columbia Business Law Review* and was earning some recognition as a scholar in the area of corporate mergers and acquisitions, better known as M&A. At age twenty-six, I became the youngest adjunct law professor ever to teach at the University of Miami School of Law.

Following my clerkship and short teaching stint, I returned to Washington, where I joined one of the top Washington law firms, Wilmer, Cutler & Pickering, as an associate. At that firm, I rejoined several of my old Columbia Law School classmates, including one who had been an editor of the Law Review. Other officemates included former law clerks from the United States Supreme Court as well as an abundance of graduates from the Yale and Harvard law schools. Wilmer was then and remains a very good firm, and as a consequence had its pick of associates with the strongest credentials from the best schools. However, the firm was somewhat different than it and most other law firms are today. For one thing, there was much less structure than you currently find in most major firms. I was not required, for example, to specialize in any particular field of law. Thus, I was able to engage in a varied practice touching on bankruptcy, corporate and securities law. Assignments I received included an appeal to the U.S. Circuit Court of Appeals for the Fourth Circuit on a bankruptcy matter and another federal court litigation matter representing the board of directors of Comsat Corporation in their defense against a hostile proxy contest launched by an activist shareholder seeking control of the company. It was a great deal of work but also a great deal of fun.

Two years after starting at my first law firm, I was offered almost double my salary to join a leading New York law firm, Cleary, Gottlieb, Steen & Hamilton, in its Washington, D.C., regional office. The real attraction, however, was the promise that I would have the opportunity to practice corporate law at a national rather than a regional level. I took the job. I soon found, however, that the job was not the one that had been described to me during my recruitment. Most of my time was to be spent documenting complex structured finance transactions backed by mortgage debt. Years later, after receiving an MBA in finance from Wharton, I would realize how important this structured finance work was in supporting the U.S. economy, and particularly in financing the residential real estate market. At the time, however, the work seemed incredibly tedious. Moreover, the environment at Cleary was far less nurturing than it had been at Wilmer. I considered returning to my old firm, but when the opportunity to lead a young Internet company came along, I leapt at the chance.

For the next two years I was busy building a small software company, PSM Global, Inc., from just four to over thirty-five employees and from zero to nearly a million dollars in annual revenue (that's revenue, not income—big difference!). As business opportunities emerged in Asia, I spent more and more time abroad. Hong Kong and Shanghai became second homes. As CEO, together with my management team, I built a multimedia lab and sales center in Shanghai and opened a small software engineering office at Chengdu, in western Sichuan Province. We outsourced much of our technology development to a firm in Hyderabad, India. As the company grew, I hired outside counsel, including a leading patent law firm in Silicon Valley and business lawyers at one of my old firms in Washington. Eventually, I also tapped these lawyers to assist me in selling the company in a cash transaction.

I briefly returned to private practice after selling the company, but soon found myself attracted by the stability, prestige, and sense of mission of working for the federal government. I went to work for the United States Securities and Exchange Commission, where one of the young partners I had worked with at Wilmer, Steve Cutler, had recently become the director of the Division of Enforcement. Over the next three years I served, first, as a staff attorney and then as a senior counsel within the Division of Enforcement, prosecuting cases that included insider trading and complex securities frauds promoted by international organized crime gangs. I traveled around the country conducting investigations and met some very interesting people on both sides of the law enforcement equation. After two years at Enforcement, one of the five SEC commissioners appointed by the president of the United States asked me to serve as his personal counsel. And so I went over the wall from career staffer to political appointee.

By this point in my career, I had accumulated some credibility in the legal world. I had published several articles concerning corporate and securities law in the *Columbia Business Law Review* and in the *Securities Regulation Law Journal,* among others. Citations to my published work had appeared in many leading law reviews. However, not being satisfied with the rigors of working in a government agency, I enrolled in a graduate program at the University of Pennsylvania. Taking primarily weekend classes while working at the SEC, I earned my MBA in finance from The Wharton School at the University of Pennsylvania. Knowing that my political appointment would end at the next change in administrations, and not wanting to go back to the staff job I had held before, I started talking to investment banks. It turned out that several I-banks thought they could use someone with my experience. However, they all took some convincing that I would be willing to work the long hours demanded of junior bankers. In addition, while it would have been easy for me to join a bank at a senior level in a legal capacity, I wanted to join as an investment banker in the corporate finance area. That took some more convincing but ended up working out nicely. Today I am an investment banker with probably the top global investment bank.

INTRODUCTION

WHY DID YOU WRITE THIS BOOK, AND WHY SHOULD I READ IT?

I HAVE OFTEN thought that, had I only known in law school what I now know about the legal profession, my legal career would have progressed much more smoothly. I have talked with dozens of my fellow lawyers who tell me they have come to the same conclusion. We all agree that someone needed to write a book that candidly spilled the beans, but none of us ever had the time to do so. I finally made the decision to research and write this book, in the process talking to nearly a hundred other lawyers, many of whom had followed different career paths, and researching the issues about which I was personally less knowledgeable.

Strategic planning is the key to a successful legal career, and planning can and should begin as early as during the second year of college. If I had had the information necessary to begin planning at that stage, I am certain I would have gotten a lot more out of my legal career, in both career satisfaction and financial reward. To pass on this knowledge—accumulated by many lawyers over decades of legal work—is the singular purpose of this book. I have drawn heavily on my personal experiences, which are probably more varied and relevant than those of most practicing lawyers. Because

> Planning your legal career can and should begin as early as during the second year of college.

I have made many wrong and right decisions in my career, it is rewarding for me that I can pass on my experience to enable you to avoid my mistakes. Many of my peers and friends who are lawyers have made their own mistakes and fortuitous choices. Their stories, experiences, and advice are also contained this book. Given this accumulation of knowledge, I am confident you will be glad you opened the cover.[1]

It is, in fact, quite common for lawyers to complain that if they had only known when starting their legal career what they know now about the legal profession, they would have made very different decisions during the course of their career. Sadly, it is too late for those of us who are already well into our careers to benefit from our own experience. This is, of course, one of the great ironies of life! You, however, can learn from our mistakes, and do so comparatively painlessly! I am therefore certain that, if actually applied, the lessons from this book can help you young attorneys, as well as those of you who are still just law students and even college students considering embarking on a legal career. These lessons should enable all of you to focus your efforts better toward identifying your realistic career and life objectives, and then working efficiently toward your goals.

BEING STREET SMART ABOUT YOUR LEGAL CAREER

DURING MORE THAN a decade of legal practice, I have observed many attorneys, young and old, who are dissatisfied with their jobs. On the other hand, I have known many lawyers who are immensely successful, and happy, in their legal careers. Some are still practicing law, and others have moved on to other professional endeavors. What divides these two groups often seems like luck. However, what initially appears to be luck is, as often as not, the result of wise (or lucky!) decision making. Some legal practitioners made good choices at opportune times, while others let those same opportunities slip through their fingers. You might get lucky. But I believe that making the right decisions at the right time about your legal career need not and should not be left to chance. I wrote this book so that you will have the insight necessary to identify the critical decision-making pivots in your legal career and enable you to understand the immediate and long-term consequences of your choices.

Making the right decisions at the right time about your legal career should not be left to chance.

There have been many articles written recently about lawyers and their careers. Some point out that going to law school does not guarantee wealth and that, therefore, wanting to be affluent is not a sufficient reason to go to law school. From the very start, it is important for you to understand that there are two vastly different legal career experiences. A small minority of students, those at first-tier schools and those who graduated near the top of their class from second-tier schools, have a reasonable chance to join a big firm paying about $135,000 to recent graduates (and significantly more later on). The reality is, however, that most law students in this country do not attend the top schools or graduate at the head of their class. For this majority of young lawyers it can be difficult to get a job at all, with starting salaries for graduates of so-called "third-tier" schools averaging around $60,000 a year.[2]

- Average 2006 starting salary for graduates of first-tier law schools and top grads of second-tier schools: $135,000
- Average starting salary for graduates of third-tier" law schools: $60,000

Some commentators argue further that even the small minority of young lawyers who earn entrance to the most prestigious law firms rarely last long enough to "enjoy it". One writer points out that while 40,000 new lawyers join the legal profession each year in the United States, in law firms employing more than 500 lawyers nearly 40 percent of associates leave within four years and 60 percent leave within six years.[3] These statistics seem about right. In fact, even in smaller firms retention is an issue with a study by the National Association of Law Placement finding 42 percent of small firm lawyers will change jobs within three years.

LARGE FIRM ATTRITION
- Associates leaving within four years: 40 percent
- Associates leaving within six years: 60 percent

The conclusions drawn by many of these articles—that lawyers are largely unhappy with their careers[4] and that going to law school is really not a great way to keep your options open for careers paths other than being a lawyer[5]—have some basis. However, there are other realities as well. For one thing, graduates of top law schools have a credential that is highly respected in law and business. It is a credential that will get them a high-paying job after they graduate and that has the potential to open doors for them during the rest of their careers. Many of the associates who leave top law firms after four to six years go on to extremely successful and noteworthy careers in areas both in and out of the law. Concluding that lawyers don't get to "enjoy" the fruits of their academic labors because they leave their initial law firm jobs relatively early in their careers (that is, within six years) misses the point. Often, the greatest career enjoyment comes from the job you hold *after* your first law firm position, which may be at a government agency, a private company, an investment bank, in politics, or even working as a lawyer for a professional sports league. I have known lawyers who have entered each of these secondary careers, and who have enjoyed them deeply.

Often the greatest career enjoyment comes from the job you hold after your first law firm position . . . at a government agency, a private company, an investment bank, in politics, or even working as a lawyer for a professional sports league.

In addition, it is not true that you must attend a leading law school in order to have a top-notch legal career. Every year, some graduates from so-called third-tier law schools get the same high-paying jobs at top law firms as the graduates of first-tier schools. In addition, many of the lawyers who find the most success in their professional careers follow unorthodox career paths that often lead them into first jobs other than with large law firms. These jobs, often in government, give them uncommon expertise in a desirable specialty.

It is important that you get good career advice as early in your career as possible so that you can take advantage of the opportunities and avoid the pitfalls inherent in the practice of law. I can give you at least some of this advice, much of it from my own experience and also from my discussions with many other excellent attorneys. My career has been unusually varied. In addition to attending law school, clerking for a judge, and working in various law firms, I have been a law professor, general counsel at a software company, a federal securities prosecutor, and in a political position with the Securities and Exchange Commission. At each turn, I have learned valuable lessons and discussed career decisions with my peers. In addition, throughout my career I have reached out to other lawyers—in private firms and in government—learning about their career expectations, regrets, experiences, and recommendations.

The vast majority of young lawyers are startlingly naive about the practice and, indeed, the business of law.

What I have concluded—and what many of my lawyer friends have concluded—is that the vast majority of young lawyers are startlingly naive about the practice and, indeed, the business of law. We know this because we too were naive when we started out. The truth is that despite the seemingly dire statistics, not all lawyers are destined to be unhappy, nor is it necessarily a bad decision to pursue a career in the law. In reality, the legal field is remarkably varied and a legal education offers tremendous potential benefits. But the pursuit of a legal career is not without pitfalls, and those pitfalls can be significant and certain bad career decisions can be irreversible. The key is to be educated about the processes and realities of becoming a lawyer. This education extends far beyond law school and begins well before the first class bell of your One L year rings. This book will take you a long way down the path to that practical education.

Based on direct evidence, I believe that the majority of law students and young lawyers are vastly—and sometimes deliberately—misinformed about the nature of legal practice. They often have unreasonable expectations about the nature of legal work and what will drive their career advancement in firms. For as long as this disconnect between expectations and realities continues, young people pursuing the law are destined for disappointment. Unless young attorneys learn in advance about the uncompromising business aspects of the profession, they will continue to fail to make the choices most likely to lead to career satisfaction.

You must be street-smart about the potential risks and rewards of a legal career.

As a young lawyer you need to gain insight—well before you accept your first job offer—into the critical decisions you and all lawyers need to make in the process of developing a legal career. You must be street smart about the potential risks and rewards of a legal career. Be mindful that a legal career is a long-term commitment that will hopefully extend over many decades. That is the case whether you go to the best law school in the country or attend a strictly regional law school. This book is designed to give you insight by providing the information you need to decide not only whether you want to pursue a legal career in the first place, but also how to craft your career and guide it during your legal education, your first years out of law school, and the decades beyond. This book is not a light read. I expect you will find that it provides a more sophisticated—that is, balanced and critical—perspective on the issues surrounding legal education and the profession of law than does any other existing reference source.

THE NEED FOR STRATEGIES

HAVING A LONG-TERM strategy in place before entering the legal profession is essential. You may not stick with the plan, but thinking through the process and having a plan in place can make all the difference. I will provide numerous examples throughout this book of the value of long-term planning. Let's start by tearing down some of the construct you have already imagined about what will be the critical decision points of your legal career.

Having a long-term strategy in place . . . is essential.

One of the happiest days of my early legal career was the one on which I gained acceptance to Columbia Law School. On that day, I imagined that I had it made, and that nothing could prevent me from achieving great things in my career. On the other hand, before I was accepted, I had convinced myself that if I did not get into a top law school, there would be no point in attending a second-tier school because I would never achieve my goals from that starting point. I was wrong on both counts.

If you are a college student, you probably believe that if you get into a top law school you will inevitably enjoy a successful legal career. On the other hand, you may feel that if you do not get into a top law school, your dreams—whatever they are—will be thwarted. Let me assure you right now that neither is the case. Let's assume that your goal is to get a high paying job, and eventually obtain a partnership, with a leading law firm. That is a common goal and one that you clearly do not need to go to a first-tier law school to achieve.

Top law firms all across the country have hired the graduates of literally hundreds of different law schools.

The reality is that top law firms all across the country have hired the graduates of literally hundreds of different law schools. While it may be that the majority of big-firm hires are from first-tier nationally known law schools and leading schools in the region, it is rarely the case that going to any particular law school forecloses any job. On the other hand, going to a top law school does not guarantee that you will achieve your initial career objectives. Partnership is denied to many alumni of the top law schools. In addition, your career objectives will inevitably change many times during the course of your career.

It is true that leading law firms predominantly hire the graduates of top-tier law schools. However, it is also true that many graduates of first-tier law schools fail to get jobs with the best firms and that, even if they do get an associate position, the majority of graduates from first-tier schools (as well as from second-tier schools) fail to make partner. Most graduates of second- and third-tier law schools, on the other hand, are unable to get jobs at leading law firms. But some do, and some of those make partner. Thus, the initial decision point most aspiring attorneys reach on the road to their legal careers—what law school to attend—does not guarantee or foreclose any particular outcome. The ultimate outcome often turns on a series of other decisions and personality characteristics, as well as a healthy serving of chance.

There are many decision points in every legal career. Unfortunately, it often takes half a career to learn where the really important decision points are, at which point the time to act on them has long since passed. I hope this book will help you identify the decision points that are important to you before they are out of reach. For now, consider the following statements you may find yourself making (at least to yourself) a decade or so into your career:

- It didn't matter what law school I went to. I know lawyers who graduated from Harvard who are now working for younger Fordham graduates!
- The best decision I made was to turn down the offer I got from that big, prestigious firm in New York. I'm much happier having made partner in a small practice in my hometown, and I would never have become a member of the House of Representatives had I not developed grassroots connections!
- The relationships I have nurtured throughout my career have been the most important secret of my success. I can trace almost every major career advance and most of my client base to personal relationships!

- If I had known as a first-year associate what I know now, I would have made far different choices about the direction of my career and been a lot happier for it!

This book is intended to give you the insight to avoid making the big mistakes many young lawyers make. The book should also help you formulate a comprehensive career strategy. Before writing this book, I spent a significant amount of time talking to the kinds of people who I anticipate will use it. I spoke with college students considering going to law school, law students, recent law school graduates, LLM students, and, of course, young lawyers.

Young lawyers and law students invariably ask me for career advice when they learn about my background and interest in career strategy. The more common questions they ask include "Should I go to law school?" "Should I go directly from college to law school or should I work for a couple of years first?" and "Should I accept a position with a particular firm or a satellite office of a particular firm?" Many of my conversations with young lawyers have been impromptu. As a result, I have often had to answer some important questions without forethought. I often reflected afterward that my answers could have been a lot better. By then, of course, it is too late to revise my answer. Writing this book provided me with an opportunity to answer more fully some of those questions.

SPEAKING TO LAW STUDENTS

AN INTERESTING EXAMPLE comes to mind. Recently, when I was taking Amtrak's Metroliner from a meeting in New York back to my office in Washington, I sat next to a second-year law student from New York University School of Law who was traveling to Washington for an interview. We spoke for nearly the entire three-hour trip about what he expected to get out of his legal career and how he might best achieve those goals. I realized that the advice I was giving him would have provided me invaluable insight had I received the same wisdom while I was still in law school. At that point I began to think about my own legal career and how I could best describe it in a book. I had quite a bit of material to work with.

When I was considering applying to law schools, and then again when

I was accepted by Columbia, all my friends and relatives recommended thatI read *One L* by Scott Turow. I took their advice and read the book over the summer prior to my first year of law school. I determined later when classes began that many of my classmates had done the same thing. *One L* chronicles Turow's first year at Harvard Law School. It is a well-written book. However, while *One L* paints a vibrant picture of what it was like for Scott Turow—a married law student experiencing his first year at Harvard Law School during the late 1970s[6]—the book does not, and does not aspire to, help law students make the major decisions they will face during the course of their legal careers. What it does is provide some insight into the pressures of law school itself. However, even here, the book is dated. It draws a picture of legal education that is now almost three decades old. The face of legal education has, in many ways, changed dramatically over that interval. Technology has had a major impact on the teaching and practice of law. The economics of law firm membership have changed profoundly. The career options for lawyers have evolved and, I believe, expanded in important ways.

Moreover, in contrast to understanding the historical practice of law you, as a future lawyer, need to understand the contours of the legal profession today and be able to predict as best you can its likely future evolution.

> The career options for lawyers have . . . expanded in important ways.

One might say this book gives you the insight of an older brother or sister who went to law school and had a legal career. But that would be an oversimplification. It is unlikely that any single person would be able to provide the insights contained in this book. First, very few individuals have had the breadth of career experiences I have had. Second, few have had the range of professional colleagues who contributed the ideas and recommendations contained in this book.

What this book gives you, then, is the insight you would gain if you had an older relative who went to a top law school, clerked for two federal judges, worked in big law firms based in Washington, New York, and Boston, joined a software company as general counsel, worked in various positions at the U.S. Securities and Exchange Commission, served as a law school professor, and interviewed many of his colleagues and lawyer friends about their own career successes, failures, and insights.

WHY DO I NEED A LONG-TERM STRATEGY?

AS WITH MUCH else in life, in the pursuit of a legal career it often helps to have a well reasoned strategy at the start. When one looks at the careers of particularly successful attorneys, such as those who have attained powerful government posts or risen to positions of leadership in private firms, it often appears that they have experienced more than their share of luck. However, be reminded of Napoleon's often-quoted remark that, when requested to promote an officer, above all else he favored the luckier general. Napoleon did not, of course, mean that he wanted a lucky general, but rather a general who made his own luck.

You must make your own luck.

Like Napoleon's generals, you, too, must make your own luck. One way to start down a lucky path is to formulate a long-term strategy. This book will provide you with much of the information you will need to do that. However, the one thing I will not do is recommend a specific long-term strategy. There are three reasons for this. First, if everyone followed the same strategy, it would not work for anyone; the path would be too well worn. A crowded path is no path at all. Second, everyone has different career goals to which different strategies are better suited. You may want to become a law firm partner, for example, and I might want to become a federal judge. The paths to these outcomes will diverge, perhaps very early in your career (though I should also note that it is entirely possible to achieve both objectives in a single career). Third and most important, you need to maintain a degree of flexibility in your strategy so that you can adjust to unexpected developments and opportunities. In the extreme case, if you are on a career path to become a partner in your local law firm and find out that your best buddy from law school is running for president, you might want to consider volunteering to work on his campaign.

Have a long-term strategy in mind but allow for a certain degree of flexibility.

One piece of advice I received early in my career, while interviewing with a law firm partner who had recently been the deputy director of the SEC's Division of Investment Management, was to keep my eyes open in order to identify and take advantage of those few extraordinary opportunities that come along in the course of a career.

So, in the best case, you start your career with a long-term strategy in mind but allow for a certain degree of flexibility. You can even break down your career strategy into microstrategies, each of which takes you to the next level of your larger plan. I am going to give you a few examples of possible strategies, but they are just examples. My hope is that you will read the rest of this book before settling on the strategies you want to use. For similar reasons, this book does not tell you "the right way to do it" but rather gives illustrative examples and then lets you find your own way once you are armed with that experiential (and anecdotal) information. It is a subtle but important distinction.

I will start with an example of a strategy focused on the goal of getting into law school. Let's say you want to get into a good law school. You know that grades and LSAT scores are the two quantitative measures likely to have the greatest impact on where you get in. You have figured out that the major you choose has considerably less impact on whether you get in than do your grades. (Unlike medical schools or business schools, which may require taking certain preparatory courses, law schools pride themselves on taking students with a broad range of academic backgrounds.) In any event, you figure that admissions counselors are not going to significantly favor one undergraduate major over another. Based on this you decide to pursue a major in English (which, let us say, is an easy subject for you) and to take a number of small seminars (which you calculate, based on your research, tend to award higher average grades at your institution than do large lectures). You may even take the objective of getting a higher GPA to another level and enroll in summer classes (because, let us say for argument's sake, you have calculated that grades tend to be inflated during the summer) and study abroad for one semester (in a program your research shows awards almost everyone A's). As long as you get a good LSAT score (which you can influence by intense studying) to match your high GPA, you will have significantly increased your chance of getting into a decent law school.[7] You may even have better material to draw on in writing admissions essays, and better teacher recommendations as a result of taking all those seminars and studying abroad. In any case, what you have done is to employ a strategy in order to achieve the objective of gaining admission to a respected law school. The downside, of course, is that you may have limited your options to pursue other career strategies—in medicine and finance, for example

You might also employ a strategy to increase your chances of making partner in a law firm. Let's say you graduate from a top law school and go on to clerk for a federal judge. You know that most of your classmates are going to large law firms and a few are going to the Department of Justice (probably through its "honors program"). Very few are going directly to the Securities and Exchange Commission. And yet, you also know that SEC experience is very valuable to law firms, and that if someone obtains a senior supervisory rank at the SEC, there is a good chance he or she can move over to a law firm as at least a junior partner. Looking at the statistics, you realize that your chances of joining a law firm right after the clerkship (like most of your classmates) and staying to make partner are very slim. Perhaps one out of ten entering associates are eventually made partner in the firm. Thus, instead of going directly into a law firm you decide to take the strategic route of joining the SEC. This decision entails initially accepting a much lower salary. However, after five years you are promoted to branch chief, and three years later to assistant director. So there you are, eight years later, and some of your former classmates are just now joining the SEC after not having made partner at their respective law firms. They are coming in as entry-level attorneys (with some step-up in pay due to the government's effort to match the salaries at private-sector employers). As a result, while they have made more money during the previous eight years in private practice, you are now ready to leave the SEC and become a partner at a law firm, making perhaps half a million dollars or more a year. At the same time, your classmates will be taking significant pay cuts, trading their $200,000 salaries for pay packages worth around $120,000. In this way you have employed a strategy whereby you made some initial sacrifices for a much more positive long-term outcome.[8]

Some will question whether it is ethical to follow strategies

Being results-oriented rather than process-oriented will usually yield a more predictable positive result.

such as these, particularly with regard to the strategy of taking classes that your research suggests are more likely to give you a higher grade. That is a decision you need to make. Let me urge, however, that as a general rule, being results-oriented rather than process-oriented will usually yield a more predictable positive result. And there are obviously a great number of other strategies, none of which will work for everyone. You will have your own objectives, strengths, and weaknesses. Reading this book will, hopefully, provide insight into selecting strategies likely to yield the results you desire.

MAKING DECISIONS

I HAVE PERSONALLY made many strategic choices in the course of my legal career. In fact, I have probably made more strategic decisions in my career than have most attorneys my age. Some of these decisions I clearly got wrong, some I got right, and some shaped the later course of my career in ways I could never have predicted. One of my earliest strategic decisions was to apply to Columbia Law School as an early-decision candidate. Applying early decision meant that, if I got in, I would be bound by an oath to accept the offer. I decided to apply early decision because I believed it would increase my chance of being accepted. Columbia was the only top law school offering an early decision-option at that time. However, as a consequence I had to withdraw my application from Harvard when I got in. With a nearly perfect LSAT score and a 3.9 GPA during my three most recent semesters, I might have gotten into Harvard. My career and life might have been very different. I will never know.

It can be hard to anticipate how decisions will affect your career, and sometimes even harder to decide which outcomes are preferable.

I have made other strategic decisions as well. In my last year of law school I had to decide between accepting a two-year clerkship with a federal judge in Miami, Florida and joining a large corporate law firm in New York. Had I joined the corporate firm in New York then I would likely have made the move to an investment banking job early in my career. About three years after I graduated, banks were so hungry for associates that the steady stream of MBAs out of business schools could not satisfy them. However, I had a great experience clerking, was able to use that clerkship to obtain a job with a leading Washington law firm, and have enjoyed a diverse and challenging career as a result.

When I was a second-year associate at my first law firm, Wilmer, Cutler, I received a call from a headhunter offering me almost double my current salary if I were to join a leading New York firm. I had a lot of school loans, so I interviewed for the job. The firm was Cleary, Gottlieb, one of the top Wall Street firms. I received an offer, and ended up changing firms rather early in my career. Had I stayed at my first firm, I might have made partner five years later, as some of my friends did. Because I went to the New York firm, I learned more about structured finance than anyone should ever know, met contacts that helped me build a software company in China, and went on to a successful career as a government lawyer. It can be hard to anticipate how career decisions will affect your long-term career, and sometimes harder to decide which outcomes are preferable.

Other strategic decisions have had a significant impact on the course of my career.

- When I was in the last year of my federal clerkship, for example, I had to decide whether to accept an offer with the Securities and Exchange Commission or join a private law firm. I chose to go with the private law firm, only to join the SEC eight years later in the same entry-level position I could have gotten straight from my clerkship!

- When I did decide to join the SEC, I had to choose whether to join the Division of Enforcement or the Office of General Counsel. I chose enforcement, which led me to meet a female prosecutor whose husband I now work for at a leading investment bank.

- When I was a first-year associate in private practice, some members of the securities practice asked me to work exclusively for an idiosyncratic new partner who had just come from a senior government job as director of the Division of Market Regulation at the SEC. I had no idea how prominent he was in his field. Because I did not want to narrow my experience, I declined the offer, and the firm hired a new attorney to fill that role. The lawyer who took the job that I declined is now the general counsel of a leading investment bank, a very desirable (and well-compensated) position. He is just a couple of years older than I am. It is possible that I would be in that position today had I agreed to dedicate myself to working for that one partner.

Thus, all of these decisions influence not only where my own career is today but also my advice to you on strategic thinking.

1. DECIDING ON A LEGAL CAREER

ARE LARGE NUMBERS OF LAWYERS REALLY UNHAPPY WITH THEIR CAREERS?

COUNTLESS SURVEYS SHOW that many practicing attorneys, particularly those that work in large law firms, wish they were doing something else. A 1998 State Bar of Wisconsin member survey found about 25 percent of all the lawyers responding were considering leaving the legal profession within the next five years. The survey concluded that, while some were retiring, a significant number were simply abandoning the practice of law altogether. Many of the respondents who said they wanted to stop practicing law indicated that they were frustrated and disillusioned with being a lawyer. The Wisconsin survey is not alone. Going back a few more years, a 1992 poll conducted by *California Lawyer* magazine found a dramatic 70 percent of respondents said they would start a career other than a legal career if they were given the opportunity to do so. A 1990 American Bar Association survey found that 23 percent of respondent lawyers were dissatisfied with their careers. Finally, a 1990 Johns Hopkins

University study found lawyers had a higher incidence of depression than workers in any of the other 104 careers surveyed.

A 1990 American Bar Association survey found that 23 percent of respondent lawyers were dissatisfied with their careers.

In fact, even among very senior lawyers there is often a sense of general dissatisfaction at the thought of being "just a lawyer." Let me tell you a quick story. I served as counsel to one of the five commissioners at the SEC. These are people appointed by the president of the United States. They are very senior people and most of them are lawyers. Once a week the commissioners hold closed meetings to which only the SEC staff are invited. Important decisions on major cases are made during these meetings. The atmosphere is generally very collegial. At one of the last closed meetings I attended there was a discussion of a complex appellate court decision. The commissioners were debating a legal point. The one commissioner without a law degree (she was an economist) said "Don't look at me, I'm no lawyer." To this, another commissioner, who had a law degree from Harvard as well as an MBA from UCLA, said jokingly, "Quit bragging!" to which a third commissioner, who had a law degree but most recently had been a partner in a leading accounting firm said "Hey, neither are we." Everyone laughed. The chairman, who had received both his JD and MBA from Harvard but who had most recently spent two decades as a U.S. representative, just nodded and smiled.

There is a mild but distinct disaffection in the profession with the thought of "being a lawyer."

I deduced from this light banter that even very, very successful people who have legal backgrounds recognize that there is a mild but distinct disaffection in the profession with the thought of "being a lawyer."

It would be natural to conclude that the practice of law is inherently flawed, thus resulting in the survey results and anecdotes suggesting that many lawyers are unhappy. On the other hand, one might assume that lawyers complain unreasonably about their careers, perhaps because the kind of person who would go to law school is also the kind of person who would complain about a job that pays over $130,000 a year to start. The bottom line is that lawyers make good money at a safe job that does not cause them to risk their necks. Perhaps these people would complain no matter what the job was. And, from experience, I can tell you that lawyers are more likely to complain—about their job, about their spouse, and about the soup they get at a restaurant—than the average person. Nevertheless, there are some aspects of the legal profession that provide ample grounds for complaint.

WHY ARE LARGE NUMBERS OF LAWYERS APPARENTLY DISSATISFIED WITH THEIR CAREERS?

BEFORE YOU EMBARK on your own legal career, it is important for you to understand why a significant percentage of practicing attorneys routinely express dissatisfaction with their jobs.. Clearly, you don't want to join a profession in which you are destined to be miserable. But I can tell you that despite all of the complaining not all lawyers are miserable. In fact, many of them (even some who occasionally complain about their jobs) love what they do. Those who do not love what they are doing have an amazing array of other careers, both in and outside the actual practice of law, that they can choose to pursue.

> Lawyers who do not love what they do have an amazing array of other career choices.

I believe that any individual can find either great joy or great disappointment in the practice of law. It is an amazingly broad field. Different specialties within the practice of law can draw on drastically different sets of skills and offer strikingly different lifestyles. There is an incredible diversity of jobs. Just look at the range of compensation, from high-paying Wall Street power brokers earning over a million dollars a year to small-town public defenders earning about fifty thousand. There were more than a million lawyers practicing in the United States by 2005.[1] These include lawyers in government, law firms, and private corporations. That docs not even count the thousands of lawyers who no longer actively practice law. Clearly, these individuals are pursuing a broad range of careers.

> There were more than a million lawyers practicing in the United States as of 2005.

In any event, let's get back to focusing on why some attorneys express dissatisfaction. What are they complaining about? Discontented lawyers have a variety of complaints. The causes of some complaints are temporary, the product of short-term economic conditions, while other complaints reflect more fundamental problems with the practice of law and relate to constants about the profession that are unlikely to change over time. I can speak directly to some of these issues based on my own history. I have experienced times of great career dissatisfaction as well as periods of intense enjoyment. For example, during the internet bubble many of us were envious of the instant millions made by net-entrepreneurs, whereas during the ensuing bust we were happy to have stable legal careers. In fact, one would expect fluctuations in level of satisfaction throughout more than a ten-year legal career.

Many young attorneys have unreasonably high expectations for their careers.

First, it is important to appreciate that many young attorneys have unreasonably high expectations for their careers. This is particularly true for graduates of top law schools who often have a strong sense of entitlement, to career success in general and perhaps to firm partnership in particular. From their perspective, having graduated from good undergraduate colleges with high grades, performed exceptionally well on the LSAT, and been admitted to a leading law school gives them an expectation of continued success. This sets them up for a particularly hard fall when they come to realize that, (a) there are many smart young lawyers just like them, and (b) only a small percentage are going to make partner in their firms.[2]

The reality that smart lawyers are a dime a dozen is particularly hard for graduates of the very top firms. At the very moment one is accepted to a Harvard, Yale or Columbia, there is a flash of the future, which includes any number of great accomplishments. The feeling is that acceptance to the school guarantees fantastic success, such becoming a judge, CEO, or even president of the United States. Therefore, even without other economic forces at work, many young attorneys are bound to feel disillusionment when they find themselves sitting behind a desk for over ten hours a day editing complex documents and reviewing endless boxes of seemingly insignificant contracts. This is not what they went to Harvard Law School for, they will tell themselves and their fellow associates. The gap between expectation and reality is, I believe, a key source of much dissatisfaction among junior associates at large firms.

ARE SOME KINDS OF LAWYERS MORE GENERALLY DISSATISFIED WITH THEIR CAREERS THAN ARE OTHERS?

CORPORATE ASSOCIATES AT large law firms seem to be more dissatisfied with their careers than are many other categories of attorneys, such as litigators generally and government lawyers in particular. Corporate associates often choose their specialization under the erroneous assumption that they will have a significant amount of decision-making authority in the context of the deals they are working on. That is, law students seeking to do corporate work believe that, at a young age, they will be sitting alongside corporate titans, helping to plan the next big merger or acquisition. The fact that much of a corporate associate's job is to serve as a scrivener who is expected only to write down the intentions of the business principals (who have already made the crucial business decisions and then passed these decisions on to the law firm's senior partners who in turn have told the associate to modify the corporate documents accordingly) comes as a rude awakening. In addition, corporate associates have a high level of exposure to mid-level employees of corporate clients, and often take direction from young MBAs whom the associates see as their social peers but who, from the associate's perspective, seem to have much more interesting and professionally rewarding job functions.

> Corporate associates at large firms seem to be more dissatisfied.

From the late 1990s until about the middle of 2000 the discontent among many corporate associates reached an apex. This was largely due to the booming economic cycle, specifically to the soaring attention and valuations applied to young technology companies. During this same period, the salaries of law firm associates increased significantly, but those increases seemed to young lawyers to be small potatoes when compared with the millions of dollars in paper profits many Internet entrepreneurs were creating and the massive bonuses other young professionals in supporting fields such as investment banking and venture capital were earning. These people who were getting rich in the new economy were about the same age as the associates and most of the new millionaires did not have the educational pedigree of the Ivy-educated lawyers.[3] Many lawyers are overly fixated on university rankings, so they took the enrichment of college dropouts and lowly engineers as a personal affront. As a result, many corporate associates felt that remaining with a law firm represented an unacceptable opportunity cost in contrast with the chance they were missing to join start-up companies or work for venture capital firms. Those associates who could leave their law firms for a promising piece of the new economy generally did so.

Many associates from the very top corporate law firms did jump to aggressive positions with investment banks and Silicon Valley technology companies, both in legal and business management capacities. One of my fellow associates in private practice, a graduate of the University of Chicago School of Law, left the firm in the summer of 1999 to work for Frank Quattrone in Credit Suisse First Boston's Silicon Valley-based technology investment banking group. Some associates even went all the way back to business school full time—including one of my former Columbia roommates, who attended Stanford Business School at the height of the tech bubble—with the expectation that after graduation they would take their newly minted MBAs and assume leading roles in emerging business fields. This exodus resulted in a brain drain that caused many top law firms to implement dramatic increases in annual associate bonuses in an effort to stem the tide of departures. For example, in 1999 and 2000, Cleary, Gottlieb, Steen & Hamilton, a top New York firm—and my employer at the time—gave annual bonuses of up to $100,000 to the more senior associates.

In any event, you can imagine that, when the market value of technology companies crashed in early 2000, and during the following three years of recession that resulted in continued weakness for the American job market, the calculus for attorneys considering alternative career opportunities was significantly altered. While some corporate attorneys lost their jobs, and some entire firms, like California's Brobeck, Phleger & Harrison LLP, were forced into bankruptcy, in general, law firm associates enjoyed much more job security than their counterparts at Internet start-ups and investment banks and other firms that formerly earned significant revenue from the new economy.

ARE LAWYERS PREDESTINED TO BE UNHAPPY BECAUSE OF THEIR PERSONALITIES?

THINK OF THE line in the movie *Legally Blonde*. Reese Witherspoon's character's father famously admonishes her that "Law school is for people who are boring. And ugly. And serious." There is a certain amount of truth to this statement. The fact is, law school is hard and mainly smart people who have spent a lot of time focused on academic work get in. In fact, the student population of law school is notably different from that of business schools, which attract and accept smart people who have focused on building their real-world business experience as much as, or more than, those who have gotten the very top grades and test scores. In any event, lawyers tend to be a serious bunch of academics not afraid to focus on minutiae and subtleties—which is practical, considering that this is what they will need to do in their legal practice.

The question is, do these character traits—academic intensity and a focus on the details—necessarily predispose lawyers to be unhappy in their careers? I don't think so. First and foremost, the range of legal careers is remarkably broad. Being a federal prosecutor is very different from being a corporate associate in a big law firm. Both jobs are difficult and require attention to detail, but they differ in many critical respects. Prosecutors interview suspects and witnesses and write expository pleadings arguing their cause, sometimes in forceful and creative language. Appearing in court, before a judge and possibly a jury, is expected. Corporate associates, on the other hand, will see a judge only if they get a speeding ticket. They are focused on reviewing contracts and spend great amounts of time editing the language of agreements and working to ensure that all possible bad conduct by the parties is anticipated in the draft. Their level of contact with the outside world, other than conversations with the employees of the big companies that are their clients, is limited. Much time may be spent in windowless "due diligence" rooms reviewing boxes of documents, and nights may be spent waiting at the printer for the final drafts of deal documents. There are many jobs in between.

IF LAWYERS ARE UNHAPPY, WHY DON'T THEY JUST CHANGE CAREERS?

I KNOW MANY young lawyers who feel trapped in their jobs. Associates commonly complain about a lack of time for themselves and their families due to the large "billable hours" requirement. They also complain about the failure of partners to communicate with them, a feeling of general isolation within their firms, and a lack of training and mentoring opportunities. That associates report these complaints is well documented. Associates tend to stay at firms despite these complaints because they feel they have no alternative. When I was a young associate, the other young lawyers and I often discussed how we had to stay with the firm because it was the only way to make enough money to pay off our significant student loans. This is legitimate. Loans are a practical concern and they do have to be repaid.

However, some associates seem to stay in positions they despise for the wrong reasons. I have read reports of young firm associates saying they feel as though they "wake up in the morning, bill, eat, bill, eat and bill at the same time, bill, go to sleep." I have personally felt this way, most notably when I was in an asset-backed securities practice in my firm's busy structured finance department—a job I found repetitive and unchallenging. But I got out. I quit. Some lawyers have described themselves as "slaves" and "hamsters," meaning that they feel stuck in an endless and futile professional routine. Money seems an insufficient reason to stick with a job that makes you feel this way. Life is short, the saying goes, and you only have one go-around. Furthermore, thanks to the diversity of potential legal careers, I see little reason to stay in a position you hate. If you are a young attorney and are unhappy with your job, you can always switch to another field, although you might have to take a significant pay cut and do some extensive research to find the right move.

Some lawyers have described themselves as "slaves" and "hamsters."

Nevertheless, many young lawyers are in fact unhappy. Surveys have shown that lawyers have among the highest suicide rates, the lowest popularity ratings, the highest pressure, and the longest hours of almost any profession. And it is not just the surveys. I can report to you that I have known many unhappy lawyers, primarily in private practice. While the pay is very good, you may be surprised to learn that the long hours and constant stress (lawyers are, after all, hired when things are not going well or where there is active conflict) take their toll. Particularly strongly affected by this are the kinds of lawyers—like you—who graduated from top-ranked law schools and went to work for the most prestigious private law firms in places like New York, Washington, and Los Angeles. These are the people who had the highest expectations for themselves and their careers. The reality that most legal practice means long hours and little glory can affect this group the most.

WHAT ARE SOME COMPLAINTS VOICED BY ASSOCIATES WORKING IN LARGE LAW FIRMS?

IN MY OWN experience counseling students and lawyers over the years, I have noticed that, ironically, it is the students who obtain the most highly coveted jobs—associates at large, prestigious law firms—who often become the most dissatisfied lawyers. The same students who were envied by their law school peers often made furtive calls to me, with their office doors closed, and whispered about how desperate they felt to get out. Life as an associate in a large firm is by almost any account highly stressful and often tedious. Many of my friends who graduated from second- or third-tier schools and went to work for smaller firms, often in mid-sized cities, seemed a lot happier.

> Ironically, it is the students who obtain the most highly coveted jobs—associates at large, prestigious law firms—who often become the most dissatisfied.

The lives of associates working at smaller firms were not remarkably different. They still worked longish hours and, in fact, usually made less money, but the big difference seems to be that their expectations were much lower. I don't know how many times I have heard someone say, "I can't believe I went to Harvard Law School for this" (though I can tell you I heard it twice on one day from two different attorneys). This statement does not take on the same weight when substituting "Indiana" for "Harvard". Thus, I have found friends who graduated from less renowned schools happy—delighted, even—to find themselves working long hours to defend insurance companies at small regional law firms for a salary of $70,000 a year.

Since a lot of you will be going to top law schools and getting jobs at large urban law firms, let's focus on the complaints of your predecessors. Lawyers at big firms commonly attribute their career unhappiness to a lack of mentors, a lack of work fulfillment, inappropriate treatment, and burnout caused by overwork. The long hours and pressure to make partner can take a serious toll. Many lawyers complain that there is no real reward for good work. In most cases, even attorneys producing good work are asked to leave after seven years of service under a firm's "up or out" policy. More often, the reward for doing good work is to get more work and more pressure.

The up-or-out system is a continuing point of conflict between associates and the firms where they work. Even if you are the best and the brightest, which young associates often are, there is no guarantee of making partner, and if you don't you eventually have to leave the firm. The volatile economy experienced in recent years added to associates' feelings of instability, fear, competition, and depression. Some common bases for dissatisfaction that have been voiced by law firm associates, and some partners, include:

- Feelings of disappointment that they get no pleasure from something they spend most of their waking life doing.
- A sense that they have other talents, most commonly interpersonal skills—that could better serve them in a field that involves more contact with people.
- Feelings that the job has grown old, that it is the same formulaic work they have been doing for years with no chance of evolving into something more.
- Concluding that they aspire to be legal strategists and that they have no real interest in the detailed and repetitive work required of practicing attorneys.
- A general sense of "Is this all there is?"

One common complaint is the long hours.

Let's now take a moment to discuss what it is, exactly, that law firm associates complain about. One common complaint is the long hours. There is tremendous pressure on an associate in a large firm to bill many hours. Understand that this is a necessary part of being a lawyer—or any job where you are paid by the hour. Your time is your product, and if you are successful in selling it, you are not going to have a lot left for your personal use. You will come to think of your time differently as well. I remember, for example, trying to find the time to spend with my family when I was a junior associate and thinking that every hour I spent was worth $295 to the firm. I calculated the cost of going to the movies for two hours at over $600, including the nominal cost of the tickets. While this will seem warped and wrong to the uninitiated, see how you feel after getting monthly and then weekly and then daily reminders of how many hours you are billing and at what rate. It will change your perspective.

Another common complaint is that the work, particularly for young corporate associates, can really be very boring. The economics of corporate legal practice are quite interesting. A good deal of time is spend doing "due diligence." This is when large companies doing deals pay law firms exorbitant fees so that junior associates can spend massive amounts of time reviewing millions of pages of contracts and other documents. It is not always clear what the associates are looking for (clauses that say the contracts change if there is a change of control are the easy case). The problem is that this is not the kind of work these associates thought they would be doing when they were at Columbia, Harvard, or some other top school. This work is certainly not what they were getting euphoric feelings about when they got accepted to the school in the first place. The large pay package that comes with these jobs, and the promise of possibly moving up one day to drafting some of the actual deal documents, is not enough to take the edge off spending years of your life doing this work. What is worse, while many associates are needed to do the low-level document review, only a very few partners are needed to interface with clients. This means that a high attrition rate (either from burn-out or being asked to leave) is encouraged, further adding to the stress.

ARE LAW FIRM PARTNERS HAPPIER WITH THEIR CAREERS THAN YOUNG ASSOCIATES?

IT WOULD BE reassuring to believe that there is a light at the end of the tunnel. And you would think that being made a partner, including its rewards of earning both the respect of colleagues and an immense pay package, would result in great career satisfaction. However, based on the many conversations I have had with senior partners on this subject, I can report that many partners, when they gain seniority, do not grow to enjoy their jobs any more than they did as associates. This seems particularly so of corporate partners. I have worked with many corporate partners over the course of my career and become friends with several. Those who have confided in me have expressed varying degrees of regret about their careers—some quite astonishing, given the speakers' success in their chosen fields.

Many partners, when they gain seniority, do not grow to enjoy their jobs any more than they did as associates.

One senior partner, who became the managing partner of a top Washington law firm, told me once that early in his career he had faced the decision of going to Yale Law School or Harvard Business School. He chose Yale, which had led to his current, well respected, position. But he said he looked back on the decision and regretted not having pursued a career in business. He made plenty of money: over a million dollars a year. The reason for his dissatisfaction was, even as he grew more senior as an attorney, he continued to have to report to the recent MBAs who were the deal makers at his client firms. No matter how much success he had as a corporate lawyer, he would never be the one making the call to close or not close the deal. Similarly, other senior corporate attorneys expressed a great deal of envy when they learned I was returning to Wharton to obtain my own business degree.

It is easy to see why some senior partners are dissatisfied. They are in close contact with clients who make a great deal of money, often much more than they themselves make. These are clients whom the partners likely perceive as being less intelligent than they are and, certainly, who work a hell of a lot less than they do. Plus, law firm partners do not have the job security they once had. It used to be that law firm partners held their positions for life and could, at some point in their careers, move to a role as a sort of senior statesman. This is largely a thing of the past. Now, the atmosphere of esprit de corps has given way to one in which there is much intense competition among partners for clients and a portion of the firm's profits. Less productive partners are more likely to be terminated by a vote of the partnership now than ever in the past. This adds great pressure to senior partners, even those who have helped build the firm's reputation and goodwill throughout their careers. It is not surprising, then, that some Washington partners have expressed the strong desire that their children not follow them into the practice of law.[4]

Lawyers like to commiserate about how hard they work. Working long hours has become a badge of honor that is shared even by senior attorneys from different firms. At the same time, as lawyers grow more senior in their careers, they are often expected to work longer hours rather than shorter ones. This contrasts with many business executives who, as they gain seniority and accumulate equity in the companies they work for, mainly decrease their hours in the office, particularly as they approach retirement age. I recently ran across an interesting exchange while reading the deposition transcript of a senior corporate executive. The deposition was taken in a fraud suit against the executive's former employer. There were at least half a dozen senior lawyers in the room. When asked why he quit working for the company, the witness answered, "I was fifty-seven years old and I was working through the nights during the last year. It was okay when I was twenty-seven, thirty-seven, maybe even forty-seven, but I'll be damned if I'm going to do it when I'm fifty-seven." To this the partner questioning the witness commented, "I can respect that." It occurred to me while reading this conversation that the comments of the witness really captured what a lot of the senior lawyers in the room must have been thinking about the progression of their own careers. A recent online exchange on American Lawyer's *Counsel Connect* Web site involved a group of lawyers discussing the condition of the legal profession. One of the items was the lawyers' apparent dissatisfaction with their profession because it "requires lawyers to take responsibility for . . . outcomes they cannot control" and also their unhappiness, because lawyers are "involved in procedures that don't tend to resolve disputes or make the world a better place." But these are aspects of legal practice that are unlikely to change. One can not always choose one's clients and, as often as not, the result they are fighting for is not going to make the world a better place.

One participant in the online forum commented that lawyers "feel that way because [they] are tired of the pressure, their everyday tasks are boring, and [their] accomplishments are not fulfilling. Remember that these are intelligent, well-educated, and often creative people who have found out that law was not all it was cracked up to be." These comments are well put and are certainly echoed by many practitioners. However, again, the essential nature of legal practice is not going to change. Reviewing the documents and drafting the pleadings required in the practice of law is unlikely to change or to become less boring. On the other hand, law has provided a career for intelligent, detail-minded men and women who might not find a better or more lucrative match for their particular skill set outside of the law. This suggests that the best defense against eventually growing to despise the profession is for young lawyers to understand both the negative and positive aspects of their chosen careers.

CAN LAW SCHOOLS AND COLLEGE CAREER COUNSELORS TAKE SOME OF THE BLAME FOR CAREER DISSATISFACTION AMONG LAWYERS?

THE ROOTS OF career dissatisfaction for lawyers may rest in the unreasonable expectations law students have for their careers. A legal career can rarely deliver the consistent excitement and glamour of the profession as portrayed in television and movies. This failure of expectations to meet reality when law students graduate and enter the work force contributes significantly to the disenchantment of many young attorneys. Law schools and college career counselors do students a disservice by not presenting a counterbalancing practical view of what it is that lawyers actually do.

A lot of the blame for associates' unhappiness rests with . . . law schools themselves.

A lot of the blame for associate unhappiness rests with the entertainment industry and, indeed, law schools themselves. The realities of legal practice are often quite different from what law students expect. It is unlikely you went to the effort of taking the LSAT, getting great grades, and enduring three years of torturous law school in order to spend three or more years as a highly paid proofreader. The media does not help. Movies and television shows about lawyers, from *To Kill a Mockingbird* to *L.A. Law* portray lawyers as having interesting, glamorous, meaningful jobs. But the actual practice of law is often none of those things. At large law firms the work done by junior associates is commonly tedious. At small firms and for solo practitioners financial and work pressures can be intense.

These forces combine to make the early careers for many attorneys extremely difficult. Law firms do not help. They teach law students about the complexities of property law and the historical import of constitutional law but do not teach that law is a business. Law schools push students off to positions with leading law firms without the heads-up that they are essentially cannon fodder, filling the junior positions where many bodies are needed but likely discarded a few years later when only a very few partners are needed to grow the business. Law schools do it for a reason: large law firms are their primary constituency. That is not a sufficient excuse, in my opinion.

Students at many top law schools become focused on eventually making partner. I remember looking over the NALP forms of interviewing law firms in Columbia's career placement office. They were bound together in a two-hundred-page, pale blue, softcover book. One of the statistics was how many associates entered the firm as first year associates each year and how many lawyers made partner in each year. We thought we could calculate from that our own odds of making partner. We assumed that no associates left of their own accord and that no laterals (See Chapter 5: Changing Jobs) moved in before making partners—assumptions that, in both cases, would have been patently wrong.

These days, perhaps, at least some students are getting the message that entering a law firm and expecting decent odds of making partner in seven years is often not realistic. Some evidence suggests that an increasing number of law students are choosing alternative—meaning non-firm—jobs following graduation. But availability of these jobs is largely dependent on a strong economy. Investment banks and consulting firms hire lawyers only when the economy is particularly frothy.

SINCE SO MANY LAWYERS ARE UNHAPPY, WHY SHOULD I EVEN CONSIDER LAW SCHOOL?

OBVIOUSLY A LOT of young people go to law school, and some of them must know the reputation that lawyers have of being unhappy in their careers. The fact that you are reading this book and asking this critical question bodes well for your chances of making an educated decision about whether to pursue a legal career yourself. Keep in mind that, despite the fact that many lawyers at some point in their lives are not content with the shape of their legal careers, there are some very compelling reasons to pursue a legal career.

First of all, the practice of law is very broad. There are many different kinds of lawyers, and in a sense it is misleading to use the term "lawyer" in a general sense. The differences between the experiences of a government prosecutor working for the U.S. Department of Justice on organized-crime investigations and a patent attorney with a doctor's degree in cell biology working for a biotech start-up in San Diego, for example, are going to be immense.

Also, many jobs that are not pure "legal" jobs are available for people with a legal education. A good example is the entertainment industry, in which a significant number of the senior business managers come from a legal background. Law also pays well. Aside from the fact that you will make more as a young associate in a large urban law firm than in almost any other career, except perhaps investment banking, there are many opportunities in the private sector and in government to pull down a more than respectable salary without having to set foot in a law firm.

WHAT MAKES LAW FIRM JOBS SEEM ATTRACTIVE DURING ECONOMIC SLOWDOWNS AND LESS ATTRACTIVE DURING PERIODS OF GREAT (OR AT LEAST PERCEIVED) ECONOMIC EXPANSION?

BEING AN ASSOCIATE in a law firm, particularly a large urban law firm, is very attractive to smart young people during a slowdown in the business cycle. We have experienced two such slowdowns in roughly the past decade—one in 1991 and 1992 and more recently from early 2000 through 2003. During such times, law firm positions are attractive because of their relatively safety and comparatively high salaries.

Large law firms appear safe during periods of economic downturn because most of them are busy during both economic booms and busts. This is true at least for those firms that maintain a variety of practice areas, including litigation, corporate, and intellectual property, and that did not dedicate too many resources to servicing the business trend that was hot during the preceding economic boom). That is, a law firm that is serving as counsel on a large number of mergers and acquisitions transactions or doing a lot of IPO work during an economic boom can usually switch its resources, particularly its more junior associates, to litigation and regulatory work when the corporate business cycle turns and the transactional work dries up. At the same time, during an economic downturn, young legal professionals see their friends at investment banks and private corporations losing their jobs in large numbers.

Most large law firms offer greater career stability than other high-level employers. The reasons for this are largely economic. Investment banks, for example, have very few fixed costs but very high variable costs. This is due to the fact that a significant percentage of their expenses relate to the variable costs of employing highly paid analysts and associates. Investment banks respond to slowdowns in the business cycle by reducing these variable costs—that is, by firing the junior (and sometimes also the more senior) staff. It is during these hard economic times that it feels pretty good to be pulling in around $150,000 as a junior law firm associate without a serious risk of being laid off (though there always remains some risk of losing your job even at a large law firm if you do not plan well, as we will discuss in the following paragraphs).

Another consideration favoring working in a law firm is the counter-cyclical nature of the legal business. It is interesting to consider, first, why the business of law can be counter-cyclical to the standard macroeconomic business cycle. As I suggested earlier, litigation and regulatory work, particularly intellectual property work, generally increase during a down market. Many lawyers account for this phenomenon by suggesting that executive clients who, during a downturn, are not busy doing deals designed to build their businesses have time to consider ways to retrench, which includes shoring up their patent rights and suing to strictly enforce their in-place business agreements.

There is also generally an increased (or at least not decreased) emphasis on regulatory matters (like drug development, antitrust law, and the regulation of consumer lending) during lean times. As a result, young lawyers whom law firms might have hired out of law school with the idea of training them as corporate attorneys get redirected by the firms into litigation and regulatory lawy. More specifically, the volume of certain work, most notably bankruptcy work, is generally inversely proportionate to the quantity of corporate work so that there is often a pull from corporate to bankruptcy (and regulatory) work during down times.

I have had the pleasure to practice law through an entire business cycle, boom to bust to boom. One interesting phenomenon I observed, particularly in my early corporate work helping companies do "roll-up" transactions, in which they buy many small companies in a given sector in order to consolidate that business segment, is that when the economy really goes south, many of the same companies that earlier engaged a firm to help them conduct multiple acquisitions (think of companies such as the Washington-based U.S. Office Products, Worldcom, Inc., and PSI Net) return as clients seeking bankruptcy protection from their creditors. This is an interesting way, as a lawyer, to experience the full swing of the business cycle. In any event, one result is that lawyers who are young enough for firms to justify retraining them can find their careers redirected into these newly hot fields of specialization.

A second economic factor making law firm jobs seem more permanent during economic downturns is the fact that most law firms are somewhat more reluctant than investment banks and other business sectors to actually fire competent employees. While during economic downturns firms may not need all of the corporate associates they trained as transactional lawyers during the boom market, and while the most senior corporate attorneys may earn too high a salary for law firms to justify retraining them for service in other fields, most firms will allow natural attrition to reduce the ranks rather than employ wholesale dismissals. This reluctance to fire generally means that law firms will simply not promote lawyers in out-of-favor areas of practice. The result is that, during periods of slow business, young lawyers will temporarily switch places with their investment banking former college classmates as the objects of envy.

It is possible to lose your job due to economic changes.

As I mentioned, however, it is possible to lose your job at a law firm due to changes in the economic climate. Sometimes even large and prosperous law firms do fire associates due to a lack of business. Despite the fact that the practice of law in a large firm is theoretically countercyclical, many firms may be unable to take advantage of this fact sufficiently to save the jobs of their corporate attorneys. Some firms are simply not sufficiently diversified to shift resources to practice areas that are more in demand during down times. Some firms have reputations for corporate service but not for litigation or regulatory expertise. Other firms do not anticipate a change in the economic climate in time to retrain attorneys. A failure to adapt often infects firms that greedily jumped to expand their practices into booming areas of law (such as, recently, technology company IPOs) without at the same time counterbalancing this development by building their litigation, regulatory, or heavy industry practices.

During the 2000–2004 tech meltdown, many firms, including notable firms in San Francisco and Washington, were crippled because they had previously jumped with too much enthusiasm on the technology company bandwagon. As a result, some firms imploded after the tech bobble burst. One example is Brobeck Phleger & Harrison LLP which, after failing to negotiate a merger with Philadelphia's Morgan Lewis & Bockius LLP, announced in January 2003 that it was dissolving. During the years preceding the bust Brobeck, which was based in San Francisco, focused heavily on the technology industry to the exclusion of developing clients in more traditional fields. When the tech sector tumbled, it was simply impossible for Brobeck to support the administrative weight of its infrastructure, including associate salaries, by building up other areas of business. Brobeck saw profits fall 37 percent during 2002 and experienced a decrease in the number of its lawyers from 900 in the year 2000 to about 550 in 2002.[5]

Economic downturns occur regularly and will, inevitably, occur again in the United States. Economists employ a number of methods to predict when a recessionary business cycle is likely to recur—a flattening of the yield curve and so forth—but that would require too much space to discuss here. Nevertheless, there may come a time when you are moving forward in your legal career and become aware of the likelihood that the economy will sour—and right at the time when you would be up for partner, no less! If you are a corporate associate, this eventuality should concern you a great deal. If you are going to be a fifth- or sixth- or especially seventh-year associate at a time when corporate deal work is slowing, then you are going to be less likely than ever to make partner. You may be told you can stick around without making partner, and that you can do some regulatory work, but more likely there will be pressure placed on you to find employment outside the firm. There will be options for you: you might go into government work (which will be hard if you have no litigation experience) or to a private company as an in-house counsel (which will also be hard if the economy is bad).

But what you should have done is planned for the change in economic conditions as far in advance as possible. The question is, how can you know and what can you do if you do know? You could start by making an effort to become more well-rounded as a lawyer, perhaps by expressing an interest during your third or fourth year in some counter-cyclical area of law such as international trade or securities regulation. That will give you some insurance, at least to the extent you will have an ally in a strong practice area and some skills beyond those of your fellow corporate associates. But this is harder to do in practice than in theory. The reality is that when there is an abundance of corporate work, it is very difficult to find time to learn other skills. Nevertheless, it may end up well worth the effort to have found the time.

WHAT AM I GIVING UP BY CHOOSING TO GO TO LAW SCHOOL?

IT IS PSYCHOLOGICALLY easy, as a college senior, to go on to law school after graduation. You have spent nearly your entire life in school—since the age of about four—and law school has the benefit of serving as a kind of half-way house between academia and the real world. But you are giving up some important things, including money and opportunities, if you make the choice of going to law school. Unfortunately, many graduating seniors are not fully aware of the various opportunities that may be available to them. They may be more familiar with the concept of law school than with other opportunities because law is a profession so heavily mentioned in the press, movies, and television.

First, consider that going to law school means giving up three years of salary and paying at least $100,000 in tuition. While you will make a little bit of money during your two summers (although probably not get a paying law firm job during your first-year summer) the financial differential between going to law school and working is quite significant. More important, you will be giving up the opportunity to pursue another professional career, such as medicine or finance, and also the opportunity to learn a lot early in your career about a particular industry, as perhaps you could gain from taking a starter job in the entertainment field, for example.

Let me focus on one alternative career choice that a number of future corporate lawyers might come to regret they had not pursued: joining an investment bank as an analyst after graduation. Now, the only opportunity to become an investment banking analyst is directly out of college. You usually need to have gone to a pretty good college and majored in economics or finance or mathematics even to be considered for these jobs. And the selection process is quite rigorous. I have interviewed literally dozens of graduating college students in order to choose a single financial analyst. Plus, after you get the job, you spend two years working at least 110-hour weeks doing detailed valuation modeling, comparable company spreads, and similar quantitative work.

But the upside is significant, and hard to recognize as a college senior. First, working as an analyst means you know how to value a business in a rigorous, defensible way. This is a highly valued skill set across banking and business more generally. Second, you will have many career opportunities after your two years in hell (which are not all that bad aside from the long hours and hard work). If you worked for a bulge-bracket (one of the four or five largest investment banks) firm, you are likely to have your pick of business schools or private-equity shops, plus the possibility of being promoted directly within your bank to an associate position that will pay you well over $200,000 a year within a couple of years.

These analyst positions pay quite well. In a very good year bonuses can reach $80,000—and that is for someone just one year out of college (though the average bonus is probably about half that amount). Let's compare the first five years of a student going on to law school who we assume works for a law firm during his second-year summer and then gets a $10,000 signing bonus upon graduation, versus someone going directly into an investment banking analyst position. The future lawyer might expect compensation of $0, $0, $20,000, $135,000 and $145,000. The young investment banker (assuming he goes on to business school after two years and works in a bank as a summer associate during his single interstitial summer before returning to the bank as an associate in year five) might project income of $80,000, $100,000, $0, $20,000 and $150,000. This may not seem like a big difference to you, but consider that the present value of the legal salaries (at a rather conservative 5 percent discount rate) is $189,589 versus a considerably healthier $235,757 for the young banker. On top of this, the salary for the banker will accelerate much more rapidly after his graduation from business school than will that of the young law firm associate. After seven years, for example, the lawyer will still be an associate earning around, at best, about $225,000 a year. The banker, by that point, will be a vice president or perhaps even an executive director earning at least $350,000 at a leading investment bank. Money is not the only thing to consider in choosing a career, but I do recommend making this kind of calculation a part of your analysis in making decisions about what to do following graduation.

WHAT PREVENTS LAW FIRMS FROM FIRING LARGE NUMBERS OF ASSOCIATES WHEN THEY FIND THEY DON'T HAVE ENOUGH BUSINESS TO KEEP EVERYONE WORKING PROFITABLY?

LAW FIRMS ARE less likely to fire associates when the economy worsens than are other businesses that employ professionals, even when there is not enough work to go around. But law firms are businesses. As in any business, if the variable costs of employing highly paid staff are greater than the revenue those staff are bringing in, there is a temptation among the equity partnership to cut costs and increase profitability by removing those employees from the pay ledger. However, law firms are more restrained in their firing practices than are other employers of expensive young professionals—and it is not because law firms are nicer. It is easy to think of some possible reasons for this willingness to keep associates around even during economic downturns. One reason may be that law firms employ lawyers, who may be more likely to find a reason to sue the firm if they are fired summarily. Perhaps more compelling, law firm associates know a great deal about the firm and its clients that would harm them if the information were made public, and law firms are likely reticent to send angry, knowledgeable former associates into the world. Giving law firms the benefit of doubt, we might deduce that law firms are aware that economic downturns are temporary, and that it is worth retaining well trained associates (at a temporary loss) in anticipation of the day when their practice area again heats up (though I doubt the economics make sense, given the constant supply of new associates and the increasing cost of paying increasingly senior associates).

Some insight can be gained from looking at the past practices of law firms. That is, law firms have not always been so reluctant to fire their associates during economic downturns. While I was still in law school one leading New York law firm fired a large block of corporate attorneys during an economic downturn. The year was 1991 and the law firm was Skadden, Arps, Slate, Meagher & Flom. The firings took place just before the Christmas holiday and they had a lasting (negative) effect on the firm's ability to attract the top law school graduates for a number of years. I remember interviewing with a Skadden recruiter (a partner with the firm) on the Columbia campus in August of 1992. He had obviously been receiving some push-back from students on his arguments as to why Skadden was such a great place to come to work. After we spoke for a while he asked me to be candid and to tell him what Skadden's reputation was on campus. I remember telling him, frankly, that there was a lot of talk regarding how Skadden had let a lot of young attorneys go just before the holiday the previous year and that this had led students to question whether Skadden had a proper sense of loyalty to its associate attorneys. The interviewer explained that it was a big concern and that the firm was aware that it might have made the wrong decision, though it had been based on valid business concerns. In fact, what had happened was that Skadden had fired too many of its corporate attorneys so that as corporate business increased during the mid-1990s, they had to hire more corporate associates than they normally would have in order to build up their ranks. That top law school graduates—the lifeblood of any leading urban law firm—were uneasy about accepting offers for a couple

Major law firms are very concerned— paranoid, even—about the reputation they have among graduating law students.

of years following the firings was a significant blow to the firm. I suspect that many of the New York law firms learned from Skadden's example, adding to the caution firms now take in making mass staff reductions.

Some firms have also become expert at getting rid of associates without actually firing them. In fact, most large firms will do everything they can to get rid of associates without actually handing them pink slips. The process of getting rid of an associate this way is time consuming, however, and can take anywhere from six months to a year. Law firms are willing to take this time so as not to earn a reputation among law students as a place from which they might get fired one day (perhaps the firms have all learned from the Skadden example). After all, it would shatter the myth that leading law firms and law schools have woven for law students of law firm life as a near utopia.

Most large firms will do everything they can to get rid of associates without actually handing them pink slips.

With some variation, here is how it is done. First the good annual reviews are replaced with negative ones, generally indicating that the subject is not meeting expectations. But no coaching is provided to help the associate learn how to meet expectations. In addition, in an artful maneuver, the review may suggest the associate do something that is practically impossible to do, such as work for other partners when the law firm has adopted a structure that strongly discourages associates from working outside their assigned practice area. This poor review will be followed by a confrontation in which two partners (always two so there is a witness in case the associate later threatens to sue) come to the associate's office, close the door, and advise him that the partnership has decided that he should seek alternative career opportunities. The associate is then given, in most cases, about six months to find another job.

This is the other side of law firm life that will be hidden from you while you are in law school. Learning about it occurs soon after you join a firm, as you begin to mix with more experienced associates. Of course, law firms also like to play the game of considering the associates they deemed unworthy of partnership "alumni" and use that term quite liberally. In the best case, an associate will happily leave to work for one of the firm's clients, thus solidifying the connection between the firm and that

client for future work. Regardless of the approach, however, it is driven by the same economics. The pie of profit earned by the firm is of limited size, limited by the amount of business the partners can attract. Only partners who bring something of great value to the firm will be admitted. Even associates who do excellent work are unwelcome unless the balance of long-term benefits is in the firm's favor.

2. BEFORE YOU GO TO LAW SCHOOL

DO I REALLY NEED TO PLAN MY LEGAL CAREER BEFORE I EVEN GO TO LAW SCHOOL?

DUSTIN HOFFMAN ONCE said in an interview "Movies are like life, everything depends on a few decisions you make at the very beginning."[1] The same can be said for your legal career. That is, while going to a particular law school probably does not foreclose any particular career path, what law school you go to and, more important, what job you first take out of law school can have a major impact on the remainder of your career. Moreover, establishing long-term career objectives early in your career can make it much easier to achieve those objectives.

For example, let's say you want to become a litigation partner at a leading law firm. You might think—naively—that the best way to achieve this goal is to join a leading law firm with a strong litigation practice directly after law school. In reality, though, very few of those entering a firm as first-year associates

> Establishing long-term career objectives early in your career can make it much easier to achieve those objectives.

will make partner. The odds are overwhelmingly against you. Moreover, you will get little real trial experience as a litigation associate. Most of your time will be spent reviewing documents and editing the legal pleadings partners have written. If, on the other hand, you clerk for a federal judge after law school and are accepted into the Honors Program at the Department of Justice, you will gain real litigation experience. You will likely first-chair your own trial within two years, something that only seasoned partners do in private practice.

Within seven years, about the time you would have been up for partner had you gone to a firm (where you would be sweating over whether you were going to be made a "junior partner" or informed that you are not going to make partner and need to seek "other career opportunities"), you will probably have an impressive title, such as "Assistant United States Attorney," and will certainly have a résumé as a trial attorney that far outmatches any litigation associate's. At this point you will have opportunities to come into a private firm as a partner or perhaps as counsel, with the understanding of being made partner within a year or two. You will be in a completely different position than the associates who came up through the ranks. First, you will have developed real litigation skills that others in the firm do not have. Second, the other partners will only see you at your polished best, unlike the associates who made their learning mistakes at the firm. Finally, since the firm hired you—an experienced attorney—instead of a raw associate, the mind-set within the firm will be to nurture you as a future practice leader, rather than use you up as entry-level labor.

This is just an example. Similar benefits can be gained by having a career strategy whether you want to be a corporate lawyer, a politician, or an investment banker. And, of course, it is not absolutely necessary to plan your entire career from the start. You can change career objectives at any time (and almost certainly will do so several times throughout your working life). However, it can be hard, emotionally and economically, to change the course of your career. In this book I provide guidance about how to make long-term planning decisions that will help you realize your career goals, and I also suggest options for changing your career in positive ways after you have gained considerable experience and expertise.

EARLY PLANNING: WHAT IMPACT WILL THE COLLEGE I WENT TO HAVE ON MY LEGAL CAREER IN THE SHORT AND LONG TERM?

WHILE GOING TO a non-top college will not prevent you from getting into a top law school and even going to a nontop law school will not prevent you from making partner at a great firm, there remains a benefit to having gone to a really top college, even if you do not go to a really top law school. Put another way, if you do not go to a first-tier law school but went to a really good college, then certain people who will have an impact on your early career will give you the benefit of the doubt and hire you, whereas they might not have done so if you had gone to a non-top college. I have seen examples of this many times, particularly when the candidate went to a school like Princeton for college and then went home to his or her birth state to attend a local law school.

If you do not go to a first-tier law school but went to a really good college, certain people . . . will give you the benefit of the doubt.

In the old *Paper Chase* television series (which you will be too young to remember) two of the main characters were law students at a school like Harvard. One had gone to a public undergraduate university and the other to a top private university. They had very different personalities based on this "class" difference. They both seemed to do well, but the public school character seemed to have to work much harder for his academic and career success. Having gone to a top undergraduate school will be a lot like that. You will find certain things easier than if you had gone to an unknown or not-well-regarded school. While you might not be much better prepared for the class work in law school, you may find that you are in a better position come recruiting time, perhaps because of the increased chance of meeting up with a fellow alum on the hiring committee or just as a result of the overall higher expectation arising from your having gone to Princeton or Brown, for example.

In the real world, when you are interviewing for jobs at top law firms, you will find that a good number of the senior lawyers went to a small number of schools for college, likely Princeton, Harvard, Yale, Cornell, Dartmouth, Penn, Brown, and so on down the list. On the West Coast the list will include Stanford and Berkeley as well as UCLA and USC. In the Southeast it might include Duke and the University of Virginia. You get the idea. Alums of these schools have a certain loyalty to other alums. They will assume that if you got into one of these colleges, you must be pretty smart—just like they are!

If you decide not to go to a top law school in favor of a good regional law school, having gone to a top undergraduate college may turn out to be very valuable to you. You can attribute choosing the regional school to circumstances other than your academic inability to get into a better school. Perhaps, for example, you were trying to save some money on tuition, or you are thinking of running for office and thought it would be a better idea to go to a local school closer to your potential constituency. These rationalizations are more believable if you went to a really well regarded college. Remember, people who went to top colleges will have an unspoken bias in favor of other people who are like them in this regard. Their bias in your favor serves as a vindication of their own right to the success they have achieved.

The relationships you form in college could very well turn into your most valuable business assets.

In the longer term, the relationships you form in college could very well turn into your most valuable business assets in the decades to come. If you go to a highly competitive college, you are more likely to be in classes with people who will become leaders in business and politics. Thus, if you go to Princeton or Yale there is a greater chance that the managing director at some investment bank or the Attorney General of the United States will have been in your junior-year philosophy course, or even have been your freshman roommate. There are innumerable examples of how these types of relationships have led to legal work or, even, appointments to high government office. The axiom that sometimes it is "who you know" as much as (or more than) "what you know," which can lead to significant career breakthroughs remains, somewhat regrettably, true.

ONE MORE TIME: SHOULD I GO TO LAW SCHOOL?

This is a central question that you need to ask yourself several times during college—at least when you are deciding on a major, when you begin the law school application process, and before you send in that big first acceptance deposit check. Reading this book and evaluating your own personality and career goals should help you. However, my recommendation, based on having gone to law school, practiced law for nearly ten years at various respected law firms, and having spoken with scores of my fellow law students and practitioners about this very question, is that you should consider going to law school if at least two of the following statements ring true:

- You want a professional career that offers a high probability of allowing you to make a good living and are not particularly risk seeking or comfortable finding innovative ways to make money.
- You genuinely enjoy reading and writing and, more specifically, analyzing the detailed nuances that can win or lose positions taken in an argument or debate.
- You have a long-term plan that involves using law as a stepping-stone to a career in politics, the foreign service, or government (such as becoming a prosecutor or public defender).
- You have a long-term plan that involves developing a legal specialty such as patent, tax, or securities law, and you have worked into that plan the details of getting another relevant advanced degree or specific government or professional experience, that you believe will help you move along that career path.

Even if you do not identify yourself with any of these descriptions, it still might be worth your while to pursue a legal education. For example, it is true that legal experience can prepare you well for certain types of business, such as real estate, business transactions, and entertainment.[2] It is also true that having a law degree can make it easier to get certain kinds of jobs that might not initially seem lawyerly, such as becoming a special agent with the FBI, joining the Central Intelligence Agency as a field agent, or becoming a Wall Street banker. But keep in mind that a law degree is fairly expensive to pursue, in terms of both time and money.

Law school is costly. In addition to tuition, you will need to pay for room and board and books during your three years of school. This could easily cost you over $100,000, and, while this amount can be financed with loans, it will burden you after you graduate. Also, there is the lost opportunity cost of spending three more years in school. Those are three years that you could spend building experience in an industry that might be better suited to your personality traits or career goals. For example, if you think you might like to be a Hollywood talent agent, you would be better off moving to Santa Monica and taking a job in the mailroom of the William Morris Agency for two years, which is essentially the only way to join that world. Or, if you have an analytical bent, you might be better suited to a Wall Street firm like JPMorgan or CreditSuisse as an analyst for a year or two or three before going to business school, after which you can head back to the Street and, maybe, make the really big bucks. Think about the opportunities, and keep in mind that after you go to law school, you are that much older, and are saddled with debt, so it will be increasingly difficult for you to squeeze into these entry-level positions.

Don't, however, get scared away from the thought of going to law school by thinking of the other options you are giving up. Law offers a solid education and a career that has a considerable upside and a downside that can best be described as one in which you may feel that you "settled" for something less than you might otherwise have achieved. But this "settling" is a matter of perspective and, in a weak economy, really no downside at all. What I mean is that, as a young lawyer, when your friends who went to Wall Street or started a new company doing business in China are making big bucks and doing exciting deals, you are going to feel like you screwed up by not taking the risks they took. Your $150,000 salary is going to look paltry in contrast to what they are accomplishing. But, when, as a young lawyer, your friends who went to Wall Street are getting laid off and the ones who started a new company are moving back into their parents' basement, you are going to feel pretty sweet with your $150,000 salary, chrome and marble lobby, and summer associate recruiting lunches at Palm. It is all a matter of perspective and, more precisely from your position as the decision maker, risk tolerance.

WHAT UNDERGRADUATE CLASSES SHOULD I TAKE TO PREPARE FOR MY LEGAL CAREER?

THERE ARE TWO answers to this question. Sorry for making your life more complicated!

The easy answer, which will be particularly welcome if you are reading this toward the end of your undergraduate experience, is that as a general rule, no one major offers you a much better chance of getting into or performing well in law school than any other. That is, law schools are full of liberal arts majors with English, philosophy, and, particularly, political science degrees. There are also law students with engineering degrees, premed majors, and degrees in other, more "substantive" disciplines, although there are fewer of them than there are of the liberal arts types, probably because the engineers of this world have more lucrative career opportunities directly out of college.

As a general rule, no one undergraduate major offers you a much better chance of getting into or performing well in law school than any other.

Some students have asked me whether they should study prelaw. I do not believe that a prelaw curriculum in college prepares you particularly well for law school, although it might give you a small initial advantage over your classmates because you may have a better feel for the general lay of the land. Note, however, that most of the better colleges—the Ivies, Stanford, Duke, Chicago—do not offer prelaw as a major. I was a political science major, which is practically useless unless you go to law school, and I did take the opportunity to study what could pass for constitutional law during the summer before I went to law school. I took these classes not at my undergraduate institution, Duke, but at Cambridge University in England. The series of three "law" classes I took did not prepare me at all for what I encountered academically in my first-year torts, contracts, civil procedure, or legal writing classes.

Some of the most rewarding jobs in law require a specialty outside of a pure legal education.

The more difficult answer is that it can matter a great deal what other degrees you hold, including what you majored in as an undergraduate, depending on what you want to do with your law degree. This goes toward formulating your long-term career objectives, which I'll cover more in Chapter 9: Pursuing Other Degrees. To give some concrete examples, though, consider that some of the most rewarding jobs in law require a specialty outside of a pure legal education. My favorite example is that intellectual property law involves biotechnology. Biotechnology is unquestionably an up-and-coming field that will employ increasing numbers of lawyers in the decades ahead.

Law firms will be hiring many more lawyers with biology and biochemistry backgrounds to file patent applications and litigate biotechnology issues, among other projects. Litigation requiring knowledge of biology may range from patent litigation to constitutional law cases involving the ethics of cloning. Already innovative biotechnology companies are fighting over the few good lawyers with advanced degrees in biology and related scientific fields.

One has only to look at online job posting Web sites to see that these companies are offering above-market salaries to mid-level lawyers with the right, very specific educational backgrounds. Moreover, many of these jobs are in desirable locations. Leading hubs for biotechnology firms include Boston, the San Francisco Bay Area, and the area just north of downtown San Diego. In order to enter a master's degree program in the hard sciences you will need, as a practical matter of gaining admission, to have studied that subject as an undergraduate. That is, if you want to get a master's degree in physics or chemistry you should have majored in these areas as an undergraduate. There are some exceptions. For example, if you were a math major in college you could probably be accepted into a graduate physics program with some additional coursework, due to the close relation between physics and mathematics.

HOW CAN I APPLY OPTION VALUATION TECHNIQUES TO MY CHOICE OF MAJORS IN COLLEGE?

THIS IS A loaded question, as I would bet you did not know that option valuation techniques can be applied effectively to help you select your college major in the context of a broader career plan that may or may not include going to law school. The answer is that it can, and the trick for me is to explain it to you without giving you a complete course in real options theory (which I would probably mangle anyway!).

First a brief note on valuing options. The bottom line is that putting off decisions that are irreversible and costly has value if, in the interim, you are able to get information that will make your ultimate decision better informed. In the world of "real" options,[3] this means the expected value of an investment by a company that can invest $10 now and learn more about a project before deciding whether to invest an additional $90 later on is greater than the expected value of an investment in the same project by a company that must invest the full $100 up front in order to initiate the project. That's pretty easy.

You can apply this technique to almost any decision, including your deciding which undergraduate major to pursue. The trick is, obviously, to keep your options open. If you declare an English major, for example, you may have limited your options unnecessarily. Certain jobs will not be open to you, or at least they will not be as open to you as they would have been had you chosen another discipline. For example, an undergraduate who majored in English will be highly unlikely to get a job as an investment banking analyst at a bulge-bracket firm after graduation, and this will in turn cut off an entire area of career advancement that some consider to be highly desirable. Declaring an economics or mathematics major, on the other hand, will leave open the possibility of virtually any career but will probably pose a higher risk of receiving less-than-perfect grades, which in turn could hurt your prospects for gaining admission to a top law school.

HOW DO LAW SCHOOLS ADMISSIONS OFFICERS VIEW GRADES VERSUS THE CLASSES IN WHICH THEY WERE EARNED?

While I am certain that some law school admissions officers will claim otherwise, I believe the raw grades one receives in college gets more weight than the subject matter of the classes the student took. If this is the case—and I will explain shortly why I believe it is—the implication is that an applicant could be better off getting an A-minus average in English than a B-plus average in physics, even though in the views of some people obtaining a B-plus average in the "hard" (by which I mean quantitative) sciences can be at least as difficult as obtaining an A-minus average in a humanities discipline.

There are two reasons for the average future law school applicant to aim for a high raw GPA rather than try to take very difficult classes and potentially earn a lower GPA.

First, a student receiving an A average in English is in a highly defensible position. There is little room for that student to have done better, and there is nothing to indicate that the student would

Any student receiving an A average is in a highly defensible position.

not have done just as well taking physics classes. A student receiving a B average in physics, however, probably did not do as well as at least several other students in his program. While he may claim that he would have done better if he had taken English classes, there is no evidence of this, and in fact, it is possible that the student is stronger in math than language and might actually have done worse in an English curriculum. The first student thus gets the benefit of the doubt, whereas the second student does not.[4]

Second, it is very difficult for admissions officers to do anything but look at raw GPA scores when considering the thousands of applicants before them, even if they wanted (and claimed) to dig deeper. Giving more weight to particular majors is a slippery slope, and is also not in the interest of law schools. Even if we assume that quantitative programs of study are more taxing than humanities subjects, how would admissions officers compare the GPA of an English major to that of a political sciences major, or the GPA of a physics major to that of a chemistry major? How do we compare schools—say, an English major at School A to an English major at School B or an English major at School X to a physics major at School Y? The added complexity would be overwhelming for admissions staffs. Moreover, the skills used in law school are often the language and reasoning skills developed in good humanities programs, and so it is not clear that the "harder" classes are a better test of whether a student is prepared for the rigors of law school.

Now, there are limits to this reasoning. A student with a B average in chemical engineering and a student with an A-minus average in fashion design would probably not be given equal credit for the undergraduate work. The perceived harder major would likely win out in that case because the grades were close and the student with the "easier" major did not receive straight A's, meaning he does not get the benefit of the possibility that he is the top student in the class (presumably someone else got higher grades than he did). Also, some weight would likely be given to the overall quality of the school. A graduate of Princeton will almost certainly receive a higher weighting than a graduate of Rutgers, for example, though the law school might also try to get at least one Rutgers graduate in for the sake of being able to advertise that the law school pulls from a large number of undergraduate institutions.

ARE THERE STRATEGIES I CAN USE TO IMPROVE MY CHANCES OF EARNING A HIGH GPA, AND WILL PURSUING THEM IMPROVE MY CHANCES OF GETTING INTO LAW SCHOOL?

THERE ARE PROBABLY strategies you can use to get better grades than you might earn without employing a strategy. This does not mean cheating, by any means. Rather, it means recognizing your own strengths and weaknesses and tailoring your course selections accordingly. You may also be able to identify inconsistencies in the grading of courses at your undergraduate institution, and to take advantage of these inconsistencies to earn a higher GPA.

At most colleges (and probably at all colleges if you are willing to do the background research) there are classes you can take that will virtually guarantee you a good grade, or at least give you a better shot at achieving an A. I remember one such class at Duke. A classics graduate student was going to teach a class in Olde English. The class qualified as a language credit (required for graduation) and focused on teaching the archaic, dead languages that were spoken in England and France around the time that the ancient story of Beowulf was written.[5]

The class was taught like a language class for a living language, with vocabulary, grammar, and reading lessons. The graduate student's goal was to have the class reading medieval texts from the period by the end of the semester. I went to the first several classes. Only a few students showed up, one of whom claimed to be taking the class in anticipation that she was going to apply for a Rhodes Scholarship to study classics at Oxford. During the introduction the teacher made it clear that this was his passion, that teaching the class was his pet project, and that the minimum grade he would give would be an A. Foolishly, I dropped the course. But if you were looking to boost your GPA, this would have been a no-brainer.

Finding classes like this with a guaranteed minimum grade is rare, though you can probably identify one or two likely prospects each year at your average large university. A more fertile approach may be to select small classes, particularly seminars where a close relationship develops between the teacher and the students. In my analysis (which admittedly is based on my own experience at Duke) small classes tend to result in a higher average grade when contrasted with large survey-type classes, such as introductory microeconomics.

Small classes are also sometimes exempt from the mandatory bell curve imposed on professors at many universities. A bell curve requires that each professor give a percentage of students (perhaps 10 percent) the lowest grade, that he or she give the bulk of students middling grades in the B range, and that he or she give a small percentage (again, about 10 percent) of students a top grade. Some professors dislike the imposition of the bell curve on their grading and prefer to teach seminars where they have more discretion. It makes less sense to impose a bell curve on a small class because the small sample is less representative of the broader school population (this is an application of basic statistics) and may result in strange outcomes such as only one student (or even a fraction of a student—think of a seminar with seven students in it!) receiving an A or a C. In my experience, many professors who volunteer to teach seminars prefer to give higher grades to all the students if the professor feels they have earned it.

Finally, as I mentioned, the best way to identify classes where the average grades have historically been high (and thus your odds of scoring well are correspondingly elevated) is to know someone who took the class in an earlier term. This is one area where membership in a fraternity, sorority, or sports team can yield benefits. Many fraternities, for example, maintain a list of professors who regularly give out a large number of top grades—that is, where the grading curve is heavily skewed upward.[6]

Consider summer programs as a way to boost your GPA.

Consider summer programs as a way to boost your GPA. Summer programs are often taught by teachers who have their own personal agenda—which may not include strict grading—and are often more relaxed in terms of student-teacher interaction and academic expectations. I recall one program at Duke that was run by a Japanese instructor. This program entailed a summer immersion in the Japanese language and culture and entailed such activities as traveling to a North Carolina factory that made the fake "krab" sticks composed of haddock fish that are used in sushi. This was a virtually guaranteed eight credits of A. (Of note, in this case it apparently helped the grading that the teacher was a visiting instructor from overseas rather than an American teacher.)

It is easiest to fit these rare classes into your schedule if you have a fairly flexible academic program, such as is the case with your standard liberal arts major. But it is very hard to do if you are, say, a premed student (in which case you have a long list of required classes including calculus, Organic Chemistry I, Organic Chemistry II, etc.) or an engineering student (in which case you might actually learn something useful). Contrast these classes with your standard engineering curriculum and you will find that, as far as academic rigor, there is a tremendous difference. The question, then, is whether law schools take into account the drastic contrast in difficulty between a transcript reflecting a number of seminar-level English and political science classes and one in which engineering and hard-science classes predominate.

SHOULD I GET ANOTHER GRADUATE DEGREE BEFORE I GO TO LAW SCHOOL?

THE MOVIES OFTEN portray students at top law schools as already holding other advanced degrees (for example, in the comedy *Legally Blonde,* the geeky Harvard Law students have mostly other advanced degrees under their belts) and, in reality, quite a few law students already hold degrees including, commonly, master's degrees in the humanities. The prevalence of law students with a masters degree in history or literature can be accounted for at least partially by the fact that decent-paying jobs for grad students in these areas of expertise are scarce. However, most graduate degrees are not going to help you much in your legal career.

While getting a master's degree in history, English, or philosophy is unlikely to make you more attractive to legal recruiters, although the education may marginally improve your writing ability), the time you spend maturing may allow you to gain a better perspective on what you want to get out of a legal education and career. Reading this book should help with that as well. However, a drawback of getting a graduate humanities degree is that you lose a few years that could be spent advancing your career and making good money. This is the compounded "opportunity cost" of delaying your law school education. Those graduate school years might be better spent doing something else, such as spending the early years of your legal career learning a specialty in a government agency (the Securities and Exchange Commission, for example).

One of my college roommates spent a couple of years after college getting a master's degree in history from Yale. He ended up joining the same law firm that I did but was a first-year associate when I was a fourth-year. I did not see that he had gained any particular perspective or advantage from getting the master's degree. He was older and more mature, but he likely ended up in the same firm that he would have joined had he gone there directly from college. Law firms do not give any credit for other graduate degrees unless they directly advance the lawyer's career, such as a master's in taxation. In retrospect, it might have been better for my old roommate to have gone straight to law school and then taken a couple of years off either to clerk for a judge or work for the federal government in an area in which he was interested.

> Law firms do not give any credit for other graduate degrees.

An exception is where the additional degree will be directly relevant to your area of practice. Obvious examples are for patent attorneys who really need to have an advanced technical degree, in engineering, medicine, biology, or chemistry, for example, in order to serve the highly specialized needs of their clients. Patent attorneys, especially those with doctoral degrees in a relevant science, are among the highest-paid class of lawyers in the country. While you will need to do your own calculations given the degree (master's or doctoral) that you might want to consider pursuing, I believe you will find that the compensation offered to recently minted JD recipients going into patent law who have an advanced degree is high enough to justify the years lost and expense incurred in getting that diploma.

WHEN SHOULD I GO TO LAW SCHOOL?

A number of college students have asked me whether they should go to law school directly, get an advanced degree or work for a couple of years before pursuing a legal education. Obviously, this question is relevant only to current college students. Therefore, I will look at this question from the perspective of an eighteen- to twenty-two-year-old college student.

Let me talk first about the option of working for a couple of years after college graduation and before deciding whether to go to law school. As a college student you have limited experience concerning either what you want—and are best suited—to do as a career and what it means to go to law school and become a lawyer. Before this book was published, students who had an older sibling or other relative or even a close friend who was a legal practitioner had a distinct advantage over those of you who did not, because the former could obtain candid answers to their questions about legal practice and career development before deciding whether to embark on the lengthy and expensive process of becoming qualified to practice law. This book is designed to replicate the experience of having a knowledgeable lawyer as a confidant and to level the playing field somewhat by giving you a better understanding of what it is like to practice law. Nevertheless, for those of you who are not certain a legal career is for you, it may be worthwhile taking one or two years off from your studies to take a job that will give you a taste of legal practice.

The reality is that most law students, at least initially after graduating from law school and perhaps after completing a judicial clerkship, find themselves practicing law in a law firm. Law students from among the twenty-or so best-regarded law schools generally gravitate to larger firms in major metropolitan areas. The experience of working in a major urban law firm offers unique pressures—high work product expectations and unusual social dynamics—and unique rewards—high salaries and considerable prestige among your peers and friends. It is difficult for me to give you a complete description of this environment to the extent that you will be able, with any level of certainty, to determine whether you would prosper in that kind of environment. Therefore, a college student who thinks he or she will likely follow the usual path and join a leading law firm after graduation would not be making a mistake by working in one of those firms for a year or two before going to law school.

There is really only one position available for bright young college graduates who want to work for a large law firm for a

There is only one position for college graduates who want the experience of working for a law firm without first investing in a legal education.

period of time after college graduation without going to law school: paralegal. All law firms hire paralegals, although the actual job description varies significantly depending on what department or practice area you end up working in. For example, a corporate paralegal will likely spend a great deal of time handling contract documents in preparation for the closing of deals, as well as spend time tracking down incorporation certificates from and making business filings to various state corporations commissions. In contrast, a litigation paralegal may spend a great deal of time organizing discovery-related documents for trial, or assisting in reviewing and summarizing depositions for the purpose of supporting attorneys in their drafting of various motions and pleadings. In either case, the work will be significantly less interesting and require less skill than that assigned to lawyers. Nevertheless, you will be working directly with attorneys and will experience first-hand the things that make them excited about their jobs and those they find discouraging. You can count on hearing complaints about the long hours, about the lack of respect they get from clients, and about their concerns over whether they will make partner. You may also be fortunate enough to work with attorneys who are genuinely excited about their work and who will enthusiastically encourage you to join the profession. You won't make a lot of money during those two years, but you will come out of the experience having more realistic expectations about practicing in a large firm.

Another benefit of working for a law firm for a year or two is that you may improve your chances of getting into a top law school. Most law students still come directly from college, in contrast to business students who generally work at least two years before pursuing their master's degree. If you make sure to impress at least one attorney at your firm, you will be able to secure a strong law school recommendation (which the attorney will probably let you draft for their signature). You will also have the basis for a strong admissions essay, which will be particularly weighty given that you will have strong and specific anecdotal material to draw upon to explain why you want to go to law school and what you expect to accomplish. Finally, when you do graduate from law school, having worked in a law firm after college will make you particularly attractive to firms because you, unlike most of your classmates, will be able to say that you worked in a law firm environment, enjoyed it, and wanted to get back into the game. This will alleviate one great fear the hiring committee has about all new lawyers, which is that they will find working in a law firm environment not to their taste and will quit before the firm has been able to realize a positive return from its investment in recruiting, hiring, training, and paying the young attorney.

There are other jobs you might consider taking after college that would prepare you for a legal career but which could lead you in an entirely different direction from the traditional large-firm path. Take, for example, working for a member of Congress, either a representative or a senator, on Capitol Hill. You will make a good deal less money than you would have made had you gone to a law school, graduated, and become a law firm associate. You will also have to work your way up from the bottom. And, to get the job, you will need connections, a lot of drive, or both.

If you do take the initiative to get a job on the Hill instead of going directly to law school, you will likely start out as a junior staffer working on an individual member's staff, making perhaps as little as $25,000 a year. Working there for a year or two will put you in a good position to go to law school, with a good recommendation from your member, and perhaps later will enable you to rejoin the congressional staff as counsel to a congressional committee or subcommittee.

On the other hand, you could stay on as a congressional staffer and rise through the ranks. After perhaps ten years you could become a legislative assistant or, better, the chief of staff for a member. At that point you would make over $100,000 a year, but not much more. Of course, the real financial reward will come after you have built your network of connections. As a senior congressional staffer you will have built a strong rapport with your member and developed a network of relationships with other staffers and, hopefully, other members. You will then have an opportunity to go into a private lobbying position and make as much as $200,000 a year.

Another possibility, if you are really lucky, is that your member may be appointed by the president to an important executive post. For example, the current chairman of the Securities and Exchange Commission is Christopher Cox, a former representative from California. When he left Congress, he brought several of his senior staffers over to the SEC and put them in senior positions. Although they do not have strong securities backgrounds, and few are lawyers, they will gain significant contacts in their new positions that will increase their marketability in the private sector.

The downside is that working for a member of Congress exposes you to significant risks. For one thing, you share the risks of your member. If he or she loses an election, you are out of a job. If he or she retires soon after you leave for a lobbying position, your value to your new employer is significantly diminished. You are also stuck living in Washington. Therefore, as with any career decision, you need to consider the pluses and minuses.

WHAT ARE THE GENERAL ARGUMENTS FOR AND AGAINST GOING DIRECTLY TO LAW SCHOOL AFTER COLLEGE?

WHILE YOU MAY benefit from getting some real-world experience before going to law school, I continue to believe that it is a good idea to attend as early as possible in your career. Much can depend on when you graduated from law school, including your seniority level in getting office space and in your pay level in many others. On the other hand, however, it is also true that you only get one shot at being a newly minted attorney. Let us focus on law firms for a moment and set aside other legal career paths, including the government route. Being a new attorney imparts a critical status in law firms. Being new does not necessarily mean that you are young. Being new means only that you graduated from law school recently (one to three years ago) and that you may have clerked for a judge between graduating and coming to work for the firm. Being new means you are being evaluated for your fitness for the partnership track.

If you are on this track, you have a shot at being asked to join the partnership within seven and ten years. If you are not a newly minted attorney and you don't have a good excuse—such as going into government and rising impressively through the ranks before leaving for the public sector—you are more than likely considered damaged goods because it will be assumed that you were passed over for partnership at other firms. No firm will want you if they think that some other firm found you didn't meet their requirements for partnership. They don't want hand-me-downs. Therefore, if you think taking a couple of years off after law school to gain experience and maturity will put you in a stronger position to make a good first impression, it may be advisable to make that somewhat costly investment.

ARE THERE JOBS I SHOULD NOT TAKE BEFORE GOING TO LAW SCHOOL?

IT IS A lot harder to advise what not to do than what to do. So, my advice is that you might want to take an unusual job between college and law school and that experience might play an important part in your career following law school. For example, let's say you take a Luce Scholarship and live in Japan for a year or so after college. Later, you may find that your familiarity with Japan and facility with the language lead to great career opportunities as an attorney. So keep in mind that any unusual experience can pay unexpected dividends.

That being said, there are some jobs that you probably don't want to do before going to law school. For example, you probably do not want to join the Foreign Service. Foreign Service officers are employees of the U.S. Department of State who formulate and implement foreign policy and are the "frontline personnel at all U.S. embassies, consulates, and diplomatic missions."[7] My roommate at Duke was considering joining the Foreign Service after graduation. An oral and a written examination are required, and they are both very difficult, demanding an in-depth understanding of global current events. In any event, at some point along the process, my roommate (who was doing quite well) mentioned that he was also considering going to law school. He was quickly advised by the young Foreign Service officers who had befriended him that he was better off going directly to law school than joining the government.

I think the Foreign Service officers were probably correct, and here is why. Getting a job with the Foreign Service is difficult, but it is not very prestigious (at least not in business circles these days) and not very well paid. You will likely spend a couple of years stamping visas at some overseas U.S. embassy before getting any real experience. It is for career diplomats who do not mind working in a massive bureaucracy. Once you join, there is a good deal of forward momentum to stick with it, and there are long-term practical time commitments. Appointments to over-seas posts can be for two or more years. Joining the Foreign Service could easily lead to a career in a low-paid, middle management job that offers unsurpassed travel opportunities. In contrast, if you were to go to law school instead, at the very least you could get a government job at a much higher pay grade. While you probably would not join the Foreign Service as an entry-level diplomat, you could find similar types of work at higher pay.

One of the guys I clerked with (for a federal judge) is a good example of what you can do in government in the international arena as a lawyer. After clerking, he joined the Department of Justice and, after a few years, applied for a posting in Romania. He is now the senior Justice Department official in that country, with a rank much higher than he would be likely to have (he got the position when he was thirty-four years old) if he had gone through the Foreign Service's system. Plus he is an attorney and can come back to the states with his experience and potentially get a job with a law firm for a salary several times what he is now earning. That is another benefit of being an attorney in high government employment: when you leave, you have a profession in which to apply the skills and relationships you have developed.

WHEN AM I TOO OLD TO GO TO LAW SCHOOL?

You are never too old to do anything in your professional career except perhaps become a professional athlete. But let's dissect this question before reaching that simplistic conclusion. First we will assume that you want to go to law school in order to get a job that pays well and that will, in turn, allow you to support yourself and, particularly if you are a little older, your dependents. The question then becomes, "At what age will law firms and other organizations that hire attorneys consider me too old to be a good candidate for an entry-level legal position?" You can imagine that any employer, in or out of the legal field, will be concerned about hiring those who may be too set in their ways to learn new skills, who will be resistant to working for someone who is much younger than they are, or who will be retiring soon and therefore won't be around long enough to add a lot of long-term value to the organization.

So it is in the context of getting a job that I am going to answer the question of when it is too late to embark on a legal career. I'll start by asserting that going to law school as an older student does not have the same stigma as going to business school as an older student. The traditional MBA employers—investment banks and consulting firms—are quite concerned about applicants' ages. It is my understanding that the leading investment banks rarely hire newly minted MBAs as associates if they are more than twenty-nine or so. Consulting firms are not quite as rigid in their age cutoff but they generally require that older applicants have established themselves as experts in a particular field that can be leveraged to develop business for the firm. In both cases, the employers' concerns appear to be that an older student will have less tolerance for long working hours, will have higher salary expectations, and will chafe at reporting to a much younger supervisor.

In my observation, the same stigma does not attach with regard to going to law school.[8] In fact, I have known many older students who went back to law school in order to begin a second career in the law. But some issues do remain. Law firms and, particularly, government employers often embrace older law school graduates. In private law firms, older lawyers can be an asset where they are required to gain the confidence of clients and the respect of opposing counsel in a way that a twenty-five-year-old associate would find difficult to achieve. In fact, it is my impression that some firms have come to recognize that newly hired associates are likely to remain with the firm for an average of only three to five years. As a result, the more value candidates can bring during that time period the better—and the fact the new attorneys may be just twenty years from retirement rather than have their careers ahead of them of forty years has very little impact on their value to the firm.

In addition, the same concerns that might face an investment bank with regard to supervising older hires do not apply as directly in the law firm context. The hierarchy/age dilemma with regard to hiring older law school graduates is not a major issue at many law firms because most work is done individually with one partner usually directly supervising one or two associates. There is very little large-team work. Partners have such a stranglehold on authority in law firms that the fact that a partner may be younger than a new associate means relatively little to their working relationship. The lines of command are crystal clear. In addition, the fact that legal practice experience is so critical to successful client representation means that even older associates must rely on the experience of a younger but more experienced partner.

Older law school graduates will need to market themselves to law firms differently from younger graduates. Large urban law firms have a particular model associate in mind. He or she is between twenty-five and twenty-eight years old, among other characteristics. Someone who has changed careers to become a lawyer is going to need to articulate the reasons for that choice. For example, the interviewer will ask, "Why did you choose to stop being an architect?" and "How will that experience help you be a better lawyer?" You will need to convince the hiring committee that with a wife and two young children at home you are willing to put in the ninety-hour weeks expected of a junior firm associate. In order to do this, you will need to express a more specific career focus and a stronger drive than will the younger candidate.

Nevertheless, older law students do find success at leading urban firms. I have personally known several new associates at firms who did not follow the path of directly entering law school after college. In fact, I have known several attorneys, hired by top Washington law firms, who enjoyed a full career in the military before going to law school. These were impressive people who spent their mandatory twenty years in the service before retiring with full pensions. They generally attended top undergraduate schools, including the United States naval and military academies, at Annapolis and West Point. Therefore, while they were about forty years old before even starting their legal education, they were able to show significant personal drive for excellence, leadership and success. While hired as first-year associates (and paid accordingly), these individuals generally are given more responsibility, particularly in dealing directly with senior officers of corporate clients, and this is generally due to the perception that clients will be comfortable taking legal advice from an older person. After all, the client is unlikely to know (or ask) how long it has been since the older gentleman sitting across from him graduated from law school.

As I mentioned, government employers can be even less sensitive to age. In fact, the agency I worked for, the Securities and Exchange Commission, gives hiring preferences to veterans, who are generally older. Therefore, if you served in the military before going to law school and wanted to get a job as an attorney with the SEC, you would have an official advantage. I believe this is the case for most, or perhaps for all, other federal employers of attorneys. That being said, when applying for any job as an older person, it is important to be able to articulate why you went back to school and got a law degree. Generally, however, the interviewer will have reason to favor any well-thought-out answer over the fact that a student went directly from college to law school and does not have any real-world experience. In that case, I have often found (and I am talking from the perspective of someone who has been both an interviewer and a law professor) that no matter what words they use, students seem to be saying that they could not think of anything else to do with their lives.

IS THERE A WAY TO EARN A LAW DEGREE IN LESS THAN THREE YEARS?

GOING TO LAW school entails a significant investment of time and money. Each year spent in school is another year of paying tuition and not earning a salary. In addition to four years as an undergraduate, law students spend three years in law school to earn a Juris Doctor degree. The American Bar Association sets the guidelines governing what an accredited law school must demand of its students. Recently, the ABA updated its accreditation guidelines to require more total hours of instruction while allowing schools greater flexibility in structuring those hours. This enabled at least one school—the University of Dayton—to announce a program that started in the fall of 2005 that would let students earn a JD in two years. The program requires that students attend classes during the summer, and it satisfies the requirements set by the ABA.

A program like the one at the University of Dayton will be tempting for some students. It costs the same in tuition as a three-year degree, but it allows students to join the workforce sooner. This theoretically reduces the opportunity cost of going to law school. However, it assumes that you can get a job after having graduated from the University of Dayton's law school. The school is not nationally ranked and you would likely be limited to getting jobs in the local area. Thus, top law school applicants should probably enroll in a regular three-year program at a school with a stronger reputation. In addition, law students usually work for a law firm during the summers between academic years. The summer job before the final third year of law school is a very common source of employment after graduation. In fact, large law firms rely so heavily on hiring from their summer associate classes that many hire very few law school graduates who were not summer associates. Thus, even if a well-regarded law school were to offer a two-year degree, law students would need to question whether giving up the summer employment opportunity is worth the possibility of getting a permanent job sooner.

There are more creative ways to decrease the amount of time it takes to become a lawyer, although they are somewhat unconventional and require a good deal of advance planning. Let's say you are a senior in an American high school. Your grades are good enough to get into a first-tier university. But, instead of going to an American university, you apply to and are accepted by either Oxford or Cambridge in England.[9] These are top, world-renowned schools.[10] With the American dollar weak against the pound sterling, you are going to pay somewhat more for your education in England. However, you are going to have a very good time, though somewhat different from your counterparts at American universities. Classes will be smaller, and some classes will be taught in one-on-one "readings" with professors. Social life will be more formal: there will be black-tie parties and dinners at the "high table." And as an American, you will be something of an anomaly. But you will be well on your way to becoming a lawyer in record time.

In England, the educational system is quite different. College is only three years long. Moreover, you can study law as an undergraduate and graduate in just three years and emerge with a law degree that is sufficient to allow you to begin down the path to practicing law. At Oxford you would receive a BA in jurisprudence; at Cambridge your degree would be a BA in law.[11] In order to practice in Britain, you need to join one of the Inns of Court in London and serve for several years as an apprentice. However, you are not going to practice in the UK. Instead, you are going to apply to an American law school.[12] And when you are admitted, you are going to request that the American school give you credit for some of your "Oxbridge" legal study, such that you can graduate from the American law school in two years. The deans may resist, but I know it can be done because one of my classmates at Columbia who had graduated with a law degree from Cambridge was permitted to graduate in two years' time. Thus, you will have obtained your American JD degree in just five years after graduating from high school instead of the customary seven.

It is worth noting that, in 2002, the University of London and Columbia University Law School established a formal "double-degree" program that mirrors, in some respects, the strategy I outlined above. Specifically, the program gives students an LL.B (Bachelor of Laws) degree from the University of London (which includes the London School of Economics) and a JD from Columbia in just four years of study. LSE students spend their first two years at LSE and Columbia students spend their first two years at Columbia, where they take their respective foundation courses. Students then switch schools for the final two years. LSE students can "waive out" of courses that are similar to courses taken at LSE. In this way, the number of years normally required to obtain these degrees (three years at Columbia and three at the University of London) is reduced. Graduates are eligible to practice in both the United States and England. However, the program saves more time for English students than it does for Americans. Americans still have to get a four-year undergraduate degree to get into Columbia Law, whereas the LL.B degree itself is an undergraduate degree. Thus, Americans will spend a total of eight years in school compared to the British students' four years.

WHAT ARE SOME OTHER UNCONVENTIONAL LAW SCHOOL DEGREES?

A FEW LAW schools, including some leading ones, offer interesting alternatives to spending three years in one law school to obtain the standard JD degree. Columbia, NYU, and Stanford, for example, each offer formal joint degree programs with Princeton University's Woodrow Wilson School of Public and International Affairs. Recipients receive a joint JD/MPA (Master of Public Affairs) from the respective schools. Other schools offer international options. Cornell Law School, for example, offers a joint JD/Master en Droit (French law degree). In this four-year program, students attend Cornell Law School for the first two years and the Université Paris I Panthéon Sorbonne for their final two years. As you might expect, students must be fluent in both English and French. In addition, American applicants must have the undergraduate training sufficient for admission to a French law school and French applicants must have a baccalaureate degree and at least two years of advanced study at a French institution.

There are a large number of alternative degrees and, if you are interested, you can probably find one that suits your specific interests. For example, if you are interested in medical policy, I am sure you can find a large number of joint JD/Master of Public Health programs. Plus, you can always design your own joint degree by going to the respective schools and explaining your interest and what you hope to accomplish by obtaining both of the degrees. As a general rule, however, schools will not lower their admissions criteria solely because you are intent on pursuing a joint degree. That is, Columbia Law is not going to let you in with a lower LSAT because you are applying to Princeton's MPA program simultaneously. But applying for the joint degree will get you noticed by the admissions counselors at both schools sufficiently for you to have an opportunity to articulate your career goals. Given that these are professional schools and are therefore interested in graduates who might make particularly beneficial use of their degrees, the admissions staff will be receptive to any particularly compelling reasons behind your request.

A separate question is whether you should pursue a joint degree. In almost all cases, you are going to have to spend another year (at least) in school. That means you forgo a year of salary and a year of work experience. You need to ask yourself, is what you want to do really so unique and specific that it justifies this kind of an investment and sacrifice? Perhaps it does. But I am betting that, for the vast majority of students, one degree is sufficient to get them where they want to go professionally. Holding two degrees is often a waste of one degree. The two most common professional degrees are the JD and the MBA. My younger brother called me a couple of years back to say he was considering undertaking a joint JD/MBA. program at the University of California at Los Angeles. I asked him what he wanted to be. He knew he did not want to be a lawyer. Why, then, I asked, was he thinking about getting an JD? He did not have a good answer. I encouraged him to just pursue the MBA. Today, he is a successful investment banker working in San Francisco. A law degree would have been a waste for him. Moreover, he might not have gotten his good banking job if the firm that hired him had seen he was getting a JD and wondered about his dedication to an investment banking career.

3. DECIDING ON A LAW SCHOOL

WHICH LAW SCHOOL SHOULD I GO TO?

IF YOU WERE to ask me "does it matter which law school I go to?" I would answer both "Yes, it will have a tremendous impact on your career" and "No, it doesn't really matter". Both answers would be right even though they seem inconsistent. I will explain.

The early years of your legal career can be affected tremendously by which law school you go to. In fact, the practice of law often seems like two different professions. Access to one of these professions is initially limited to graduates of top law schools while access to the other is open to everyone but generally is the domain of graduates of law schools known only locally or regionally. If you graduate from a top law school—for example Harvard, Columbia, Stanford, or Yale—you will be channeled toward the large urban law firms that hire almost exclusively from these schools. You will work there for a few years, a small

Which law school you went to has a much bigger impact on your career just after you graduate. Later on, it is what you have done with your degree rather than where you got it that matters.

number of you will make partner, and the remainder of you will go on to practice in smaller firms, join a government agency, or go in-house at a corporation.

If, on the other hand, you are a graduate of a less well-regarded local or regional school—Rutgers, or perhaps the University of Maryland—there is a much smaller chance you will find a job right out of law school with one of the more prestigious urban law firms. Of course, there are some notable exceptions. One excellent example is Valerie Caproni. A 1979 graduate of the University of Georgia law school, she clerked for a U.S. Circuit Court judge, worked as an associate at one of the most prestigious law firms in New York—Cravath, Swain & Moore—became a respected Assistant U.S. Attorney in New York, and then headed the SEC's Los Angeles office before becoming the FBI's general counsel. So, if you go to a second-tier law school but graduate at the very top of your class and work very hard, there is a chance you will land a job with a leading law firm. But this will require persistence, and a degree of luck that is difficult to bank on.

Leading law firms recruit on the campuses of a small number of top law schools.

The reality is that leading law firms recruit on campus at a small number of law schools. These are invariably the top national schools. Most of the firm's hiring comes out of this on-campus recruiting. Therefore, from the very start, the odds are against you if you go to a second tier school. Some good urban law firms hire from local law schools in addition to those with a strong national reputation. For example, the best New York firms (like Davis, Polk & Wardwell and Cravath, Swain & Moore) will hire the top graduates from Fordham University in Manhattan, and the top Miami law firms (like Greenberg, Traurig) will hire the students with the best grades at the University of Miami. This is due, at least in part, to the momentum that results from some of the partners having gone to those schools. In fact, many law firms go through a cycle in which they begin as smaller firms founded by local lawyers and only over decades grow to positions of national prominence. In such cases, the early partners may have gone to second-tier schools and have a propensity to hire at least the occasional graduate of their alma mater. But for the most part, graduates of lower-ranked law schools should plan to find positions with smaller, less prestigious, less well-paying law firms. On this basis, then, what law school you go to can have a major impact on your legal career.

The importance of which law school you attended has a "half life." After a few years, the law school you went to tends to have less of an impact on your job prospects. If you were a top graduate at Fordham and you went to a top law firm in New York, the fact you graduated from Fordham rather than Yale has very little—and, over time, even less—importance. It is, rather, what you accomplished in your job (Did you make partner? Did you win a big case?) that becomes more relevant. Law school success is, after all, a proxy for employers to gauge the probability of your success as a lawyer and, if you have succeeded as a lawyer, you have de facto proved your ability.

The importance of which law school you attended has a "half life."

Another thing to consider is that very few people stay at the same firm for their entire careers. In fact, firms will force out most associates after seven or eight years. Many of these individuals will go on to government agencies, where they will have the same jobs as (and maybe even report to) the graduates of other law schools, including second- and third-tier law schools, who might not have had the option to join prestigious private practices in leading firms. Because graduates of second-tier law schools are more likely to have gotten a government job directly after graduation from law school, due to the fact they were unable to land high paying associate positions in firms, they are more likely to have gained some level of seniority. So what you tend to have is former Columbia and Yale graduates who went to work for Davis, Polk finding themselves reporting to lawyers who graduated from Rutgers Law School the same year that they did but who went to work for the government agency directly.

WHAT ABOUT GOING TO YALE?

YALE IS THE best law school in the country. It is better than Harvard and it is better than Stanford. It is better even than Columbia! One can say all of this with complete confidence. It is better because it is harder to get into and because graduates of Yale—whether the law school or the undergraduate colleges—do extremely well in business, politics, and in particular the law. It is also reportedly a school that offers a solid learning environment that is largely free from the academic pressures of Harvard and Columbia. There are no real grades. Everyone is apparently brilliant, though, and the personal drive to learn seems to be enough to get the work done, or at least that is the official story. But, again, the school is very small, and competition for admission is among the fiercest of any school in the world.[1]

If you want to build a career in politics, and you can get in, then go to Yale Law School.

Certainly, if you want to build a career in politics, and you can get in, then go to Yale Law School. Yale University has dominated the upper echelons of politics in America for at least the last half century. Take as an example the 2004 presidential election. Both candidates were Yale men: John Kerry is a member of the class of 1966 and George W. Bush graduated in 1968. Howard Dean, the former governor of Vermont who was a leading contender for the Democratic nomination, was a member of the class of 1971. Vice President Dick Cheney attended Yale University for two years. Graduates of Yale Law School have met with similar success. Vice President Gerald Ford, who became president after Watergate forced Richard Nixon out of office, graduated from Yale Law School in January 1941. Bill Clinton was also a Yale Law School graduate, class of 1973.

Of course, graduates of other top schools like Harvard, Stanford, and Columbia do pretty well. John Roberts, the lawyer and judge whom President Bush picked to replace Chief Justice William Rehnquist on the Supreme Court, graduated from Harvard Law School in 1979 (and had clerked for Rehnquist after graduating and clerking for Judge Friendly). With his appointment, five members of the Supreme Court graduated from Harvard Law School. Stanford Law School has seen its share of Supreme Court Justices as well, including the former justices Sandra Day O'Connor and William Rehnquist. But if you want to have the most prestigious law degree, there is no substitute for Yale. Columbia Law School only has one Supreme Court Justice: Ruth Bader Ginsberg, and she started law school at Harvard before transferring to New York to join her husband. However, Columbia holds its own in the ranks of elected officials. George Pataki, a governor of New York State, graduated from Columbia Law in 1970, though he graduated from Yale as an undergraduate in 1967.

IS IT WORTH GOING TO LAW SCHOOL IF I CAN'T GET INTO A REALLY TOP LAW SCHOOL?

DON'T BE OVERLY focused on what law school you can get into. It seems important now but, in the future, it will seem much less critical. Let me give you an example. I went to Columbia Law School. After nearly ten years of working in law firms and running a small business, I found myself working at the Securities and Exchange Commission. My colleagues at the SEC included someone who went to Yale Law School, another who went to Ohio State University, a couple of women who went to Howard University Law School, and a dozen other people who went to various schools, including Columbia and American University. We all got paid the same. Our promotion prospects were all about equal, and certainly based on daily performance rather than academic pedigree. Many people who went to less-well-regarded law schools and who got worse grades than me do the exact same thing that I do and some have higher seniority and get paid more than I did. Thus, I can tell you that while the law school I went to felt important when I was applying to law schools and during the first two years after graduation, now, ten years later, it is just a footnote and an entry on a résumé that rarely gets read by anyone.

You can often accomplish as much—and sometimes more—from a third-tier law school as you can from a first-tier one. Many have.

That is not to say that it is not better to go to a top school than a poorly regarded one. It will be easier for you, for the rest of your career, if you go to Harvard versus Rutgers. However, you can often accomplish as much—and sometimes more— from a third-tier school as you can from a first-tier one. What you do with your career depends most on three things that have nothing (or at least very little) to do with where you went to school: how well you make a long-term plan for yourself, how determined you are to succeed, and your "luck." Luck is the most frustrating. And, of course, there is really no such thing. Luck is the intersection of opportunity and taking advantage of that opportunity.

DO I NEED TO GO TO AN ABA-ACCREDITED LAW SCHOOL?

I STRONGLY RECOMMEND that you go to a law school that is accredited by the American Bar Association (ABA). Most states (including New York) require that you graduate from an ABA-accredited law school before sitting for the bar. Many firms will only hire associates who went to an ABA-accredited law school (top firms will only hire associates who attended a nationally recognized law school or who graduated near the top of their class from a strong regional law school). One exception is in California, where some law schools are accredited by the California Bar Association (CBA) and not the ABA. In California, the CBA is very strong and you can sit for the California bar if you graduate from a CBA-accredited law school that is not ABA-accredited. However, I strongly recommend that you attend an ABA-approved school, if only to maintain as much professional flexibility as possible.

Consider, for example, where you may be five or more years from now. You want to join a firm in another state. Normally, you might have the option to "waive into" the bars of that other jurisdiction. Some states allow experienced attorneys to "waive into" their bars if they have, generally, at least five years of practice experience and are in good standing with their original state bar association. For example, Pennsylvania Bar Admission Rule 204 permits certain out-of-state lawyers to be admitted to the practice of law in Pennsylvania without having to take and pass the Pennsylvania state bar examination. But you probably won't be able to do this unless you attended an ABA-accredited law school. Sticking with the example, Pennsylvania requires any attorney who seeks to join the bar under Rule 204 to have graduated from an ABA-accredited law school, among other requirements. Thus, if you don't go to an ABA-accredited institution, the mark will follow you around for the remainder of your career.

It is not as though you do not have a large number of choices. You do. There are many ABA-accredited law schools. As a result, it is hard to imagine an excuse for not going to one of them if you intend to be a practicing attorney. As of February 2006 there were 193 law schools in the United States approved by the American Bar Association (up from 187 civilian law schools approved as of early 2004) plus the U.S. Army Judge Advocate General's school, which is also listed as "approved" but serves the specialized function of offering an officer's resident graduate course, which is a specialized program beyond the Juris Doctor degree and is available only to military attorneys. You can find a current list of the ABA-approved law schools at www.aba.org.

The Law School Admissions Counsel (LSAC) provides updated versions of the list of ABA-approved law schools as well as an online ABA-LSAC Official Guide that contains information about themselves provided by the ABA-approved law schools. You can view both the updated list and this guide at http://officialguide.lsac.org. If the LSAC site is not operating, or if you want a second opinion, you can also get information about ABA-approved law schools, including a list of approved schools and information about law schools that are "provisionally" approved, at www.abanet.org.[1] Note, however, that the ABA does not provide rankings for law schools and takes pains to distance itself from any rating system. The following disclaimer appears on the ABA's Web site, www.abanet.org:

> No rating of law schools beyond the simple statement of their accreditation status is attempted or advocated by the official organizations in legal education. Qualities that make one kind of school good for one student may not be as important to another. The American Bar Association and its Section of Legal Education and Admissions to the Bar have issued disclaimers of any law school rating system. Prospective law students should consider a variety of factors in making their choice among schools.

Nevertheless, law schools are obviously ranked—by applicants, by students, and by the employers that hire law students. Of these three, it is the opinions of the employers that hire law students that should be the most important to you. Law school is, after all, a professional school, and getting a law degree is usually the first step in embarking on a career as an attorney. You want to be able to get a job when you graduate and have as many avenues open to you as possible.

As a general rule, you should go to the best law school you can get into. Consider that no matter which law school you attend, you are going to be making about the same investment of time and money. Sure, some law schools are less expensive than others. State universities usually offer tuition breaks for students who have lived in-state for a period of time. And where two schools are nearly equally ranked and one is much more costly than another, the cost consideration might be determinative. But in general, take into account that law school is an investment, and a long-term one at that. You are only going to go to law school once. If you get into Harvard or Stanford, for example, you should bite the bullet, take out loans, and do whatever else you need to do in order to go to that top school over a local or regional law school. Short-term hardship will be rewarded with the increased opportunities you will enjoy over the length of your career.

While not all graduates of top law schools rise to the top of their professions, they have an initial advantage.

Elsewhere in this book I point out going to a top school is not a guarantee of success. In fact, many graduates of less-well-regarded schools do as well as or better in their careers than graduates of leading law schools. This is undeniable. But when you are considering what law school to go to, at that time you do not know what path your future career may follow. It is highly unlikely you will become an appellate or a Supreme Court law clerk or, eventually, a judge or justice unless you go to a top school. It will be much harder to get a job as an associate at a leading law firm in New York, Chicago, or Washington unless you graduate from a nationally ranked law school. While not all graduates of top law schools rise to the top of their professions, they have an initial advantage. The stakes are high enough that convenience and money alone are difficult bases on which to rationalize not going to the best law school you can get into.

WHAT ARE THE GENERAL CATEGORIES OF LAW SCHOOLS I CAN ATTEND IN CALIFORNIA?

FOR PRACTICAL REASONS, let's divide the world of law schools into three categories: those accredited by the ABA, those accredited by the California Bar Association, and those that are not accredited at all. We will tackle them in reverse order.

Unaccredited law schools are the least prestigious. While you can take the California bar examination after having attended an unaccredited school, you can't take the bar in most other states or waive into those states' bars unless you attended an ABA-accredited law school. There were eleven unaccredited law schools in California plus nine correspondence schools registered with the state bar as of mid-2006.[2] Despite the fact that these schools focus on training students to pass the California bar examination, only about 15 percent of such graduates usually do. Moreover, you are unlikely to get what most lawyers would consider a "real" legal education if you go to an unaccredited school. These schools often focus exclusively on training their students to pass the bar examination. This means the curriculum of these schools generally does not include instruction on legal theory and clinical, or practical, legal skills.

A second category of law school, which is unique to the State of California, is that accredited by the California Bar Association. While these schools are certainly more prestigious than are unaccredited law schools, they are generally not considered as good as ABA-accredited law schools by most legal practitioners. You can take the California bar examination but not the examinations of most other state bars if you go to a CBA-accredited school. At last count, there were twenty law schools accredited by the California Bar Association,[3] and about 30 percent of the students from these schools passed the California bar. Certainly, that is better than the unaccredited school pass rate. However, it is far below the results achieved by ABA-approved school graduates.

ABA-approved law schools are considered the most prestigious.

ABA-approved law schools are fully accredited and are considered the most prestigious of all general categories of law schools.[4] I cannot say it more simply: you should aspire to going to an ABA-accredited school. As I mentioned, most states will not let you take the bar examination unless you graduated from an ABA-accredited school. In addition, the legal education is far better. Despite the fact that ABA-accredited law schools do not focus exclusively on training their students to pass the bar examination, in California, as many as 80 percent of the graduates of ABA-accredited law schools end up passing the California bar exam. Keep in mind that ABA-accredited law schools in general and nationally ranked law schools in particular expect students to study for the bar examination on their own or with the help of a professional test preparation service, while focusing on a broad general legal education during class hours.

WHAT IS THE FUTURE OF THE UNACCREDITED LAW SCHOOLS?

UNACCREDITED LAW SCHOOLS, a class most common in the State of California, are under siege. An April 2006 cover story in the *California Bar Journal* bears the heading "Unaccredited law schools targeted in Sacramento."[5] The article highlights the fact that unaccredited law schools, despite focusing on training students to pass the California bar examination, have abysmal pass rates. It reports that at one unaccredited school, UC Irvine College of Law, only two graduates have passed the bar exam during the last nine years.[6] At another law school, Southern California Institute of Law in Santa Barbara, which is accredited by the California State Bar Association, the article reports that over the past nine years nine graduates passed and thirty-four graduates took the exam at least once. The bar exam pass rates for ten unaccredited California law schools discussed in the article were similarly disheartening. I have included those statistics in Appendix B.

Despite the obvious shortcomings of unaccredited schools, students continue to attend them. Some graduates of unaccredited law schools have resorted to litigation to try to obtain the right to sit for state bar examinations. These efforts have not met with much success. For example, on February 7, 2002, the Montana Supreme Court issued an order upholding the state bar's policy of allowing only those individuals who had graduated from an American Bar Association-accredited law school to sit for the Montana bar examination. The Montana law, Section 1(b) of the Rules for Admission, provided that an applicant for the bar "must have a Juris Doctor or equivalent degree from a law school accredited by the American Bar Association at the time of graduation." Note that this means the law school had to be accredited when the applicant graduated. If the school became accredited *after* the candidate graduated, that accreditation would not apply retroactively.

The petitioner in the Montana case had attended the University of West Los Angeles School of law (UWLA) located in Inglewood, California. UWLA was not accredited by the ABA but was accredited by the State Bar of California and regionally accredited by the Western Association of Schools and Colleges (WASC). In support of her application, the petitioner submitted a letter from UWLA's acting dean that stated, among other things, that UWLA graduates had a cumulative bar passage rate of approximately 70 percent, and that UWLA had not sought ABA accreditation because it wanted to focus its resources on helping students pass the bar examination in order to keep tuition costs down. The Montana court rejected the petition, finding that it could not independently determine whether schools not accredited by the ABA provided a quality legal education and also noting that UWLA was actually more expensive than many California schools and much more costly than the University of Montana's law school. (The court found that annual tuition and fees at UWLA totaled $14,260 while at UCLA the cost was $11,156, and at the University of Montana about $7,550.)

In addition to serving as a lesson as to why not to go to an unaccredited law school for practical reasons, the Montana Supreme Court case described above reveals something interesting about the true function of unaccredited law schools in California. The Montana decision attributes to the acting dean of UWLA the statement that UWLA's "freedom from ABA rules dictating the allocation of resources allows UWLA to keep tuition costs low and to *commit all the resources necessary to ensure that our graduates achieve commendable bar passage rates*" [emphasis added]. If you haven't figured it out yet I will tell you. These schools are first and foremost just three-year-long bar exam preparation classes in which students are taught specifically the topics that are tested on the California bar examination. This curriculum focus is in sharp contrast to the education received at top-ranked law schools, particularly at Yale, Chicago, Stanford, Harvard, and Columbia, where legal history, legal theory, and complex legal reasoning are taught and where students are mainly left to study on their own during the two-month period between their graduation in late May and the bar exam in July.

Studying for the bar exam does not prepare you very well to be an effective lawyer and may, ironically, not help you pass the bar exam any more than a broad legal education would. Unless you go to a school where you will be educated to be a lawyer, and not just taught to pass the bar examination, you are not doing yourself a service. I have observed firsthand students who went the route of just studying for the California bar examination. In January 2003, I sat for the California Bar Examination, which I took in San Diego over a three-day period. Many—it seemed most—of the other candidates taking the exam with me (and staying in the same hotel) had graduated from unaccredited or CBA-accredited schools. Some spoke freely about how their studies had focused specifically on strategies to pass the California bar. They had memorized relevant California codes and taken innumerable practice examinations. And yet, I observed two things. First, they were less able to discuss the practice of law and the theory of law than I would have expected. Second, most were taking the exam for at least the second or even the third time, having previously failed to pass. The California bar is a very difficult test, generally acknowledged to be the most difficult state bar exam in the country. In addition to the Multistate Bar Examination (which is multiple choice) there are two days of California-specific testing, including a day of essay questions. While many of the students who attended unaccredited schools in effect studied for the exam for three years, I passed the California bar on my first try after having studied for just three weeks. I attribute this, in part, to the benefits of a traditional legal education, which teaches candidates to think and not simply to memorize.

CAN I PRACTICE LAW WITHOUT EVER HAVING GONE TO LAW SCHOOL?

THERE ARE A couple of ways. A handful of states let individuals who have not gone to law school take the bar examination. Four states—California, Vermont, Virginia, and Washington State—let students apprentice for three or four years at private law firms or in a judge's chambers instead of going to law school. Of course, they still need to pass the state bar examination. People who study the law in this manner are called "law readers" and, while it may be attractive to think about avoiding high law school tuition and difficult law school exams, the practice remains uncommon. Published estimates show that fewer than 150 people are currently getting their legal education from programs that do not require law school, contrasted with more than 140,000 students who are attending ABA-approved law schools.[7] Results are also uncertain. Despite the fact that candidates have the option to spend most of their time just studying the topics tested on the bar examination, only a small percentage of law readers end up passing bar examinations. For example, only one out of nine law readers passed the Virginia bar examination in 2004.[8]

In addition, New York, Maine, and Wyoming provide for non-law school graduates to take bar exams, but generally require that they have at least some formal classroom legal education. For example, the rules for taking the New York state bar examination, set forth in the Rules of the Court of Appeals for the Admission of Attorneys and Counselors at Law, provide four ways that you can qualify to sit for the bar. First, as in any bar exam, you can graduate from an ABA-approved law school. Second, as in most states, you can graduate from an unapproved law school and practice for five years in another domestic jurisdiction to which you are admitted.[9] Third, more uncommonly, you can have the equivalent of a three-year legal education from a foreign law school that is approved by the relevant foreign jurisdiction or be admitted to practice law in a foreign jurisdiction and also receive the equivalent of an LL.M degree in American law.[10] Fourth, you can combine law school and law office study.[11] This last is what interests us here.

Under Section 520.4 of the New York Rules of the Court of Appeals, you are qualified to sit for the bar if you meet the following criteria: you began the study of law after your eighteenth birthday, you successfully completed at least one year of study in a full-time program or the equivalent in a part-time program at an ABA-approved law school and at the conclusion of that year were eligible to continue in that school's JD program, and after that year of legal study you continued to study law in a law office located in New York State under the supervision of one or more attorneys admitted to practice law in New York State, for a period of time, together with the time spent studying at an approved law school, totaling four years. Thus, for example, if you finish two complete years of law school, New York allows you to sit for the bar if you then skip your third year of law school and instead spend two years studying law in a private law office in New York State.

Of course, if you consider pursuing this course to New York bar membership, you need to carefully review all of the relevant provisions of the Appellate Rules. The Court of Appeals is very particular that its rules be followed. For example, upon commencing law study in a private

Fewer than 150 people are currently getting their legal education from programs that do not require law school, contrasted with more than 140,000 students who are attending ABA-approved law schools.

office, your supervising attorney has the responsibility of filing a Certificate of Commencement with the Clerk of the Court of Appeals certifying that your clerkship is about to commence and disclosing the amount of credit you are entitled to for prior law school class time. If this certificate is not filed and you discover it only after you have spent some years in an apprenticeship, you may find that the Court of Appeals will not give you credit for time served. The same warning of carefully complying with the rules applies to any state in which you consider pursuing a nontraditional route to bar membership.

In general, as with unaccredited law schools, I recommend against pursuing an apprenticeship as a means to obtaining bar membership. You will learn a lot in law school that is not tested on the bar examination but that is invaluable for your career development. You will have the opportunity to debate important Supreme Court decisions with fellow students, absorb varying opinions and approaches from diverse faculty members, and participate in events such as mock trials and law review editorial boards that will sharpen your thinking and writing skills. Upon graduation, you will have a network of classmates and fellow alums who may become your greatest resource. In contrast, if you study in one small law office, you may learn enough about the specific subjects tested on the bar to pass that test, but you will not receive the well-rounded education that is really required of any decent lawyer today. You will also be highly influenced by the individual attorney or attorneys who instruct you and may not be challenged into thinking for yourself. Nevertheless, it remains true that some great Americans, including President Abraham Lincoln, learned the law through an apprenticeship rather than through formal academic legal study. But times have changed since the mid-nineteenth century. Employers today expect associates to have earned their JD. It is difficult to imagine that any respectable law firm today would hire a lawyer who had not graduated from law school. An exception might be a family-run firm in which the candidate studies under the tutelage of a parent, with the knowledge that he or she will inherit the family practice. Even then, however, one has to wonder whether the family firm's clients will be adequately served.

You will learn a lot in law school that is not tested on the bar examination but that is invaluable for your career development.

4. SOME SOCIAL ISSUES TO CONSIDER

I AM A WOMAN. WHAT SHOULD I TAKE INTO CONSIDERATION BASED ON MY GENDER?

TIMES HAVE CERTAINLY changed for women in the law. Fifty years ago there were very few opportunities for women to advance in the legal profession. It was only in 1953 that women were first admitted to Harvard Law School, for example.[1] Ruth Bader Ginsberg, who started her legal education at Harvard Law School, made Law Review there, transferred to Columbia Law to be with her husband, made Law Review again there, and graduated tied for first in her class. Even so, she could not find a job with a New York law firm upon graduation. In fact, the future Supreme Court justice reportedly could not even get a clerkship interview with any of the Supreme Court justices.[2]

Women have made great strides in the legal profession over the past several decades. Whereas before about 1980 the practice of law was by and large a male-dominated arena, today a significant number of female attorneys work in both private firms and government agencies. This trend is likely to continue. In fact, about half of all law school graduates in 2005 were women. A 2003 study by the U.S. Equal Employment Opportunity Commission entitled *Diversity in Law Firms* illustrates the point.[3] The EEOC study found that, since 1975, the representation of female lawyers practicing in large law firms has increased substantially. Specifically, the percentage of female attorneys working in law firms grew from 14.4 percent in 1975 to 40.3 percent in 2002. The EEOC study also found that the percentage of female law students increased from 33 percent of students in 1982 to 48.3 percent of students in 2002.

The percentage of female attorneys working in law firms grew from 14.4 percent in 1975 to 40.3 percent in 2002. The percentage of female law students who were female increased from 33 percent of students in 1982 to 48.3 percent of students in 2002.

While the number of women practicing law has increased, they continue to face issues and obstacles that are unique to their sex. There are several reasons that women face different concerns from men. Most obviously, in our society, women continue to play a more active role in raising children then men do. Women still reportedly provide 70 to 80 percent of child care.[4] A male attorney who has a child may be out of work for a week, whereas a female attorney is more likely to be out of the office for a longer period of time during her pregnancy, and after giving birth she may want to dedicate comparatively more time to rearing the child. This translates into longer maternity leaves than paternity leaves and a greater tendency among female attorneys to seek part-time work schedules while their children are young. This, in turn, has an impact on the career development of some female lawyers.

Scholars have concluded that the maternal obligations of women can have a deleterious effect on their careers in a number of disciplines, and law is no exception. Joan Williams, a 1985 graduate of Harvard Law School and a professor of law at American University's Washington College of Law wrote in 2000 that twice the percentage of men as women from her class reported both having children and making partner in a law firm. She also found that, of the graduates of her class who entered academia, one out of three men but only one out of twenty women were teaching at elite law schools.[5] Williams attributed this inequity largely to men needing less time off in connection with the birth of a child and the inflexibility of employers, whether law firms or academic institutions—in not providing special career tracks for women seeking to work part time during the approximately twenty years needed to raise a child.

Law firms are generally pretty flexible in dealing with female attorneys who want to reduce their workload after having children. Most firms allow women to work part-time schedules. Certain practice areas, such as regulatory work or intellectual property law, are more conducive to part-time schedules than other disciplines, such as litigation and M&A transactional work. However, female lawyers complain that part-time firm work often evolves into full-time work for part-time pay, as client demands cause them to work the same hours they did before the schedule change.

Some women make partner, have children, and eventually give up their partnership positions in order to be stay-at-home parents. These women decide that it is simply untenable to both work for a firm and care for young children. Compelling arguments can be made that having your children raised by the nanny is not in the children's best interest. In cases such as this—and in one case in particular that I observed directly—senior female associates expressed great distress that a woman recently made a partner would give up her position to have children. These associates felt that it would reduce the chance of other women in the firm to be seriously considered for partnership. However, after a couple of years of women regularly being made partner in this leading Washington firm, it is now safe to conclude that one young female partner giving up a partnership in order to raise a family had no effect on the decision-making processes of the partnership committee with respect to female candidates.

IS GOVERNMENT SERVICE AN ATTRACTIVE OPTION FOR WOMEN?

An EEOC study identified several interesting trends. First, the study found that white women[6] specifically are more likely to be employed by the government than are white men. The study reported that, as of 1995, 20.7 percent of white women lawyers were employed by the government compared with just 7.6 percent of white men.[7] The study did not provide data showing the percentage of attorneys at various government agencies who were white females, nor did it address the employment of nonwhite women.

Several factors may help to explain why a larger percentage of female than male attorneys choose to enter government service. For one thing, women may be more willing than men to take the pay cut that comes from leaving the private practice and entering government employment. That pay cut can be significant—from over $200,000 for a mid-level attorney at a private law firm to about $100,000 for a government staff attorney. Also, new mothers may value the flexible schedule of government jobs more than do men. Many government jobs require only regular nine-to-five business hours. Federal government jobs also allow for "flex" schedules that give a day off every other week. Men may not be as willing or able to trade their high private-sector pay for a more flexible schedule.

As of 1995, 20.7 percent of white women lawyers were employed by the government compared with just 7.6 percent of white men.

DO WOMEN DO BETTER IN LARGE FIRMS THAN IN SMALLER FIRMS?

WOMEN HAVE GENERALLY done better in large, urban law firms than they have in smaller, less urban firms. This conclusion is supported by both anecdotal and quantifiable information. Some of the likely reasons for this may be the same reasons women have excelled in public-sector legal jobs. Elite law firms, like the government, tend to be more progressive, more responsive to social changes, and larger and therefore better able to absorb the risk that any given woman might be more likely than a man to leave after receiving expensive job training in order to raise a family than are smaller firms.

Large, nationally known law firms generally have a higher proportion of women than do smaller, regional firms.

A 2003 study by the EEOC found that large, nationally known law firms generally have a higher proportion of women than do smaller, regional firms.[8] This study found that whereas in 1980 only 23.2 percent of associates in elite law firms were female, by 1990 36.2 percent of associates in such firms were women.[9] This shows an increasing trend over a fairly short period of time. The trend has, moreover, continued such that today, at least half of all associates entering elite law firms are female.

There are several reasons that elite law firms are hiring and promoting a greater percentage of women than smaller and less prestigious law firms. Generally, though, the most elite law firms are also large, urban law firms. These firms tend to hire a large portion of the top graduates of the most well-respected law schools. Since about half of the graduates of these law schools are women, it is practically inevitable that the top firms would hire associates representative of the overall law school population, or else lose out on half of the potential applicants.

Large firms depend upon the constant inflow of new associates from law schools. Their business model demands a constant replenishing of junior-level attorneys. Some firms hire as many as thirty graduates of top law schools each year, far more than will eventually make partner. Smaller firms, however, have much more modest hiring needs. They also have less of a chance of tempting graduates of the top law schools. In addition, their turnover rate is much lower. As a result, they have a greater opportunity to hire only a small number of associates, usually male.

But why would they want to do this? Female attorneys are, by any observable measure, at least as capable as men. The answer may lie in economics. Large law firms expect a high rate of turnover in their associates—indeed, they depend upon it. They can easily absorb the cost of training associates only to have them leave a few years later. This is a cost—and a risk—that most smaller firms can not support. Smaller firms generally hire just a small number of associates—perhaps just one or two—in any given year. A smaller firm may not want to take the risk of training a new associate only to have that associate leave soon after.

For various reasons, a firm may calculate that the risk of a twenty-five-year-old female associate leaving after working for a few years is greater than the risk of a male associate doing so. Smaller firms, because they can't afford to train people and then lose them, may put significantly more emphasis on evaluating whether a prospective associate is likely to stick around for the long term. A female associate leaving to have a child might ask to work part time, or might decide to cease practicing law altogether. A smaller firm that has experienced the early loss of a valued female associate may be much more likely to hold this against future female applicants than a larger firm. This may well lead the smaller firm to disfavor hiring additional female associates.

WHAT IMPACT DOES HAVING A CHILD HAVE ON A WOMAN'S LEGAL CAREER?

HAVING CHILDREN DOES not need to end or even significantly interrupt a woman's legal career. In fact, give the increasing number of women entering the legal profession (and progressing to partnership), most firms have already addressed the fact that they need to focus on retaining valued female attorneys after they have children. In addition, it is becoming increasingly common for men to take on a significant burden in rearing children. If you are a female attorney and have a strong career trajectory, you and your spouse might want to consider having you continue working while your husband stays home with the children. This might work particularly well if you can alternate sabbaticals.

Firms, particularly large ones, commonly allow female attorneys to take on a part-time schedule so that they can participate in raising children. As with anything, however, firms take various approaches. If you are female and think you may want to have children while continuing in your career, then you should talk to female attorneys who work for the firm you are considering joining. Ask how the firm accommodates women who want to work part time to raise children. Are the other partners receptive to this? Will working part time take you off the partnership track? How long can you take a sabbatical? If you are already a partner, ask whether going part time will mean that you have to surrender part of your partnership earnings. Get comfortable with the answers before you accept the offer.

While the legal profession can be highly—even notoriously—demanding, many firms have found that it is worthwhile to grant female attorneys the flexibility they need to simultaneously work and raise children. Consider that more than half of all law school graduates are now women. Large firms compete actively with each other to recruit the top law school graduates. Receiving poor marks on associate surveys in the category of being a good place for women to work could make it difficult for a top firm to recruit its share of top law school graduates. Half the graduates could write off such a firm. No leading law firm would take such a risk. Moreover, many women consider having children at the time they are reaching a level of authority in their firms. From positions as junior partners or partners, they have the ability to directly influence and even shape firm policies regarding adopting flexible schedules for working mothers. Given these factors, it should not be surprising that some of the nation's best law firms are also some very good places for professional women to work.

Whether a firm is likely to grant a working mother flexible office hours depends on several factors. One of them is the size of the firm. Larger firms will have a greater capacity to grant flexible schedules because there will always be other lawyers who can fill in when clients' demands arise. A second factor is the practice area. Women who are litigators, for example, will have a hard time working on a flexible schedule because judges tend to set hearings based on their own busy dockets rather than on the schedules of the counsel appearing before them. Moreover, trial deadlines are set under the applicable (civil or criminal) rules of procedure. Thus, in litigation and other time-sensitive practice areas, it is often simply not an option to work part time. In other areas, such as appellate, trusts and estates, and intellectual property work, it can be quite easy for a lawyer to work on a part-time or flexible schedule.

However, working part time can have one major pitfall. While firms frequently grant part-time work schedules at part-time pay, it is more than usual that part-time work expands to full-time very quickly. This is a product of the significant demands clients commonly place on their favorite lawyers. As a result, many female lawyers who start working three or four days a week find themselves migrating toward a much fuller work load. Three days a week becomes four days plus nights and weekends. Billable hours increase from 1,000 to 1,800 hours a year. And, often, salaries are lower, as they remain pegged to a part-time schedule. Women who are looking forward to having families may want to investigate the part-time scheduling policies of the firm and in particular to understand whether there is real dedication to allowing "part time" to remain "part time," including whether other partners will help to insulate female partners from the demands of overly aggressive clients.

ARE LAW FIRMS REALLY INTERESTED IN CREATING AN ETHNICALLY DIVERSE WORKFORCE?

LARGE FIRMS CERTAINLY are interested in creating an ethnically diverse workforce, for a number of reasons. First, many lawyers at large firms think it is the right thing to do. Second, large firms face potential legal liability if they do not have minority attorneys because this opens them up to charges that they discriminate in hiring, whether or not that is actually true. Third, if law firms do not hire minority applicants, they are missing out on a large segment of potential associate candidates. Minority law school students may take a greater interest in firms that already employee a number of minority attorneys. Fourth, having certain minorities as employees can open up business development opportunities, such as having a Chinese-American partner make a pitch to a company based in China, or bringing a Hispanic associate to a meeting with potential Latin American clients. The diversity of the American work force is a key competitive advantage that most large law firms have not failed to recognize.

One testament to the increase in interest in minority hiring is an e-mail I recently received promoting a seminar titled "Achieving Diversity in Your Law Firm: Hiring and Retaining the Best." This seminar (for which I was to receive continuing education credit) urged that "Failing to meet corporate diversity requirements can mean the difference between winning and losing business" and promised that my colleagues and I would discover:

- "Proven strategies to recruit and retain a diverse workplace;
- Best practices of law firms that have been successful in creating diversity;
- Which and how much firm resources to dedicate to diversity efforts; and
- How to protect your best diversity associates from poaching."

That such a seminar can attract sufficient interest from lawyers to be commercially viable suggests that increasing or maintaining ethnic diversity is a priority among firms. The example also shows that firms compete for the best minority applicants, particularly after they prove themselves as junior associates. This is the reason for the seminar's emphasis on preventing firms from "poaching"—stealing away—minority employees.

ARE THERE PARTICULAR TYPES OF EMPLOYERS OR FIELDS OF PRACTICE THAT OFFER BETTER OPPORTUNITIES FOR MINORITY LAWYERS?

MEMBERS OF MINORITY groups practice in every area of the law today. Nevertheless, there are some areas in which minorities have had greater success than others, though much of the information on this is anecdotal.

First, consider that minorities have increased their representation in the legal field significantly over the last several decades. A 2003 study conducted by EEOC found that, since 1975, the number of African-American, Hispanic, and Asian-American lawyers practicing with large law firms increased substantially. The study found the percentage of law degree recipients who were African Americans increased from 4.2 percent in 1982 to 7.2 percent in 2002, that the percentage of Hispanics increased from 2.3 percent to 5.7 percent over the same time interval, and that the percentage of Asian Americans rose from 1.3 percent to 6.5 percent.

The fact that more minorities are graduating from law schools today does not, of course, necessarily mean they are distributed evenly among all legal fields and all types of legal employers. It might be anticipated, for example, that a greater number of minority lawyers would go back to practice law in the underserved communities from which they came, perhaps as solo practitioners, rather than going to work for large corporate law firms. However, while some young lawyers certainly are returning to serve their birth populations, statistics suggest that many minority law school graduates are joining larger law firms. A 2003 study entitled Diversity in Law Firms conducted by the U.S. Equal Employment Opportunity Commission found the percentage of practicing attorneys who are ethnic minorities has increased in recent years across the board, including at law firms. The study found the number of African Americans working as lawyers in law firms increased from 2.3 percent in 1975 to 4.4 percent in 2002, that the number of Hispanics rose from 0.7 percent to 2.9 percent over that period, and that the number of Asian Americans increased—perhaps the most significantly—from just 0.5 percent to 5.3 percent.

> The percentage of law degree recipients who were African Americans increased from 4.2 percent in 1982 to 7.2 percent in 2002, the percentage of Hispanics increased from 2.3 percent to 5.7 percent, and the percentage of Asian Americans rose from 1.3 percent to 6.5 percent.

The number of
African Ameri-
cans working as
lawyers in law
firms increased
from 2.3 percent
in 1975 to 4.4
percent in 2002,
the number of
Hispanics rose
from 0.7 percent
to 2.9 percent,
and the number of
Asian Americans
increased from
just 0.5 percent
to 5.3 percent.

In fact, the EEOC diversity study found evidence that the hiring of women and minority lawyers was unevenly distributed between large and small firms. The study showed that law firms that were larger and had more offices hired significantly greater numbers of female and minority lawyers. This finding is not particularly surprising considering that many smaller firms are essentially family-run, multigenerational enterprises, or else dominated by a small cadre of senior lawyers. Larger firms, on the other hand, may tend to be more representative of the broader population, or at least the population of law school graduates, and are generally run more democratically and with, perhaps, more of a profit maximization objective in mind. Large law firms competing with other firms to hire the few top graduates of the most prestigious law schools simply have no choice but to hire minorities and women graduating from those programs or else to artificially diminish the pool of potential associates. Consistent with that theory, the EEOC study found the locations, prestige, and earnings rankings of firms had an effect on both the number of minority legal professionals and the number of female lawyers, with the more prestigious and higher-earning firms hiring more of both, but that these factors had more of an effect on the percentage of minorities hired than on the number of women.

Taking this into account, if you are a minority and are graduating from a top legal program, you should consider your chances of landing a job at a top urban law firm on a par with your white male counterparts. Moreover, you should consider that there will be many mentoring and networking opportunities involving members of most any major ethnic group. While it may remain true today that there are disproportionately more white male partners at major firms, considering the long gestation period for maturing young lawyers into partners, it seems likely that the ranks of minority partners will grow as minority associates gain experience and seniority.

I AM GAY. WHAT IMPACT WILL THAT HAVE ON MY LEGAL CAREER?

THE ANSWER IS that it depends—maybe not at all, maybe a lot. I have practiced with a number of attorneys who are homosexual and have spoken with them about their experience. In general, gay attorneys report that the cultural environment at large law firms located in major urban centers on both coasts—including Washington, New York, Chicago, San Francisco, and Los Angeles—is generally quite liberal and accepting with sexual orientation basically a nonissue. In my experience, I have observed that being a homosexual does not appear to have posed an insurmountable obstacle to advancement for at least some of the gay attorneys I have known, particularly at the larger, more prestigious law firms.[10]

For example, there were two associates at my first law firm in class years close to mine who were openly gay and who both made partner. Many heterosexual associates in those same class years did not make partner. This should not be surprising if you keep in mind that law is a business. The fact that the homosexual attorneys contributed to the business success of the firm likely weighed much more than their personal lives in the decision about whether the partnership was willing to admit them.

However, note that in January 2007, & associate who is gay sued one of the largest New York law firms—Sullivan & Cromwell—for sexual orientation discrimination (see "Gay Lawyer: Firm Mistreated Me, Legal Powerhouse Sullivan and Cromwell Rocked by Sexual Orientation Discrimination Suit," abcnews.go.com, January 18, 2007). While the law firm denies the allegations, the suit raises concerns. (Sullivan & Cromwell has been a supporter of the Lesbian and Gay Law Association of New York, has other openly gay associates and partners, and generally enjoys a good reputation among gay attorneys.)

Regionally, and firm-by-firm within any region, there will be a great deal of variability with regard to how well homosexuality is received. Fortunately, there is an easy way to compile a list of law firms that are gay friendly. NALP, the Association for Legal Career Professionals,[11] compiles a significant amount of information on law firms. Among other things, it maintains a Gay/Lesbian/Bisexual/Transgendered Contact List that you can access at www.nalp.org. This list contains contact information for a large number of gay-oriented professional and law school organizations and is maintained by NALP's GLBT Committee. NALP also publishes *Resources/Organizations for Building Relationships with the GLBT Community.*

However, what may be of most direct use to you may be the NALP forms themselves. These are the single-page forms that every law firm completes. These should be on file with your law school's placement office. An example of a real NALP form is attached as Appendix B. Most law schools even print a book for interviewing students that compiles the NALP Forms of the law firms that are coming on campus to interview. Among the information reported is the number of openly gay attorneys who are partners, of counsel, and associates. Thus, the form lets you determine whether attorneys at the firm feel free to state openly that they are gay, gives you a picture of whether associates who are openly gay are being promoted to partner, and gives you information about whether, in the future, there may be greater acceptance of homosexuality (for example, if there are multiple openly gay associates but no gay partners yet).

5. IMPROVING YOUR CHANCES OF LAW SCHOOL ADMISSION

HOW CAN I IMPROVE MY CHANCES OF GETTING INTO LAW SCHOOL?

THERE ARE SO many law schools out there that you are virtually certain to gain acceptance to one of them. But the real question here is how to get into the best law school. Another, related, question is whether you need to get into a law school of a certain caliber in order to justify the time and effort of going to law school. The answer to the second question hinges on your career goals and expectations.

First, the easy answer. Most law schools—from top national schools like Yale and Columbia to regional schools like New Jersey's Seton Hall—care a great deal about the raw statistics of applicants. These statistics come in two forms: LSAT scores and undergraduate GPAs. Statistics on the students accepted by law schools are tracked and reported by various authorities, including the popular *U.S. News & World Report* surveys, that rank law schools against their peers. What this means for you is that law schools are going to base their admissions decisions largely on your LSAT score and GPA.

You need to view your LSAT score and your grades as the bedrock of your law school application. Also keep in mind that law school admissions officers will take into account any upward trend in your undergraduate GPA. For example, if you had a C average during your freshman and sophomore years when you were a premed major but you then switched to a political science major in your junior year and improved to an A-minus GPA, you can argue that you should be judged as an A-minus student rather than as a B-minus student for the purpose of law school admissions. Make certain, if you can show this kind of upward trend, that you articulate the reason for it in your law school essays. Also, in the event you are fortunate enough to be planning your law school ascension while still an undergraduate, take some classes in which you are naturally strong in order to push up your GPA in those last few semesters. Remember, you can always put off law school for a year so that your senior year grades will be counted (they won't be considered if you apply and are accepted during your senior year). And keep in mind that the weight placed on freshman year grades can almost always be minimized by arguing that you were adjusting to college life.

> The weight placed on freshman-year grades can almost always be minimized by arguing that you were adjusting to college life.

WHAT IMPACT CAN COLLEGE INTERNSHIPS HAVE ON MY CHANCE OF GAINING ADMISSION TO LAW SCHOOL?

YOU CAN ALSO increase your chances of gaining admission to law school if you have the right kind of summer or school-year internship experience during your junior year before you graduate. This may take some networking, but it can be done if you are willing to do the legwork and are financially able to work without pay. Also, keep in mind that the right internship may make more of a difference with law schools that are not in the very top tier. First-tier schools are going to be more concerned with your having the threshold academic credentials; it may make the difference if you are on the cusp of admission at a first-tier school and you otherwise have the requisite good grades and LSAT scores.

The internships I have in mind are with known regulatory agencies, judges, and top law firms. An internship at the Securities and Exchange

Commission, for example, shows a level of understanding of a very important area of regulatory law (that you know the SEC exists and generally what it does is a big step above what most law school applicants know) and can be leveraged if you know how. For example, if you were to get an internship with the SEC and befriend some of the attorneys there, you might find out where they went to law school. Ask them who their securities law professor was. Then, when you apply to that law school, call up the law professor and introduce yourself. Say you got to know so-and-so, their former student, who is now at the SEC (or whatever regulatory agency you were able to get an internship with). The professor may not know that his former student is at the SEC—or even remember his former student—but he will feel good that someone he has taught is out in the world in a position of authority making a difference. Tell the professor you are looking forward to the prospect of taking his class, and ask him if he has any admissions advice. Perhaps he knows someone in the admissions office; don't be shy about asking if you feel the conversation is going well. Perhaps you will even be on campus and you could stop by and talk to the professor in person (if you do be sure to read up on their latest law review publications and be prepared to discuss the issues that are important to that professor in an informed and intelligent manner). The professor will likely become your strongest advocate from inside the institution and your chance of gaining admission will increase exponentially.

HOW IMPORTANT ARE GRADES WHEN APPLYING TO LAW SCHOOL?

GRADES ARE ONE of the two factors, the other being your Law School Admissions Test (LSAT) score, that admissions committees give great weight to in considering your law school application. In general, grades are a more important part of a law school application than they are of applications to other professional schools, a case in point being business schools. This is because going to law school, and pursuing a legal career, is more of a pure academic pursuit than going to business school or entering into a business career, in which case worldly skills, such as natural leadership ability, play a more crucial role in determining success. In addition, law schools are ranked primarily in terms of how competitive they are to get into, and this competitiveness is defined largely in terms of the average LSAT and undergraduate GPA of the school's admitted students.

But you knew that grades were important. The real question is, how deeply below the surface do most law schools look in analyzing the quality of your undergraduate academic program rather than simply looking to the end result, your GPA number? Specifically, you might ask whether it is better to have a 4.0 GPA and a Bachelor of Arts degree in sociology or a 3.0 GPA and a Bachelor of Science degree in physics. Similarly, you might ask whether it is better to have a 4.0 GPA at the University of Wisconsin, a good but not great school, or a 3.0 GPA at the significantly more prestigious Princeton University. These are, after all, the real questions that may affect your long-term decision-making, particularly if you are fortunate enough to be planning early on from the position of being a high school senior or in your first couple of years at college. You will likely find that my analysis, though practical, raises considerable controversy when mentioned to law school admissions officials and undergraduate academicians.

While, undeniably, the combination of a 4.0 GPA in physics from Princeton conveys the strongest impression of academic aptitude of any of the scenarios I set forth above, the reality is that a 4.0 from the University of Wisconsin in sociology is nearly as unassailable, as long as you have the LSAT score to back it up. Keep in mind that your immediate objectives in supplying statistics to the law school of your choice are to convince the admissions committee that you have the intellectual capacity to perform well in their school and that you have the statistics to improve, or at least not harm, the GPA and LSAT averages for admitted students.

It may also be a positive attribute of your application that, as long as you have the grades and test scores, you are from a school that does not traditionally send a lot of students to a particular law school. Top law schools like to be able to advertise that they draw their students from a large number of undergraduate colleges and universities. These schools do not want all of their students to come from a handful of Ivy League and Seven Sisters schools, even though a large block of the students inevitably will come from those institutions. Admissions counselors know that many brilliant students cannot afford to attend any but a local or state school and they will therefore give you the benefit of the doubt about your institution so long as you have top grades and scores. Moreover, as long as you can articulate a reason for choosing that sociology major—or whatever major—it does not really matter to the law school what you chose to study as an eighteen-year-old. They are going to look at your raw statistics, and your GPA is always going to be one of those two key numbers.

That is not to say that the caliber of your undergraduate school, or the rigor of your undergraduate major, will not be taken into account at all. There are reasons that a large number of Columbia Law School students were educated at Harvard, Princeton, Yale, and Columbia itself as undergraduates. However, part of the reason for this concentration of students from this small club of schools is that it was difficult to get into those schools and the vast majority of the students there are very intelligent. Other schools may have only a small percentage of students with the same academic ability. Law schools would like to accept those small numbers of qualified students. Since it is hard to compare grades received at a school like Princeton with those from a school like the University of Wisconsin, law school admissions counselors are going to likely put a greater emphasis on LSAT scores in comparing the applicants from diverse backgrounds. Nevertheless, a top law school is only going to take a close look at a University of Wisconsin applicant who has very good grades.

Let me provide an illustrative example before moving on. My cousin attended Monmouth College in New Jersey during the mid-1980s. That school was later renamed Monmouth University, but it remains, at best, a third- or fourth-tier college and at the time my cousin was applying to law school was just slightly above a community college in terms of academic reputation. I don't believe that many, or perhaps even any, other graduates of Monmouth College have ever gone on to attend Columbia Law School. However, my cousin had earned close to a 4.0 GPA and had gotten a very high LSAT score: 46 out of a possible 48 points on the scale in use at that time. He was accepted at Columbia, and waitlisted at

Harvard. He eventually was accepted off the waiting list at Harvard but by that time had committed himself to Columbia, from which he graduated as a Harlan Fiske Stone Scholar, which is a very respectable academic honor. The lesson is that it was not the kiss of death for him to have attended a very mediocre regional college because he was able to present the necessary GPA and LSAT scores. Moreover, he was sufficiently prepared to perform well at Columbia—a fact that likely will have made it easier for the admissions committee to accept future qualified applicants from Monmouth College/University.

WHAT IS THE LSAT?

THE LAW SCHOOL Admissions Test (LSAT) is administered by the Law School Admissions Council (LSAC), a nonprofit group based about thirty miles north of Philadelphia. LSAC counts among its members about 200 law schools, primarily in the United States but also in Canada. Taking the LSAT is a little like taking a really hard version of the Verbal part of the SAT. About 150,000 LSATs are taken each year. The test is given four times a year at test centers around the United States and abroad. All law schools that are members of LSAC require applicants to take the LSAT, with the majority requiring that it be taken by December of the year prior to that in which admission is sought. However, most college students take the test in the summer prior to their senior year of college so they have time after classes end in the spring to dedicate all of their time to studying for the LSAT.

About 150,000 LSATs are taken each year.

Law schools claim that the LSAT helps them make informed admission decisions by providing a standard basis on which to judge applicants. It is designed to test basic reading and verbal reasoning skills that law schools use to determine an applicant's general ability to do law school work. Since applicants come from a broad range of backgrounds and majors, the test is a useful standard measure of preparedness. While law schools are always quick to point out that the LSAT is not the only criteria considered for admission, in reality it is often the most important one, particularly where a school is keen to maintain or rise in the rankings of what law schools are "best."

In any ranking system, it is necessary that the "best" law schools have the highest average LSAT scores for admitted students.

The test has 100 questions and takes three hours and twenty-five minutes. It consists of five thirty-five-minute multiple-choice sections followed by a thirty-minute writing sample. It is a standardized test designed to measure an applicant's ability to read and understand complex factual scenarios; organize information; draw reasonable conclusions; and evaluate the strength of various arguments. Only four of the five multiple-choice sections are actually graded; the fifth serves as a basis for determining the fairness of possible future test questions. However, students taking the test never know which section will not be graded (otherwise no one would complete this section, instead saving their mental energy for the graded parts). Copies of the writing section are provided to the law schools to which a candidate applies but are not graded by LSAC.

The LSAT is scored on a scale from 120 to 180. The score has several components. . First, there is a "raw" score, which is the number you answered correctly out of 100. LSAC compares your raw score with all others taking that LSAT to calculate your "scaled score" of between 1 and 180. LSAC then calculates your Percentile, which ranks your performance against all others who took that particular exam. For example, a Raw 77 might equate to a Scaled 175 and a Percentile of 95. This means you got more correct answers than 95 percent of the other test takers on the LSAT that day. The Percentile is the number used by law schools in reviewing your application.

HOW IMPORTANT IS MY LSAT SCORE?
Your LSAT score is probably the single most important factor in whether you get into the law school of your choice. I know this is a strong statement, and some admissions counselors may disagree with it, but if you think about it, it makes a lot of sense. Grades, activities, and essays certainly also play a role in law school admissions decisions. And where a group of candidates have LSAT scores that are nearly the same, say, within a standard deviation of each other, these other factors will be determinative. However, activities and essays—and even grades—are

considerably "softer" than are LSAT scores, which means they are more subjective, and harder to compare against a broad group of candidates.

Law school admissions counselors want to pick students who will, above all, be able to perform exceptionally well in the academically rigorous environment of law school. To succeed in law school, a student needs to be both smart and hardworking, in that order. Incidentally, these are the same characteristics—smarts and work ethic—that are required for success as a practicing lawyer. As a result, the criteria for law school admission line up quite nicely with the criteria for employment by leading law firms. Law schools have found that good performance on the LSAT is a very good predictor of aptitude for law school performance, and thus for admission. In short, law schools see the LSAT as the litmus test for law school performance and law firms see law school performance (grades) as the litmus test for legal practice performance.

While it is important to have top grades—particularly for the very best law schools—top grades without a correspondingly high LSAT score may not be enough to get you in. Those of you with very good college grades may disagree with the statement that the LSAT is the best predictor of academic success in law school. You may reason that past academic success is the best predictor of future academic success, and you would have a defensible argument. However, law school classes tend to be very different from most college courses. The Socratic method—in which teachers call on students unannounced to discuss complex issues of law on the spot—requires very fast thinking. The logic behind many legal subjects—including, notably, subjects like property, tax, and securities law—requires strong reasoning skills. Law schools believe the ability to handle this kind of thinking is best tested by the LSAT.

Law schools also recognize that every college and every academic major is so different that they can not reasonably compare, say, the grades of an engineering major from MIT with a public policy major from Duke. The LSAT gives schools a standard basis for comparison. Finally, you need to recognize that the LSAT is an institution. Everyone who has gone to law school has taken it. Law schools have the benefit of having compared how law students who received high versus low LSAT scores performed in law school. Schools have been able to establish a statistical correlation showing performance on the LSAT predicts performance in law school (though they may be reluctant to share their findings).

HOW CAN I PERFORM BETTER ON THE LSAT?

The bad news is, it is much harder to guarantee a high LSAT score than it is to guarantee a high college grade point average. To get a high GPA with minimal risk, you can always go to a college that is not academically rigorous and take an easy major in small classes with teachers known to reward students with an average of a high grade. The LSAT, in contrast, is administered in a timed, controlled environment in which effort is made to ensure that no candidate has an advantage.

The good news is, there is quite a lot you can do to prepare for the LSAT. Most applicants use a professional test preparation service and, if you do not do so, you will be at a disadvantage. The LSAT is a test for which you simply must prepare. I am not going to give you specific pointers on how to study for the test. I will tell you, however, that I did study very hard for the LSAT and received a very high score. In my day, the highest score was 48. I got two questions wrong and received a score of 47.

There is quite a lot you can do to prepare for the LSAT.

I attribute my high LSAT score to the fact that I completed every old LSAT I could find. I took each test under timed conditions—just as I would in the exam. I also dissected each question so that I understood what ability or approach the question was trying to test. I found there were only a finite number of different types of questions in each section and that understanding where the question was leading was very helpful in understanding it and finding the correct solution. I also took a course given by the Princeton Review, which was a great help in providing me with extra practice tests (some are available directly from the Educational Testing Service in Princeton, New Jersey) and giving me insights about the test that made me feel less nervous on the day of the exam.

I recommend using either Princeton Review or Kaplan test preparation services. Both are sophisticated programs and will give you a good feel for what it is like to take the actual exam. As I mentioned, I took a Princeton Review course and did quite well on the LSAT. My brother taught for Kaplan and later served as an executive with Kaplan supervising their operations in France. I disclose this so that you know I am not without bias. Both programs are quite expensive. You should expect to pay over $1,000 for either program (in late 2005 the cost of taking a Princeton Review LSAT review course in the Washington region was $1,349). Given the overall investment of time and money in law school, though, I believe this cost is well worth it.

Here are some Web sites that you might want to review in considering various LSAT preparatory courses:

http://www.lsac.org
www.kaptest.com
www.princetonreview.com
http://home-lsat.com
www.testmasters180.com
www.prepmaster.com
www.powerscore.com

HOW IMPORTANT ARE LAW SCHOOL APPLICATION ESSAYS, AND WHAT SHOULD I WRITE ABOUT?

WITHOUT GOOD GRADES and solid test scores, your application will not make it into the "possible accept" pile on the admissions counselor's desk. However, if you have sufficient statistics and submit an application with a materially deficient essay—such as one containing multiple spelling and grammatical mistakes or one that evidences severe emotional instability or an extreme lack of social tact—you could torpedo your chances of gaining acceptance. In other words, great essays alone won't get you in (unless perhaps you are writing about the two Olympic gold medals you won and even then you would need the bare minimum acceptable academic numbers for the school) but a careless or improper essay probably will keep you out. Fortunately, your essays are completely within your control. There is no excuse for screwing them up.

You are not supposed to let anyone help you on your admissions essays. Most, if not all, law schools require that you sign a statement attesting to the fact that you have received no help in writing them.

However, in practice, a significant percentage of law school applicants get some kind of help writing their essays. I personally wrote my law school essays alone the night before my applications were due. They could have been much better. In fact, I recall vaguely writing one essay for Yale (the one asking generally about why I wanted to be a lawyer) in the form of a very bad poem. I did not get accepted by Yale (I withdrew the application!) but I did get accepted by other schools, including the University of Pennsylvania and Georgetown. Nevertheless, I do not recommend my complete go-it-alone strategy unless you are either a superb writer or you just don't care that much about whether you get in and are confident you can live with the feeling, if you don't get in, that you could have if you had just gotten a little bit of feedback and/or help on your essays.

ARE THERE ANY UNCONVENTIONAL ROUTES TO LAW SCHOOL THAT I SHOULD CONSIDER?

THE HARDEST WAY to get into a well-regarded law school is to apply during your senior year of college. If you do this (as I did) you will be competing against a very large number of very similar applicants. In order to gain admission, you will need to have very good LSAT scores (at least testing in the 95th percentile for a top-ten law school) and at least respectable grades (at least a 3.3 GPA).

If you want to have a better chance of getting into a very well-regarded law school, then you might consider changing the rules of the game by trying something markedly different. If you are in high school right now, then your options are broad. On thing you might consider doing is going to college at a top foreign university rather than in the United States. Specifically, I am thinking about Oxford University and Cambridge University in the United Kingdom (you might also consider McGill University in Canada but, since I attended Cambridge for a term, studying law as an undergraduate at Emmanuel College, I am somewhat more familiar with the English system).

Going to Cambridge or Oxford for college is certainly unconventional, but it will put you in a different class of law school applicants for at least two reasons. First, and obviously, you will be applying as a candidate from an old and elite English university. Law schools list the different colleges from which their first-year students came. Admissions people will like the idea of having someone educated at Oxford in their admitted pool. It will make them look like they did a good job of promoting the law school to a broad, even international, body of students. Second, you will have an opportunity at Oxford to concentrate your legal studies in the law, rather than having to study something less relevant to the profession of law like political science or English. In England—and many other countries—legal education is obtained at the undergraduate level. English lawyers study law in college and then continue their education through professional Inns of Court after graduation. You will have a compelling story for admissions officials about why you want to study law—you already have, and you wish to continue your legal education at a graduate level in America.

Also, keep in mind that you can actually finish your undergraduate education earlier in England, where a BA degree is generally obtained in three rather than four years. This will give you an additional year of lead time over your peers if you elect to go directly to law school in the United States.[1] In addition, if you want to stay in England for an additional year, you can always pick up a master's degree in the same time you would have earned only a BA in America. This will make you even more attractive to admissions personnel and could yield additional dividends. Specifically, you might waive out of some law school classes if you have already covered them in your professional curriculum overseas. This is not a hypothetical scenario. During my second year at Columbia Law a new student joined our class. He had received his initial law degree at Oxford (his background was that he was of Indian extraction and had lived from his childhood in South Africa) and had convinced the Columbia deans to allow him to use his transferred credits for most of the first year core curriculum. He thus effectively completed Columbia Law School and obtained a JD degree in two years of study. He went on to be quite successful in obtaining work after graduation. As I recall, he went on join Sullivan & Cromwell, one of the top law firms in New York, if not the world, as an associate.

6. WHAT TO DO IN LAW SCHOOL

HOW IMPORTANT ARE GOOD GRADES IN LAW SCHOOL?

GRADES ARE VERY important in law school, particularly during your first year. In fact, getting good grades is more important for law students than it is for students in most other professional degree programs, such as business and medical school. This is so because law school grades directly affect the student's eligibility for certain honors, such as joining the staff of the school's law review, which determines the student's eligibility for certain types of postgraduate jobs, such as appellate clerkships. These jobs, in turn, can play a significant role in shaping the remainder of the lawyer's professional career.

Grades are the single most important factor that your likely first employers—law firms and judges—consider when they select summer associates or law clerks. Firms also look primarily at grades when hiring full-time associates. In fact, achieving good grades is at least as important as which law school you attended. Consider the case of a law firm looking at a New York University law student with consistently top marks and a Columbia University law student with middling to lower grades. Both are very good law schools, but Columbia, an Ivy League school, probably has the edge over NYU in terms of reputation. However, I believe most law firms would still hire the NYU candidate because of his proven ability to do excellent legal work, albeit in an academic setting. The Columbia student has only proven, by getting into Columbia, that he had the aptitude during college to get good grades in whatever major he pursued and to score well on the LSAT. Law school academic performance is both the most recent and the most directly applicable indicator to how well the candidate is likely to perform at a law firm.

Grades are particularly critical during the first year of law school. Getting good grades during the first year is critical to getting onto law review. That accomplishment—joining law review—is clear-cut. Either you are a member or you are not. It is, in many ways, better to get great grades the first year and get on law review and then get middling grades the second and third years than it is to get good grades all three years but not make law review. Your grades will not follow you through the rest of your career—they will not appear on your law firm biography, for example—but whether you made law review will. Clerkships, jobs, and even career advancement will turn, to some degree or another, on whether you can say you made law review. Some schools, like Columbia, provide academic benchmarks other than whether you made law review. This is a good thing, because such a small percentage of the class (maybe about 10 percent) can actually get on law review. At Columbia, if you get grades in approximately the top 20 percent of the class in any one full year, you are designated a Harlan Fiske Stone[1] Scholar. If you get basically perfect grades for a year you are designated a James Kent[2] Scholar, which is extremely prestigious among the small group of Columbia graduates who understand what it signifies.

HOW CAN I GET GOOD GRADES IN LAW SCHOOL?

ONE OF THE most important things you will learn during your first year of law school is how to learn about a legal subject. When you start your first year you will be amazingly inefficient. You will want to read every line of text and each footnote of every legal decision. You will try to devour every hornbook and textbook you are assigned. This is tremendously time consuming and is not the best way to master your subjects. You will learn this, painfully, in the first semester, when lack of sleep begins to reduce your ability to learn in class. In time, you will learn that working with a team of your classmates to prepare outlines and discuss ideas outside of class is the best way to get the material into your head. Usually, you get this process down just in time for your third year of law school. Given that grades during the first year are so critical, it will serve you well to get organized within a few days after law classes begin, scout out some promising (that means smart) classmates to start a study group, and get to work.

HOW IMPORTANT ARE STUDY GROUPS IN LAW SCHOOL?

CHOOSING GOOD PARTNERS for study groups is critical, especially during the first year of law school. Some graduate business schools assign entering students to a study group that they use for all their first-year classes. Law schools, on the other hand, usually leave it up to the students to network and find their own groups. This means there is great value in getting to know your classmates—and their strengths and weaknesses—as early as possible. While there are several strategies to choosing good study group partners, in general one wants to choose individuals who are smart, hardworking, and a good match for your personality. In study groups there is always the conflict that all students thinks they are doing more work than everyone else. The answer is for all students to agree to do their share of work, and divide the work as evenly as possible. Neat and highly organized study group partners can be of additional benefit.

HOW CRITICAL ARE GOOD OUTLINES AND HOW DO I MAKE ONE?

ONE THING THAT good study groups do together is to make good outlines. Given the large quantity of information to be learned in each class, and the fact it is nearly impossible for a single student to read all the assigned cases, creating group outlines is critical. However, I am not going to try to teach you how to write a good outline. Some books try to do this, but I think it is a silly exercise because what makes a good outline depends so much on your own learning style and the manner in which the teacher teaches the class. Nevertheless, a good outline will distill the large mass of information you learned through class and the assigned readings to a manageable volume, preferably less than twenty pages. Moreover, the best thing you can do is to listen carefully to what the professors emphasize during class presentations and to make certain that your outline fully addresses those areas that seem of greatest interest to them.

I did not create great outlines in law school. However, I recall one instance where a professor made a point in a class to emphasize one issue. I included a comprehensive analysis of that particular point in my outline, anticipating the various scenarios that could be used to test knowledge of the point. I was rewarded when a third of the exam reflected this point, echoing one of my proposed scenarios. I did very well on that exam, and many other students had missed the teacher's tipoff altogether. Keep that in mind when you are tempted to use some Property Law outline you find on the Web or inherit from an older student. You may best serve yourself by creating a shorter, more targeted outline that reflects what was actually covered in the class.

HOW IMPORTANT IS IT TO MAKE LAW REVIEW?

FOR A SELECT few jobs you need to make law review. For most jobs you do not. Specifically, if you ever want to clerk for a Supreme Court justice then you must become a member of law review while you are in law school. But if you just want to make partner eventually, or clerk for a District or Appellate Court judge after graduation, then you may not need to make law review. An exception is if you go to a school that is not well ranked, in which case you had better make law review to be considered for any judicial clerkships or positions with top law firms.

Making law review is a gateway to a narrow set of highly competitive jobs.

There are generally two ways to get onto law review. One is to have the grades and the other is to write your way on. I have known people who have done both. Being accepted onto law review based on your grades means you did very well during your first year of law school. This is why first-year grades are so important. Law review decisions are made during the summer after your first year. You can get lousy grades during your second and third years and it will make little difference—you were still a member of law review and will be for the rest of your life. It will be the second thing on your firm biographies, right after which law school you went to and before the name of the judge you clerked for.

The other way to get on law review is to write a student article for publication. If you write such an article and it is accepted, then you will become a member of the law review just as if you got on because of your grades. This is much harder and is subjective. If current members of the law review staff, including those who made law review based on their grades, don't like you, you may have no chance of getting on even if you create an outstanding piece of legal research and commentary.

ARE THE OTHER JOURNALS GOOD SUBSTITUTES FOR LAW REVIEW?

WHEN I DISCUSS law review I mean the single publication that is the foremost student-edited legal publication at a particular school. At some schools this periodical is referred to as the law journal. Any other publication is a secondary journal, regardless of its name. Secondary law journals include such titles as the *Business Law Review* and the *Journal of Transnational Law,* for example. These are not as prestigious as being on the real law review.

If you are unable to make law review, it is a good idea to join a secondary journal. However, be aware that secondary journals are all significantly less beneficial to your career than law review. While being on a secondary journal will give you some writing and editing experience, which employers will recognize and reward, you will not be eligible for certain jobs that only membership in law review can provide. For example, you will not be clerking for a Supreme Court justice unless you are on law review, even if you went to a top school like Harvard or Stanford. You also will have a difficult time getting certain competitive U.S. Circuit Court of Appeals clerkships and will likely never be the Solicitor General of the United States.

That being said, I was not a member of my school's law review. And yet, I got a great deal out of serving as an editor of the *Columbia Journal of Law and the Arts* and writing for the *Columbia Business Law Review.* Both were secondary journals. One thing to keep in mind is that not all secondary journals are created equal. Some are more difficult to get on and more prestigious than others. At Columbia, the *Business Law Review* and the *Journal of Transnational Law* had the reputation of being serious law journals that attracted meaningful contributions from law professors and legal practitioners. They were harder to get on than, say, the *Journal of Law and the Arts*. Nevertheless, any secondary journal experience is better than none.

WHAT ARE CLINICS AND SHOULD I DO ONE?

A CLINIC IS a law school experience in which students get some form of credit for spending a period of time during a semester going to a place where legal services are provided and participating in the supervised provision of legal advice. Most law schools have some kind of legal clinic program. At Columbia, there was a clinic in which you could spend three hours a week at the office of the VLA—Volunteer Lawyers for the Arts— answering the phone. The VLA serves the arts community in New York City—painters, writers, actors—and provides them with any range of legal services for very little or no money. Potential clients would call with anything from a copyright issue to a landlord-tenant dispute and ask for advice. As interns we were not lawyers yet, and could not legally provide advice. That would be considered practicing law without a license. However, we could take down the client's information, get their financial data to make sure their income qualified them to get our services for free, and then refer them to the right staff attorney.

A clinic can be a great learning experience, or it can be a waste of time. You should look carefully at the particular clinic you are considering. Find out what, exactly, you will be doing before signing on. Will you be making a difference? Will you learn something? Will you be able to study while you are there? Some clinics are graded. They are usually an easy A. This can be a great GPA boost, though most employers will recognize that it was not a competitive class. In general, you are better served by taking a structured class in which you will learn something substantive. Taking an extra tax law class will teach you a lot more than sitting in a room waiting for the next destitute client to call. However, you will have no better chance to have direct contact with real-life clients while you are in law school than through a clinic. It can provide a human side to the practice of law.

WHAT SHOULD I DO DURING MY FIRST-YEAR SUMMER?

IT IS DIFFICULT to get a law-related job during the summer after your first, or One L, year of law school. This is so for a couple of good reasons. First, at the time potential employers will need to make a decision regarding whether to hire you—at the latest toward the middle of your spring semester—you will only have one semester's worth of grades to show. Employers, particularly those who are going to pay you for your time, are usually very focused on grades as a measure of aptitude for completing legal work and will be nervous about your lack of a track record. Second, employers know that you are very unlikely to go back to your first-summer employer when, after graduation, you finally choose a permanent place of employment. The main reason—almost the only reason—law firms hire summer associates is to reserve a body of young lawyers whom they can tap for permanent placement among their associate ranks. Law firms do not make any money from their summer associates, much of whose time is spent in training, socializing, and conducting background (that is, unbillable) research projects. At many firms, most of the time that a summer associate spends working on client work is written off as part of preparing the final bill. Therefore, consider yourself very lucky if you manage to convince a law firm to hire you (and pay you) during your first-year summer.

That being said, some law firms do hire summer associates during their first year summer. However, there needs to be some form of catalyst for this to happen. Let me give you an example from personal experience. I went to Columbia Law School in New York, having grown up in New Jersey, where I attended high school and belonged to a number of civic organizations, including a volunteer fire department. I was therefore able to present a fairly convincing picture of someone who looked as though they might return to practice law in New Jersey. Now, it is hard for New Jersey law firms to attract Columbia law students, even during the worst of economic times. This is because most Columbia law students go to work for big Wall Street firms, which offer salaries almost twice as high as New Jersey firms (particularly if you look at how salaries increase in later years of practice) and bonuses that can be four times greater. Therefore, when as a first-year law student I managed to get some interviews with the larger New Jersey firms, at the end of each of my interview sessions I was asked one question. That question, presaged by an explanation of how much they liked me, was whether, if offered a summer-associate position, I would be willing to commit to return to the firm as a full-time associate after graduation. You will likely recognize that such an agreement would be unlikely to be held enforceable by any court, at the least because of its effect of constraining trade. Nevertheless, I would not make that commitment and did not secure a paid job offer during the summer following my first year.

I did have a law school classmate who was successful in landing a paid summer-associate position after his first year. Again, however, there were unusual circumstances involved. Specifically, my friend returned to his native Los Angeles during spring break and went to a couple of smaller regional offices. He introduced himself as a Columbia One L (I don't believe he had any prior relationship with any of the firms) and was promptly told that they were not hiring any first-year law students to fill summer-associate positions that year. Undeterred, Richard told them he was willing to work for nothing and was confident that he would be returning to L.A. after he graduated. One of the firms hired him—and not for free. Apparently impressed with his tenacity, they paid him a decent salary (almost what he would have gotten from a larger national firm) and he was one of the few law students in our class to secure gainful employment that summer.

It is much more common for first-year law students to obtain unpaid internships or clerkships during their first summer. In fact, there are enough unpaid positions available in the law that virtually any first-year student—particularly those from a nationally ranked law school—should be able to obtain such a position. While many of these positions are in government, some are in the private sector. For the best positions, it helps to go the personal route and tap someone you know or perhaps one of your professors to make an introduction. This is what I did when my law firm advances were rejected. Specifically, I turned to my aunt, whose neighbor was a New York State Supreme Court judge. His good friend was a United States District Court judge in the Southern District of New York. It turned out that this judge always hired one law student to serve as an unpaid summer law clerk in his chambers. The duties were essentially a watered-down version of what the full-time law clerks did, which meant drafting decisions and conducting legal research demanded by the cases before the judge. I worked from late May through mid-August and got paid nothing, but I was able to add a valuable law-specific line to my short résumé. The actual value of that line has certainly diminished with the passage of time and the addition of other jobs to my curriculum vitae. Nevertheless, I do believe that the experience was more beneficial than spending another summer as a lifeguard. I do know, for example, that having worked for a judge during the summer after my first year of law school significantly increased my chances of being offered an official clerkship from a judge in the Southern District of Florida after I graduated from law school. For one thing, the two judges were good friends, dating back to when they were both nominated to the federal bench. I did not know this when I applied for my postgraduate clerkship, but it worked out nicely.

In fact, an unpaid summer internship can contribute to your success in building a workable five-, ten-, or twenty-year career plan. For example, I have known law students who were interested in public health to obtain unpaid internships from the National Institutes of Health (NIH) and those who were interested in securities law get jobs with the Securities and Exchange Commission (SEC). The Federal Trade Commission (FTC) and the Department of Justice (DOJ) also generally offer opportunities for students to come in and work for free during the summer. For students in Washington, D.C., law schools (such as Georgetown, George Washington, and American universities) there are opportunities to get this government experience during the school year through various clinical programs with government institutions. (I know, for example, that here at the SEC we regularly hire area law students to spend one day a week attached to one of the Enforcement Division's branches.) However, for law students studying outside of the nation's capital, the first-year summer may offer an invaluable opportunity to get some brief agency experience. This experience, in turn, may form a solid foundation of interest in a particular area of law when it comes time to interview for a position as a first-year associate.

Consider, for example, that law students—even third-years—generally know very little about what it means to actually practice law. While they study core courses such as contracts, torts, and constitutional law, there is really very little basis for understanding what it means to seek the approval of a new drug application before the FDA or argue for a decreased penalty before the Securities and Exchange Commission. However, if you spend a summer working in one of these agencies, you will acquire a potent weapon for your interviewing arsenal. Unlike many of your classmates, you will gain the ability to speak with some level of authority about what it is like on the other side of the negotiating table, even if your duties at that agency were limited to following the staff attorneys around and doing discreet research assignments. This will put you in a different, far more favorable, light with potential employers.

WHAT SHOULD I DO DURING MY SECOND-YEAR SUMMER CLERKSHIP?

IF YOU WANT to work for a law firm after graduation, you should make every effort to work for a law firm during your second-year summer. If you can't find a job with a large national firm, you should try to get a job with a smaller regional or even a local firm. If you can't get a position with a small local firm, you should consider working for a government agency such as the SEC or the DOJ. These agencies sometimes run paid internship programs and almost certainly will accept unpaid interns.[3] If you can't get a position as an intern with a government agency, you should volunteer at the local public defender's office. They are likely to need the extra body to do the important but largely unappreciated work they do.

You also might consider volunteering for a political party, working for the summer at your home-state congressman's office in Washington, or finding anything else that is related to the law or government. What you do not want to do, no matter what, is to take a paying job in a position entirely unrelated to law (you don't want to wait tables or tend bar). I know that this can be a significant imposition if you are trying to pay for law school yourself. It seems unfair that affluent students can more easily take on an unpaid position without making a major financial sacrifice. But, if you want to develop your legal career, it is critical that you use your second-year summer as strategically as possible to show your dedication to legal practice and thinking. For this reason, you may want to start early in your first year of law school coming up with contingency plans in the event you are unable to get a standard summer-associate position the summer before your last year of school.

WHAT IF I CAN'T GET A LAW FIRM JOB FOR THE SUMMER?

IT IS NOT a big deal if you can't get a law firm job during your first-year summer. In fact, it's quite likely that only a minority (and perhaps a very small minority at that) of your class will work in law firms during the summer between their first and second year of school. Of my classmates at Columbia, I know of only five who landed paid first-summer jobs with law firms, and those were unusual situations in which the students went out of their way to track down and secure positions. The rest of us had to settle for unpaid legal internships with government agencies, judges, or nonprofit organizations. However, not having a paid law firm job during your One L summer will have absolutely no effect on your attractiveness to future full-time employers. No one expects first-years to get law firm jobs. It is good for you to work in the law in some capacity during your first summer, however, though this could be anything from taking an unpaid internship with a federal judge (which is what I did) to volunteering at your local small-town prosecutor's office.

It is a much bigger problem if you do not have a law firm job during the summer following your second year of law school. Not spending your Two L summer working for a firm is a problem if you hope to join a prestigious law firm after graduation. Even if you don't end up working for the firm you clerked with during the summer, whether you worked for a firm and whether you had a successful summer will weigh heavily with other firms' view you as a candidate. Law firms are more confident hiring law students who have been selected as summer associates by other top firms, and they gain even greater confidence if the students were successful summer associates—which translates into their having been offered permanent employment by the firm with which they summered.

It is easy to appreciate the impact of having received an offer from Firm X will have on how Firm Y views you as a potential hire. Law firms have only a small amount of information on which to base their decision to hire you permanently. They only know you from a handful of half-hour interviews. They don't know how you interact with others, how fast you work, or how detail-oriented you are. Grades and writing samples do not tell the whole story. And hiring an associate who is not able to do the work—or who has a serious personality flaw—can be very costly. Firms need some assurance that a new hire is likely to work out, which means that the person ends up being a productive worker for at least five years. Having received an offer from a firm that observed your performance at close range for three months is about the best attestation of fit the firm can hope to get. Getting a Two L summer job with a firm is, therefore, an important first step toward getting the all-important return offer.

Fortunately, if you are a law student at a leading law school (by which I mean any law school in about the top twenty-five ranked law schools), almost your entire class will find positions with law firms for their second-year summer. At Columbia Law, for example, I know of some law students who had as many as ten offers from various law firms for Two L summer employment. That is not to say, however, that some students, even those from top schools, do not have a difficult time finding law firm jobs. For every student who has ten offers there exist at least two students who have only one offer and are very glad to have that. In fact, in some cases, students from even top schools receive no offers at all after the initial round of on-campus interviews are completed. Luckily, since on-campus interviews take place in the early fall of the second year, there is usually plenty of time for these unfortunate students to reach out— usually to secondary firms that did not bother to send representatives to recruit on campus—in the hope of securing a summer position. Most will be successful, if they put in the effort.

One thing you should consider is what distinguishes the law student who receives ten summer internship positions from the student who receives few or none. Generally, grades have a big impact on Two L summer hiring. Since second-year students have a year of grades under their belt that form the basis for hiring decisions, it is possible for students with the lowest grades to have a very difficult time finding law firm jobs. But personality can play a role as well. A candidate who comes across as overly cocky or just plain crazy will have a hard time finding a job. Being reserved is not the kiss of death, however, because firms usually consider that either the candidate will mature out of their shyness or, if not, still be a productive associate doing the detailed behind-the-scenes work required of many legal disciplines (i.e., they can stay in their offices writing briefs while the partners interact with the clients).

Now that I have scared you, I need to disclose that I personally did not get a job during my Two L summer with a top New York or Washington law firm, yet I have enjoyed quite a successful legal career ever since. In fact, I got no offers from on-campus hiring at Columbia at the start of my second year. I knew this could be a significant handicap later on when I looked for full-time jobs. Therefore, what I did was to use the Martindale Hubbell lawyer directory (which was then in book form but which can now be easily navigated online) and Columbia Law's own databases to determine which alumni were working at what regional law firms. I also looked for law firms that had not interviewed on campus but that had particularly well-regarded corporate practices, since I was most interested in pursuing a career in corporate law.

My methods for finding a Two L summer job outside the normal interviewing structure worked out well. I discovered an interesting intersection, in that a Columbia Law School graduate was a senior partner at a mid-sized law firm in Wilmington, Delaware. The firm had a couple of hundred lawyers and was perhaps the leading law firm in this small city about two hours south of New York by train. What is more, I discovered that the firm was written up in legal periodicals as one of the most well-regarded firms practicing in the area of Delaware corporate law. Since most large companies are incorporated in the State of Delaware, partly because the Delaware Corporate Code and related Chancery Court case law are extremely well developed, most large corporate disputes—including those involving hostile tender offers and other corporate takeovers—end up in Delaware courts. This firm ended up being at the epicenter of many of the largest and most famous takeover battles, including most of the ones I had learned about in my corporate law classes.

To get the job, I employed a direct and aggressive approach. I called the alum partner and told him I had read about the firm's work, was duly impressed, and had a strong interest in practicing in the area of Delaware corporate law. He was flattered and more than happy to help me get an initial round of interviews. I got the summer job, gained a firsthand opportunity to learn about Delaware corporate law, and received an offer from a firm that many top national law firms use on a regular basis as their Delaware counsel. Although references to this summer job have long since been deleted from my résumé, working for the Delaware firm contributed directly to my obtaining employment with a leading law firm after my judicial clerkship. Moreover, the personal relationships I formed during that summer have been particularly useful over the years.

HOW IMPORTANT IS IT TO GET A PERMANENT JOB OFFER FROM MY SUMMER CLERKSHIP?

IF YOU WORK for a law firm during your second-year summer, it is very important for you to get an offer of permanent employment. Prospective employers—particularly law firms—do not like to take risks. This is one of the reasons they spend so much money on their summer-associate programs. The fact is that law firms never make money from summer associates. Most of the work summer associates do for clients is written off. In addition, summer associates are very expensive to recruit, train, provide office space for, and pay. The reason the programs are still worth their high cost is because hiring a full-time attorney without knowing their abilities and personalities firsthand is an enormous risk. As expensive as it is to recruit top law students for summer-associate jobs, it is even more expensive to get rid of junior associates who do not work out.

Getting an offer of permanent employment is a stamp of approval from the firm that gave you the offer. If you worked at the firm as a summer associate, getting an offer is confirmation to both the partners at that firm and to all other firms of a similar caliber that you performed well enough—and were, let's face it, "normal" enough—to be asked to join the firm family. In contrast, if you worked at a firm as a summer associate and then did not get an offer, the conclusion drawn by other firms is that you either did not meet expectations or that you are somehow abnormal in your personality. Partners doing the hiring at other firms will consider the possibility that you do drugs or hit on the partners' wives at summer associate events. (In fact, these are among the more colorful reasons some summer associates have gotten into trouble!)

You simply do not want prospective employers to be imagining all the terrible things you could have done to warrant not receiving a permanent offer of employment from your summer firm. For this reason you want to be very careful not to accept a summer-associate position with a firm that is facing economic hardship. A firm that is having trouble bringing in business may decide not to hire any of its summer associates. This is actually better than if the firm decides only to hire half of its summer associates, however, since a firm that hires none of its summer associates will be noted by other firms and there will be no way to differentiate between the performances of the various summer associates. However, if some summer associates do get hired, you will be fighting the uphill battle of explaining why they got hired and you did not, when at most firms only the very worst summer associates do not get asked back. Indeed, since most firms hire summer associates with the expectation of hiring all or virtually all of them as full-time associates, it remains a very difficult task to convince other firms that you were not hired based on factors beyond your control.

WHAT DO I DO IF I DON'T GET A JOB OFFER FROM MY SUMMER EMPLOYER?

THERE IS NO way to hide the fact that not getting a job offer from the law firm where you spent the summer before your third year of law school is a bad thing. (If you do not get a job offer from the law firm where you spent your first-year summer, it is not such a bad thing because there is generally less of an expectation that you would necessarily return to that firm.) The entire purpose of the second-summer internship is to determine whether the law student is a good fit for full-time employment. Usually, firms are very reluctant not to offer positions to summer associates because failing to offer a job will signal to all future prospective law school hires that joining this firm presents a high risk of not getting an offer.

So, what do you do? First, I recommend talking to the hiring coordinator at the firm. She may be willing to give you feedback as to why you were not given an offer. Is it due to a poor economy, or because you danced drunk on the table at a firm outing? Is there any room to negotiate and reach a deal that would benefit both you and the firm? Keep in mind that it is not in the firm's interest not to give you an offer. Ask whether they can give you a "soft" offer—that is, formally an offer to return with the understanding that you will not take them up on that offer. Some firms have done this. You would be a fool to accept such an offer knowing they would make your life hell and probably fire you within a year anyway. But it gives both you and the firm cover. You can go to other prospective employers with the truthful story that you were made an offer to return and the firm can report to prospective future hires that they gave everyone in their summer class an offer last year. If the hiring coordinator is not enticed by your offer, go up the chain to the partners you worked with or even to the firm's managing partner. You have nothing to lose, given that they have already blackballed you.

You also need to think about how you will convince other employers to hire you since you did not get a firm offer. Other law firms are going to be very concerned about why a firm with which you worked for a summer did not extend you an offer. Government employers are not going to be as focused on this issue. You might want to consider joining a government agency directly out of law school. If you are at a top law school, this will be a relatively easy path, as very few graduates of top law schools elect to give up sky-high associate salaries for the relative pittance the government pays. In addition, such a move could set you up for a much more rewarding long-term career. If you are set on going to a law firm, however, you will have your work cut out for you. You need to explain exactly why you were not given an offer. The assumption will initially be that you did a bad job. If it is because the firm is thinking of closing that practice or office, or because a particular partner with whom you were working is leaving the firm, then this is a good, specific reason that may get you over. However, saying "I don't know" is probably the worst answer of all. It shows that either you were not motivated to find out the reason or you are lying. You don't want let your prospective employer's imagination run wild.

HOW DO I WRITE A MEMO?

As A SUMMER associate you will invariably be asked to write a memo about some area of the law, likely applied to a particular fact scenario that is relevant to a case your supervising attorney is working on. This is an opportunity to make a good impression, which in turn will have a big impact on the recommendation you receive from the attorney and whether you get an offer from the firm or agency you are working for. There are two requirements for writing your memo. First, get it done on time, and second, do it well. Neither of these is straightforward, however,

Let's focus on the timing issue first. Keep in mind that things always take longer than you think they will. The attorney who gives you the project may have a deadline in mind. He may say, "Do your best, but I need this by tomorrow afternoon." In that case, be sure to get him a finished project by his deadline, even if you have to stay up all night to get it done. If he asks, "How busy are you?" or leaves it up to you to set your own deadline, be reasonable. It will take longer than you think, so don't promise to have it completed within a day. But don't take a week. Get an idea from the attorney when he needs the finished product, and do this by asking him outright. Is it something he needs as soon as possible, or can it be drafted over a period of a week or so? Find out the purpose of the memo: does it need to be incorporated in a larger document? But the worst thing to do is to promise to finish the project in a short amount of time and then not be able to deliver on your promise. Once you set a date or agree to a deadline, you must not miss it.

Regardless of your time line, it is also important to do a job that meets or exceeds the expectations of the assigning attorney. The best way to do this is to ask the assigning attorney for an example of a memo to use as a model. Then use that model; look at the formatting, the level of detail, and the types of materials cited. Did the model memo rely on cases, on legislation, or did it go all the way to a review of congressional testimony on passage of the bill? If there is a question about any aspect of the assignment, go back to the assigning attorney as early and as often as necessary. The worst thing is to hand in the assignment on the appointed deadline only to find out that you researched the wrong topic. In addition, for more candid insight, you might want to ask around among the more junior associates who have worked for the assigning attorney. They may have valuable insights into what that particular lawyer expects.

Legal memos themselves are fairly standardized. While every attorney and law firm has its own variation, the underlying theme remains the same. A good legal memo should clearly and succinctly set forth the question presented, followed by a brief summary of the law, followed by a more detailed application of the law to the facts presented in the case you are considering. I am not going to try to teach you how to write a good legal memo (or a good paragraph) here. However, keep in mind a couple of cardinal rules. First, use strong topic sentences. The supervising attorney should be able to understand your argument by reading only the first sentence of each of the paragraphs in your discussion section. Second, when dealing with a factual chronology, describe the events in order and start each sentence with the date on which the event occurred. For example, your discussion may read: "On May 1, 1999, this happened. One June 1, 2000, that happened." Don't be afraid of repetition and don't embed the dates in the middle of the sentence. The purpose of this writing is to convey information, not to create great literature.

WHAT IF I ALREADY KNOW I WANT TO BE A BANKER AFTER I GRADUATE?

I AM APPENDING this short section to the end of the what-to-do-in-law-school section because, chronologically, it would be great to identify your interest in banking when you are a One L rather than after you had graduated and started at a law firm. That is, if you are at a good law school and know you want to be an I-banker instead of a lawyer after you graduate, we can do something about it if you still have a year or two of law school in front of you. If you have already graduated and are working in a law firm, the task of making the transition to banking is a bit more arduous.

As you may already know, I joined an investment bank as a finance professional (a true investment banker) after I had had a fairly long career as a practicing lawyer. Making this transition is very difficult to do and, even today, it is difficult for me to shake the stigma of having been a practicing lawyer. The expectation is that I will not have the quantitative (think math) skills of someone who went directly from school (either undergraduate or MBA) to the banking life. And I have an MBA in finance from Wharton, probably the most quantitative major at the most quantitative business school in the country! What has impressed me, though, is the number of investment bankers who hold law degrees. In the group of about a dozen bankers with whom I work most closely, four have law degrees. But I am the only one ever to have actually practiced law. The rest went directly into banking after law school, and this is the path that I recommend most highly to you if you are able to get a banking offer.

Luckily for you, investment banks will interview law students at the schools where they are also interviewing MBA candidates. Also, I am on the recruiting committee for my investment bank and recently had conversations about what kinds of law students it is worth our (quite valuable) time to interview. By and large, investment banks are more comfortable hiring MBA candidates than they are hiring lawyers. This is because the MBA candidates are self-selected to have an interest in banking or business (rather than the more academic and risk-adverse legal discipline) and to have the basic training needed to do quantitative banking work.

If law students want to have a shot at getting a banking job, they should keep the following in mind: First, banks are not going to come knocking on the door. Interested law students will have to reach out to the banks, including by finding the right contact person at the banks interviewing MBAs on campus (the best would be a banker who either graduated from their law school or one who is on the hiring team for the business school at the university where they are attending law school) and putting together a convincing package that includes a banking-specific résumé and cover letter.

Second, banks are going to want to see some historical interest in banking or finance. As a first-year law student interested in going into banking, you should prepare by taking quantitative classes—accounting, finance, statistics and corporate valuation to start—as early and as often as possible. This will usually mean taking classes at the business school and may require that you take an overload of classes so that you can also complete your law school core requirements. Many investment banks have a policy of not interviewing lawyers for banking positions unless they have taken a certain number of quantitative classes while in law school.

Third, you should try to get a summer-associate internship at a bank instead of at a law firm. This will be difficult and may also make it more difficult for you to get a top law firm job if you change your mind. However, it is essential that you establish your banking credentials as early as possible if you want to make the difficult move from law school student to investment banker.

Another choice, of course, is to stay in graduate school another year and pick up an MBA. At schools where the law school is better than the business school, such as Yale, it will be easy to tack on an MBA. At schools where the business school is better than the law school, such as the University of Pennsylvania, it may be the case that most law students do not have the quantitative credentials to gain admission to the business school. As a general matter, however, law students have an opportunity during their first year of law school to apply to the university's business school. If you get in, then you spend another three years (four total) taking alternating business and law school classes. This program gives you a total of three summers during which you can try different internships in the law and business and gives you a strong credential for joining a law firm, an investment bank, or a strategy-consulting firm. However, it is time consuming and expensive in terms of both tuition and the opportunity cost of postponing entering the workforce for another year.

7. ■ JUDICIAL CLERKSHIPS

WHAT IS A JUDICIAL CLERKSHIP?

IN MANY WAYS, a judicial clerkship is an important continuation of your legal education. In the United States, lawyers are not required to serve as legal apprentices before practicing law, as they are in many other countries, including the UK. Serving as the law clerk to a judge provides a transition between law school and judicial practice, during which you can learn how judges and juries interpret and apply the law in real situations, observe different attorneys with varying practice styles ply their trade before your judge, and generally mature under the tutelage of a senior legal professional.

Clerking for a judge, particularly for a federal judge or a state Supreme Court justice, is prestigious and can significantly increase your marketability to firms. For salary purposes, firms will generally give you credit for the time spent clerking, effectively considering former judicial clerks as second- or third-year associates and adjusting their salaries to reflect that seniority. In addition, most firms will give you a clerkship bonus, which can be $10,000, or even more. Nonlawyers, however, often do not understand the importance of a clerkship. I remember having a conversation with a telephone operator at my credit card issuer where this played out. During my clerkship with a federal district court judge, I had applied for a credit card. The records of the credit card company had my job title as "clerk," and my salary, which at that time for federal law clerks was about $35,000.[1] In my first year of law practice, just one year later, I was making several times that salary. The operator could not fathom how a "clerk" making a small salary one year could be a corporate lawyer earning a salary in the six figures the next.

WHAT DO FEDERAL LAW CLERKS DO?

THE ACTUAL TASKS law clerks perform depend on both the type of court in which the judge sits and the characteristics of the individual judge. Federal district court judges, for example, preside over hearings and trials in which the factual record of the case is determined and the law is applied to those facts for the first time. The trials themselves may be bench trials, in which the judge determines the outcome, or jury trials, in which the jury determines who wins. A great deal of a district court law clerk's time is spent reviewing pretrial motions filed by the litigants, including, as examples, motions for extensions of time, motions for summary judgment, and various motions relating to discovery. Some judges give their law clerks a great deal of responsibility, even allowing them to draft entire opinions in some cases. Other judges limit their law clerks' input to researching individual legal issues and processing incoming motions. This may depend on both the judge's personal work style and the confidence he or she has in the ability of a particular clerk. However, regardless of the degree to which law clerks contribute to the final written opinion issued by the court, it is important that law clerks be very discreet with regard to the work they do. Officially, all written opinions that come out of a judge's chambers have the judge as their sole author.

United States Court of Appeals judges serve a very different function from federal district court judges. They are appellate judges, meaning they hear appeals that primarily claim that the legal determinations made by the district court judges were wrong. It is somewhat more prestigious to clerk for a federal Court of Appeals judge than it is to clerk for a District Court judge, though in my opinion it is more fun to clerk in the district courts. Some district court law clerks will go on to clerk for a Court of Appeals judge following the conclusion of their initial clerkship. Law clerks to Court of Appeals judges spend a great deal of their time researching the law, studying the factual record developed at the district court level, helping their judge prepare to hear oral arguments from lawyers, and preparing draft opinions. The Court of Appeals focuses more on the law and its interpretation than the district courts, and Court of Appeals judges have the responsibility for judging whether the district court judges did their job correctly. Therefore, there is perhaps a greater effort by Court of Appeals judges to make sure they hire as law clerks only individuals who have proved their exceptional aptitude for legal research and writing. Thus, very high grades and law review membership are particularly prized.

While appellate clerkships certainly offer greater prestige, keep in mind that appellate clerks do not get to observe the same kinds of practical legal skills that district court clerks see on a daily basis. District court clerks have a chance to observe many cross-examinations of witnesses, as well as the way various lawyers select juries and interact with them, while Court of Appeals clerks only get to read the trial transcripts and then listen to oral presentations by lawyers expounding on their proposed interpretation of the law. Thus, unlike district court clerks, appellate clerks do not have an opportunity to observe the various approaches and styles employed by different lawyers in the trial context. Of course, appellate court clerks do get to observe some very gifted attorneys present legal arguments in the context of appeals, and there is a certain degree of art in that. But the experience of seeing lawyers cross examine witnesses before a jury, particularly a very good lawyer in a high-profile case, can be an unparalleled learning experience. Lawyers who believe they are more likely to enter a practice requiring them to appear regularly before trial judges, and conduct trials, may be better advised to serve as district court law clerks regardless of the fact Court of Appeals clerkships offers greater prestige.

WHAT IS THE DIFFERENCE BETWEEN CLERKING FOR A JUDGE ON A U.S. COURT OF APPEALS AND CLERKING FOR A U.S. DISTRICT COURT JUDGE?

THERE IS QUITE a significant difference between clerking for a judge in a U.S. District Court and clerking for a judge sitting on one of the U.S. Courts of Appeals.[2] These differences stem largely from the fact that the U.S. District Courts are trial courts and the Courts of Appeal are, of course, appellate courts. Therefore, the job of a District Court judge involves deciding motions under the federal rules of civil procedure and presiding at a large number of judge and jury trials each year. These trials can be quite interesting, as they often involve serious criminal activity and concern significant issues of commercial law. Appellate judges, on the other hand, do not preside at trials but rather review appeals from earlier trials and sit on appellate panels that may ask questions of counsel based on those briefs.

Clerking in an appellate court is generally considered to be more prestigious than clerking in a district court.

Clerking in an appellate court is generally considered to be more prestigious than clerking in a district court. One reason for this is supply and demand. There are a good deal more district court judges than there are U.S. Circuit Court judges. Another reason is that appellate courts are a higher legal authority than district courts. If a district court judge gets the law wrong, the appellate court has the power to overturn the decision. Only the United States Supreme Court is a higher authority on the law than the judges at the various courts of appeals. There is also a perception, certainly among appellate judges and probably among most law students, that the law clerks to appellate judges must be of the very highest academic quality. It is for these reasons that the law review editors at leading law schools generally aspire to clerk for a well-regarded U.S. Court of Appeals judge, for example.[3]

However, there are certain advantages to clerking for a U.S. District Court judge. I personally enjoyed my experience clerking for two U.S. District Court judges. In fact, I am probably biased in my opinion due to my positive experience. If you are planning to pursue a career as a trial lawyer, you should get a district court clerkship directly out of law school and then, for a second year, apply for an appellate clerkship. In this way, you will get hands-on experience in the trial environment and also gain an understanding of the legal points that can be argued on appeal. The combined experience will make you a very formidable trial attorney later in your career. On the other hand, many of the very best law students— those on law review and with nearly perfect grades—aspire to clerk for a United States Supreme Court justice. The best way to achieve this is to clerk for a federal Court of Appeals judge who is known for sending clerks to the Supreme Court. Such feeder judges do exist, and your law school's career counselor can let you know who they are.

There are some basic facts you should know about the federal court system before you begin conducting research into clerkships. First, there are twelve regional U.S. Circuit Courts of Appeal. Lawyers refer to these courts as the First Circuit, Second Circuit, and so on. Each circuit covers several jurisdictions. For example, the First Circuit covers Maine, Massachusetts, New Hampshire, Rhode Island, and Puerto Rico, and the Eleventh Circuit covers Florida, Georgia, and Alabama. There are ninety-four judicial districts in the United States, each having a U.S. District Court. These courts cover a much smaller region than the Courts of Appeal. For example, in Florida there are three separate judicial districts: the Southern District of Florida, the Middle District of Florida, and the Northern District of Florida. Some states, such as Nevada, have only one district court.[4] Of course, there are multiple judges within each Court of Appeals and each U.S. District Court. The number of judges largely depends on the size and number of cases within that region (although judges often complain that there are not enough judges to handle all of the work). Since all federal judges must be nominated by the president of the United States and approved by the Senate (under its "advice and consent" authority) there can be quite a long delay in filling judicial vacancies.

SHOULD I CLERK FOR A FEDERAL JUDGE AFTER GRADUATION?

I CLERKED FOR a federal judge for two years after graduating from law school. I would recommend it and believe most lawyers who clerked for a federal judge would do so as well. Among lawyers who did not clerk, not having had that experience is often one of their chief laments. One of my law school classmates, who became a corporate partner at Wilson

Sonsini, a leading Palo Alto, California, law firm, answered my question about what was the career decision he regretted most as follows:

> I should have taken the federal clerkship that was offered to me. I took a pass on the opportunity because I knew I planned to go into corporate and securities work, and didn't want to continue delaying my entry into that line of endeavor. Nonetheless, I've wished many times since then that I had done the clerkship, both in order to preserve the ability to become a litigator if I had so chosen, and potentially to hold open the possibility of someday becoming a judge.

All this positive information about the clerkship experience does not, however, make the decision a complete no-brainer. The answer to whether you should do a clerkship is that it really depends on your specific career goals. But considering that you are facing a long career that may take unexpected turns, it is good to pursue a clerkship.

Let me first explain my own experience. I had every intention, after graduating from law school, to practice as a corporate lawyer. Nevertheless, I applied for about fifty federal clerkships during my second year of law school, interviewed with a half dozen federal district court judges, and in the fall of my final year of law school accepted the single offer I received to clerk for a federal judge sitting in Miami. I clerked for the Chief Judge for the Southern District of Florida for two years (which was what he required, rather than the more standard one-year clerkship) and learned a great deal, both about how the courts work and how decisions are made by people in power.

I have often referred to my clerkship experience, most recently when I was discussing with a colleague here at the SEC how to communicate with a federal law clerk on an insider trading case we are about to try in the Southern District of New York.

WHEN SHOULD I CLERK FOR A JUDGE?

THE MOST COMMON time to do a judicial clerkship is directly after graduating from law school. In order to do that you will need to apply for judicial clerkships during the fall of your third year. If you plan to clerk right after graduating, you need to be mindful that the timing rules are quite strict. For example, law students who applied for clerkships starting in August 2005 had to apply to those clerkships on or after September 7, 2004, and were not allowed to apply before that date. The federal judges receiving those résumés were required to observe a "reading period" from September 7 through September 19, and then on September 20 were allowed to begin interviewing candidates and making offers.[5] Given this schedule, it is important that you begin your research into potential judges by the end of your second year of law school. If you miss the application deadline, you risk losing the opportunity to clerk the next year.

> A good argument can be made for clerking in the second year after you graduate.

However, a good argument can be made for clerking in the *second* year after you graduate. While the salaries paid to federal judicial clerks change roughly every year (in 2005 the salary was about $51,000 for clerks directly out of law school), in general, the salary paid to clerks who have worked in a law firm for a year are much higher than for clerks just out of school. This is due to the federal government's policy of attempting to match civilian salaries. First-year associates can earn more than $125,000 in base compensation. While you will not get paid this much as a judicial clerk, if you accept a clerkship after earning a high salary in a firm, the government will do its best to match it, which could mean a salary of $70,000 or more. You should research the difference in compensation and calculate the present value of the salary differential to determine the benefit of pursuing a clerkship after working for a firm for a year.

WHAT ABOUT CLERKING FOR A STATE COURT JUDGE?

CLERKING FOR A federal judge is almost always more prestigious than clerking for state court judges. In fact, for a graduate of a top law school it is difficult to justify clerking for a state court judge, unless perhaps the clerkship is with a justice on a state supreme court (in New York State called the Court of Appeals). For graduates of second- or third-tier law schools, it may make more sense to clerk for a state court judge. This is primarily because of the different career track that graduates of those schools are likely to take.

While graduates of top law schools tend to gravitate toward law firms in major urban centers with a national and international practice, graduates of regional law schools tend to work in smaller law firms on state or local matters. They are far more likely to appear regularly before particular state judges throughout their practice. Therefore, it can be of great benefit for them to build relationships in the local court system.

HOW DO I GET A JUDICIAL CLERKSHIP?

IT IS IMPORTANT to send clerkship applications to a large number of judges, even if you have very good grades and attended a highly regarded law school. Do not assume you are going to get the clerkship of your choice just because you went to a top school like Harvard or Columbia. The process is highly competitive and will require a great deal of research, preparation, effort, and luck.

First of all, know how your application is likely to compare with those of other candidates. This requires a candid assessment of your grades and familiarity with the track record of your law school for placing students in clerkships. Keep in mind that having been on law review will have a significant impact on judicial clerkships. In general, law review members from the top ten law schools are most sought after by judges. After this, law review members from the next ten best schools are desired. Only after judges have looked at all of these law review members do they seriously consider graduates who did not make law review, even when they are from one of the top ten schools.

It should not be surprising that judges consider law review—a proxy for top grades—important. While judges may make borderline decisions based upon soft characteristics such as personality or shared interests, intelligence remains the primary selection factor for law clerks. This is because judges believe that the smartest clerks will produce the highest-quality work. Since this work is researching and even writing the decisions issued by the judge, it is extremely important to the judge that the work be done right.

One interesting thing is that having gone to a top law school better guarantees getting a job at a large urban law firm than it does getting a federal judicial clerkship. Top law firms primarily hire from the top law schools, and their partners consequently tend to have graduated from the top law schools. There is a strong feeling among many graduates of top law schools that they are the anointed ones. I have found this to be particularly true of Harvard graduates. This results in a tendency among partners in large firms to hire associates primarily from top schools.

In contrast, many federal judges, particularly U.S. District Court judges, did not go to the very best law schools. They are just as likely to have gone to strong regional schools. Therefore, while judges recognize some law schools are much more competitive in admissions than are other schools, they also understand that there are very bright graduates of many regional law schools. Judges may be particularly likely to give a law review member who graduated from a regional school a shot if the judge graduated from the same school.

The reason judges are more likely than partners in top law firms to have graduated from strong regional schools is that judges are often drawn from the local bar. The process for selecting federal judges involves individual senators recommending a lawyer for elevation to the federal bench, the president nominating the individual, and the full Senate voting on whether to approve the nomination. Senators tend to recommend judges who live in the district they represent, so there is momentum for local lawyers to enter the pipeline that leads to a federal judicial appointment.

HOW CAN I IMPROVE MY CHANCES OF GETTING A CLERKSHIP?

FROM THE PERSPECTIVE of judges, choosing law clerks is highly personal. Most federal law clerks serve for either one or two years. Occasionally a law clerk will stay on with a judge on a permanent basis, at the judge's discretion, but this is rare. Mostly, the law clerk position is a revolving one. Fresh young lawyers come in, work very hard for a judge for a year or two, and then go on to build their own legal careers. Often, the judge and his or her clerks will have a parent-child relationship. To illustrate this, I recall that I once called one of the federal judges for whom I clerked Dad by mistake. For many young attorneys it is their first real experience practicing law of any sort, and it is a heady time, given the immense power wielded by judges and, by proxy, their clerks. Clerks serve as much more than researchers for their judges—they are confidants and trusted advisers. Thus, it should not be surprising that judges view the clerk selection process as a highly important and personal process.

WHAT ARE SOME TACTICS THAT BACKFIRE IN SEEKING CLERKSHIPS?

THE CASCADING PRINCIPLE, whereby the desirability of something (such as an IPO share) is determined more by who else wants it than by objective information about it, has been applied to the search for a judicial clerkship with disastrous consequences.

This principle has been used by law school students for at least the last decade in an effort to get law firms as well as judges to take an interest in them. Here is how it works. A law student sends his résumé to a number of law firms or judges in a given city. Let's say for argument's sake that the law student is in school in New York and that the firm or judge is in Miami. The law student then calls up one of the firms or judges, says he is going to be in Miami for an interview with Firm X or Judge Y on a given morning, and asks whether he can have an interview that afternoon. The student does not have an interview with any firm or judge in Miami; he is just trying to get his foot in the door. Although he has never heard of the cascading principle, he is trying to enhance his attractiveness by making it seem that another firm or judge is interested in hiring him.

This approach has worked with law firms. For one thing, it is unlikely that one law firm will call another to ask whether it is really interested in hiring a given law student, unless the two firms are splitting the cost of having the student fly in to be interviewed. After all, law firms do actively compete for the best law school graduates and they would tend not to tip their recruiting hand unnecessarily. However, judges are a different story altogether. What law students may not realize is that judges sitting on the same bench—for example, federal district court judges in a given jurisdiction or federal appellate judges on a given circuit—are extremely close personally, even if they do not see eye-to-eye on political or policy issues.

That is, judges have lunch together, talk to each other about their cases, they go to baseball games together, and they discuss their clerks. Of course they are going to ask each other if they are interviewing a particular law student.

Here is what happened in one instance. I clerked in the Southern District of Florida for a federal district court judge for two years. While I was there, a law student from a top New England law school played the game I have outlined with a federal judge sitting in Miami. This law student called the judge, said he was interviewing with another judge in the district (whose office was just down the hall) and asked if he could come in for an interview. Always a reasonable man, and since the résumé was apparently quite presentable, the judge said yes and set up an appointment. In fact, I am led to understand that the student probably would have gotten an interview anyway. But the student did not have an interview with the other judge and, not surprisingly, the two judges spoke and learned quite quickly of the student's deception.

When the law student showed up at the judge's chambers everyone knew what he had done, but they did not let on. Instead, the judge's secretary asked the student to wait for the judge, saying that he was in court. Now, in the Southern District, as in, I suppose, many federal courthouses, the judge's personal chambers have two doors. One leads to the anteroom where his clerks and secretary work. The other leads to the courtroom. The student arrived at about two in the afternoon. The clerks and secretaries ignored him as he waited. The judge never came out (he eventually left through his courtroom). Our law student could not complain. This was, after all, a federal judge. Eventually the secretaries left for the day, and shooed the law student out the door. He never got to see the judge.

There is no situation in which honesty is more important than in the relationship between a law clerk and a judge. A law clerk acts, in many respects, with the power of the judge. A judge relies on the law clerk to be absolutely honest and accurate to the best of his ability. This particular law student was branded. I suspect that the story of his bad conduct traveled throughout the community of federal judges. I would be surprised if the student received even a single judicial clerkship interview.

8. THE BAR EXAMINATION

WHICH STATE BAR EXAMINATION OR EXAMINATIONS SHOULD I SIT FOR?
THE GENERAL RULE is to sit for the bar examination of the state in which
you are interested in practicing. If you are from Alabama and plan on
practicing law in a firm in Montgomery, then take the Alabama bar.
However, some of you will be going into corporate law firms in places
like Washington and Philadelphia. In addition to taking the Pennsylvania
bar exam, you might also want to take the New York bar. Many large
firms will pay for their associates to sit for the New York bar under the
theory that New York is a major commercial hub and a New York bar
license is a worthwhile credential. You should check with your future
employer and, if possible, with lead partners in your group to see
whether they have a strong preference.

SHOULD I SIT FOR THE BAR IN MORE THAN ONE STATE?
SOMETIMES IT IS possible to take more than one bar examination at around
the same time. The multistate bar examination is given twice a year, once

in the winter and once in the summer, usually in late July. For example, you might be able to take the New York state portion of the bar examination in Manhattan on a Tuesday, take the multistate part of the bar examination in Manhattan on Wednesday, and take the New Jersey state portion of the bar examination on Thursday. In this way, you can use the multistate portion of the bar exam (which is the long multiple-choice part of the exam that tests for federal law or universal legal concepts) toward both your New York and New Jersey state exams. You just need to make sure that the state portions of the exams are not being held on the same day. Since there is generally some overlap between the subjects tested on any single state's bar exam, there can be some economies of scale in taking both tests at the same time while the material is fresh in your head. In addition, you have reduced your risk such that if you happen to fail one state test you still have a chance of passing the other. But there is some extra stress. You will likely find that you are fairly worn out by that third day of testing. Also, keep in mind that you will likely be unable to do this if you are sitting for a state that has a three-day bar exam, such as California.

SHOULD I PREPARE MY ESSAYS ON A COMPUTER OR WRITE THEM OUT BY HAND?

MOST STATES NOW seem to offer the option to prepare essays on a computer. You provide the computer but the bar association provides security software that does not let you access any of the files on your computer. I did this when I took the California bar examination in January 2003. I recommend it because your work will be neater and more professional-looking, and most of us are now so used to typing that we can actually type (and think) faster at a keyboard than with a pen and paper. You can also go back and correct your mistakes on a computer, a much better solution than crossing out lines of wrong-minded text and scribbling in the margins.

CAN I BELONG TO TOO MANY STATE BARS?

I RECENTLY WITHDREW as a member of the New Jersey bar after paying bar dues for about ten years. I never practiced law in New Jersey (I joined the bar because I grew up there and my family still lives there). I estimate that I spent over $2,000 paying dues to the New Jersey State Bar over the years. Today, I'd rather have that money back (and the time I spent studying for and taking the New Jersey bar was obviously not productive time). Therefore, be careful about which bar exams you choose to take. As a corporate lawyer, you should be a member of the New York State Bar Association. If you think you might want to live in California, take that state's exam.

There is also the subject of having to meet state continuing legal education (CLE) requirements and mandatory pro bono guidelines. These are classes you need to take every year in order to remain in good standing with the state bar. These requirements vary by state but can be quite burdensome in terms of the number of class hours you need.

HOW CAN I IMPROVE MY CHANCES OF PASSING THE BAR EXAM?

IN ORDER TO pass the bar exam—any bar exam—you need to study reasonably hard and, critically, focus on the specific areas of the law that you will be tested on. You should take a bar review class. Many students take test preparatory classes with "BarBri," and you should ask your law school's career counsel or dean of students for advice on what program is best suited for your state's bar exam. Inevitably there will be presentations made on your law school's campus by the various bar preparation services. I took three bar exams: the New York and New Jersey state bar exams at the same time, and later the California bar exam. I studied for the first two using BarBri, and for the California bar I used an outline I had found on the Internet (posted by a Berkeley student). I passed all of these bar examinations easily (I think I studied for the California bar exam a total of about three weeks). However, everyone gets nervous before taking a bar exam—and people have even been known to pass out from the stress during the exam! My advice is to study hard given the time you have and stay relaxed. If you fail, you can always take it again. There are no limits to how many times you can try. Chances are that if you got into a top law school and put a reasonable amount of time and effort into studying, you are going to pass. I do not know of any of my classmates from Columbia who failed the bar exam on their first attempt.

9. PURSUING OTHER DEGREES

SHOULD I GET AN MBA AT THE SAME TIME THAT I AM GETTING MY JD?

MY FIRST REACTION when confronted with this question (and I have been both in the position of the person asking the question and the person answering it) is that, if you are asking, then the answer is probably yes. A wise person once gave me that advice and I am passing it on to you. However, as with many things, the analysis is a little more complex.

First, let me tell you my story. When I was starting my second year at Columbia Law School I had the opportunity to get my MBA from Columbia Business School through the University's joint degree program. In 1992 it was not very difficult to get into Columbia Business School. About half of all applicants were accepted, compared with around 15 percent now. I know I would have been accepted into the program (in fact, years later I was granted admission to Columbia Business School), particularly because a couple of my classmates, who had about the same qualifications as I, actually did go ahead and enter the four-year joint program.

I can tell you that I did not have the information or experience needed to make a good decision about whether to enter that joint degree program. I was twenty-three and still living off the high that comes with being accepted into a top-rated law school. I was thinking about the program because I had an interest in business (I had started my first business, selling reflective sun shields for cars at the beach, when I was in grade school) and because the students in my class who were pursuing the joint degree seemed to have a solid plan for their careers after graduation. That is, they wanted to go into investment banking rather than join a law firm.

I was fortunate in that my cousin had graduated from Columbia Law School five years before I started and some of his classmates were in New York. I was further fortunate that one of these classmates, David, who was then a senior associate at the largest corporate law firm in New York, gave me good advice on whether to pursue an MBA at the same time as the JD. He said, "If you are thinking about it now, you should just do it." Stupidly, I did not listen to him. He was right.

David said, "Look, you don't know what you want to do with your career now. If you wanted to be a judge or a prosecutor you should just stick with law school, go work for the Department of Justice, and work your way up. But I know you. You are like me. You are interested in doing business deals. You think you are going to do business deals if you work for a big corporate law firm. I work for a big corporate law firm. All I do is edit contracts. I want to get out of this and work in business, but it is hard to make that transition as a lawyer. So get the MBA and go directly into a business job without ever having practiced law." No better advice has ever been given.

It took me nearly ten years to learn how right David was when he said that the time to pursue the MBA was then if I was even thinking about it. He understood what it generally takes half a career to understand: If you have the desire to be in the business world—by which I mean doing deals, making sales, and building economic value—you are not going to be happy in a corporate law career, where you are, at best, assisting clients to do deals and make sales, and at worst, performing minor tasks like checking that all the contracts are in order before the deal closes. The problem is, you get stuck. Once you find yourself a senior associate or a junior partner, you are making too much money to make a career switch. It is rare for an attorney to find a real business-sector job and be willing to take the pay cut. Once you start down the path of being a lawyer, it is increasingly hard to deviate from it.

There is also the other thing we do not like to talk about. It is one of those dirty little secrets that seem implausible but are absolutely true. I have gone to both business school and law school and I have a number of friends who have done the same. Some of us went to business school after we practiced law for a few years. But we all feel we are business people at heart (we have a big-picture view of deals, know marketing, are gregarious, etc.). Everyone tells us, when they learn that we have both JDs and MBAs, "That is such a strong combination. You can get any job you want."

The secret is that it isn't true. Think about it. Businesses want to hire either bright young people they can train or more senior people who have developed specialized skills. Investment banks and operating companies are used to hiring MBAs in their mid-twenties for entry-level jobs. They may even hire some JD/MBAs right out of school. But they don't know what to do with a thirty-year-old lawyer who also has an MBA. In fact, having a JD can be a detriment if you are an MBA student seeking employment in the business sector. The skills you picked up studying and practicing law may be useful when you get to a senior level in the business but as a junior employee the expectation is that you will focus on a specific business role in finance, marketing, or strategic decision making.

So if you want to go into business instead of law, you need to act as early as possible in your career, whether it is by getting a joint MBA degree or by entering a business job rather than a legal job directly after law school. Practicing law forever brands you as "a lawyer." Business people employ lawyers but they view them in a somewhat negative light—lawyers are too risk averse, too steeped in the minutiae of legal issues, and unaware of larger business concerns.[1] This stigma becomes harder to shake—even by going back to business school—as time passes. Actual results illustrate what I am talking about. Of those of my law school classmates who successfully went into business careers, nearly all did so immediately after graduation. One college classmate of mine who went to Harvard Law School held out for an investment banking job following graduation (he never worked in a law firm) and is now a managing director at a leading Wall Street bank. Of my two Columbia classmates who got their MBAs, one went directly into investment banking and the other joined Wachtel, Lipton, the top New York boutique law firm specializing in sophisticated business transactions. (This is a unique firm, paying the highest associate salaries and bonuses in New York and acting in a broader advisory function than most law firms.)

My friends who practiced law for a number of years and then decided to go back to business school either full or part time had strikingly different results. Not one has had success obtaining top-quality business-sector jobs. A Columbia classmate who practiced law for five years before going to the Anderson Graduate School of Management at UCLA went back to practicing law after he got his MBA—at a salary higher than any of his MBA classmates, but back where he started from nonetheless. A fellow attorney who went to Wharton before I did found it very difficult to obtain employment in an investment bank. He echoed the comment from an associate of mine who went back to Harvard Business School full time: banks felt he was too old to start as a banking associate and that, in any event, they did not know how to use his legal expertise. The banks offered him positions within their compliance and legal divisions, but these were positions he could have gotten even without an MBA.

That is not to say you can't transition from law to business, but it is hard. One of my Columbia suitemates was able to get a job at Booz Allen Hamilton after practicing law with the top New York law firm Simpson Thacher & Bartlett for a couple of years, after which he went to Stanford Law School. Upon graduation from Stanford he went to work for a technology start-up in Austin. Another college classmate of mine currently works at McKinsey & Company, after having graduated from Harvard Law, practicing with Davis, Polk & Wardwell in New York for a couple of years, and then going on to graduate with an MBA from the Massachusetts Institute of Technology. In fact, it may be a little easier to get consulting jobs than banking jobs for lawyers with MBAs because the consulting structure (partners, hourly billing, written reports) is somewhat analogous to the way law firms work.

SHOULD I CONSIDER GETTING AN LL.M?

GETTING AN LL.M can be a good choice for some people, particularly if you are going into a specialty, like tax or bankruptcy law, or if you are five to ten years out of law school and want to change your practice area. An LL.M—essentially a master's degree in a specialized area of the law—can be either a good way for a young lawyer to quickly gain knowledge of a specific legal field or can serve lawyers with greater seniority seeking to get a flagging legal career back on track or, perhaps, on a different track.

First, let me define an LL.M degree. LL.M is Latin for *Legum Magister*, which can be translated roughly as "Master of Laws." In Latin abbreviations, plural words are indicated by double letters. An LL.M degree usually takes just one year of full time study to complete (or perhaps two or more years of taking night classes). Because the degree is intended to impart specific expertise to the student, it is usually stated in terms of the specialty, such as LL.M in Taxation or LL.M in Securities Law.

It is most useful to get an LL.M degree in a field that requires unique and specific knowledge, and that is in high demand by the legal profession. The two specialties that come to mind are taxation and securities law. I have known lawyers who have received degrees in both of these areas. One was a U.S. Bankruptcy Court judge who had received his LL.M in Taxation from New York University. NYU has one of the premier bankruptcy LL.M programs in the country, if not the best. While the degree was not directly applicable to his service as a bankruptcy judge, it was a prestigious degree that tagged him as someone comfortable with a highly technical body of law. I am confident that having the degree helped him to achieve the recognition necessary to be named a federal judge.

I also know a young lawyer who received an LL.M in Securities Law from Georgetown University's Law Center. Georgetown offers one of the most respected securities law LL.Ms in the country. It benefits from significant regional resources, particularly as many classes taught by former and current senior SEC attorneys. How this young lawyer I know used the LL.M is instructive on how such a degree can help push the career of a young lawyer forward. This young lawyer, who had not gone to a very well-regarded law school, wanted to get into securities law in

Washington. But no major Washington securities law firm would hire him, nor would the SEC. He was, however, able to get admitted to Georgetown's LL.M program in securities law. Upon graduating, he was able to get a job with the SEC's Division of Enforcement. After a few years at Enforcement, he was able to get a job in a private securities law firm. Today he is a partner in one of the leading Washington securities firms, specializing in securities enforcement work. This is an objective he was only able to achieve by using the LL.M as a stepping stone.

One thing you should take away from my anecdotal stories is that selecting the right LL.M program is critical. Both of the individuals I have told you about did two things in common: first, they both chose to undertake an LL.M in a specialized technical field that fully justified obtaining that degree. (Other fields that might also qualify would be patent and copyright law.) Second, they both chose a law school with the reputation as the preeminent school for that subject (NYU for tax and Georgetown for securities law). You should do the same.

Most of all, do not settle for second best in pursuing your LL.M degree. If you are going to do it, select a degree that will get you a job when you are done. Do not get an LL.M degree in an area like constitutional law. While it is an interesting and important subject, there is just not the demand from the legal profession for lawyers having that specialty. If top firms want a constitutional law expert, they will hire a Supreme Court law clerk. Also, you should research very carefully the reputation of the school you are considering with regard to how strong they are in your chosen specialty. It is a lot easier to get into a top LL.M program than it is to get into a top law school for a JD. You should be going to the best school in your field. This will greatly enhance the probability of your getting a job in—and advancing in—the area of specialty you have adopted.

WHY ARE THERE SO MANY FOREIGN LL.M STUDENTS?

FOREIGN LAW STUDENTS who come to American law schools are here for a different kind of LL.M than the one that American lawyers obtain. Many law schools offer a one-year master's degree program in general American law that is open to foreign-educated lawyers who have, usually, several years of experience practicing in their own countries. Law schools make a good deal of money through these programs—students or their employers generally pay cash for tuition—and also expand the ranks of their international alumni. The value of this alumni network should not be underestimated, though few law students appreciate its potential at the time they are in school.

You should buck the trend and make an attempt to develop friendships with foreign LL.M students while you are in law school, as they will be among the most interesting people—well traveled, multilingual, cultured —that you are likely to meet. The practice of law, particularly corporate law, is becoming increasingly international. If you look in the financial press, you will see that a great many transactions involve a foreign acquirer, target, or at least foreign operating divisions. Building relations with foreign LL.M students, who will often go back to their home countries and obtain prominent positions in law firms, government, or industry, can open unusual and valuable career opportunities for you. You will be one of the few American lawyers they know well, on a personal level, and they may tap you or encourage one of their colleagues to tap you to represent them in a major transaction. In addition, it is almost certain that, at some point in your career, you will be in need of a reliable attorney in a foreign country and have the opportunity to return the favor of referring business to them. These are, simply, the kind of relationships on which you can base your professional career.

It is not always easy to form friendships with foreign LL.M students. They are mostly in their own classes, only stick around for a year, and tend to socialize primarily with each other. But you can do it and it is worth the extra effort. Get to know these students when they first arrive at school at the start of the year. If there are no events planned at which JD and LL.M students socialize together, ask your dean if you can help to organize a mixer; the school will likely pay for it. Organizing such an event will give you the entrée to approach foreign LL.M students freely and ask them what kind of event they would prefer. Would they like to have an event at which the foods from their various countries are sampled? Or, better, the beers? The opportunities are wide open. If you are a second- or third-year student, you can help them get to know the campus or the town. Your efforts are sure to be appreciated and recalled. Remember, never again in your career are you going to have the opportunity to develop relationships with such a broad cross-section of the international legal community.

I AM A FOREIGN LAWYER INTERESTED IN GETTING AN LL.M DEGREE IN THE UNITED STATES. WHAT SHOULD I KNOW?

THE TOPIC OF what foreign lawyers seeking to obtain an advanced law degree from a U.S. law school need to know could fill an entire book; I will provide an overview here. I have known and worked with a number of lawyers who received LL.M degrees from American law schools. When I attended Columbia, the LL.M students lived in the same dorm that we did—Hogan Hall, at 113th Street and Broadway—and we talked a lot about why they had come to the program and what they expected to get out of it. I have also worked with a number of LL.M students and have known other LL.Ms who worked in other firms. Finally, while working in Washington in the late 1990s, I owned a language translation business that employed a number of LL.M students, from Georgetown, Stanford, and Harvard, among about a dozen other schools. Through those relationships I was able to gain some insight into how the various LL.M programs treat their students, including, critically, the extent to which obtaining the degree from various schools positioned the foreign lawyers to obtain employment in the United States.

My general conclusion is that if your objective is to get a job at a U.S. law firm after receiving your LL.M, you need to go to a very well-regarded law school and also do an effective job at networking. American law schools that offer the most highly regarded foreign LL.M programs include Columbia, Harvard, the University of Pennsylvania, Yale, NYU, UCLA, and the University of Chicago. However, don't expect to get a job in the United States even if you graduate from one of these schools. Practicing law in the United States still requires that you pass a state bar examination, and most states require that you attend law school in the United States—that is, receive a JD degree—before they will allow you to sit for the bar exam. Exceptions are New York, which allows foreign LL.M recipients to sit for the bar, and California, which does not require that a bar exam candidate attend law school at all (though other requirements apply).

You may not want to join a U.S. law firm after you graduate. This is common, as many foreign LL.M students are sponsored by law firms in their home countries and will return there after graduation, but it still makes sense to attend the best American law school you can. The programs at the schools I listed in the previous paragraph will provide you with the highest prestige factor and also place you in a distinguished group of alumni, which connections may be the main benefit you receive from attending the program.

However, the top legal education programs can be difficult to gain admission to. For that reason, you might want to consider what I believe most practicing lawyers would categorize as credible but not first-tier schools. Cornell is one example. An Ivy League law school, it has not quite kept up with the other Ivies in terms of academic reputation. However, it remains an Ivy and that will always hold considerable weight, particularly among graduates of the other Ivies. Another school you might want to consider is Georgetown University. Located in the heart of Washington, D.C., the law school is not near the main campus, which is beautiful, but rather in a modern facility closer to the historic Union Station. Georgetown is well regarded, though not a top-ten school. A benefit is that it is in the nation's capital, which will afford you close access to government and international institutions, including the World Bank and the International Monetary Fund, places where you might get an internship and also where you might find employment after graduation. You could also practice law in Washington if you first obtain admission to the California or New York bars (though there has been talk of changing this reciprocity rule). A downside is that you may have difficulty getting a job in New York or California from this school because there will be fewer alumni in those regions, although the university does have a national reputation and is respected throughout the country.

You might also want to consider whether your home country has any particularly strong connections to a given school. It is fairly common, in some regions, to find that senior government leaders have received degrees from particular schools. The University of Chicago was well represented, for example, among senior elected officials in several Latin American countries for a time. Also, UCLA and UC Berkeley continue to be very well known throughout Asia, a dividend of their geographic location on the Pacific Rim. It could make a good deal of sense for a Japanese candidate, for example, to choose UCLA if this school is particularly well known in his home country (though if the candidate can get into a truly top school like Harvard or Stanford, that would remain a better pick). As this is a big investment of time and money—and a one-time event—it is worth investing considerable research in the decision.

10. BUILDING A LEGAL CAREER

THE BIG LIE (PART I)

THERE IS SOMETHING that a group of us former law firm associates have come to call the "big lie." The big lie is simply the proposition that a legal education provides you with a golden ticket to achieve significantly more than you would have been able to without the degree. I remember that when I was accepted into Columbia Law School, everyone, from professors to friends to my parents, was very impressed. Many said that I had it made and could write my own ticket. But I have since come to believe that getting into a top law school was as much a handicap as it was a benefit. Put it in historical context. I graduated from college, and then spent three years in law school. After that I spent two years working for a federal judge for about $35,000 a year. That was five years I spent making little or no money in order to get my basic qualifications as an attorney. What if, instead, I had gone to work as an analyst on Wall Street? Though Wall Street jobs were scarce when I graduated from college, had I gotten one (I didn't even try, since I got into law school) I could have gotten an

MBA by the time I was twenty-seven and by now be fairly senior in my chosen business field. Or, better yet, what if I had looked at the economy and said, "There is an interesting company in Redmond, Washington, called Microsoft that looks like it might be doing some great things. I think I'll go up there and get a job." That would have been a very good decision.

Despite being prestigious and hard to get into, law school is costly—tuition, surely, but also the opportunity cost of forgoing real-life experience in the business world. Going to law school brings more certain results—you will likely spend some time working for big dollars at a large law firm—but it does not mean your career accomplishments will be any greater than if you had chosen another path. When you are in college, you know about only one thing—going to school. Taking the next step—going to law school—is an achievement you can understand in your experiential context. Going out and finding a job in a promising industry is a little more risky. It is an unknown. But sometimes it is the unknown that will yield the most satisfying rewards. To answer the question on your mind, yes, looking back I do wish I had flown out to Redmond and taken a job—any job—with Microsoft in 1991 (the stock has gone from about a split-adjusted buck a share to about $30 a share since 1991).

THE BIG LIE (PART II)

The second part of the big lie is that going to work for a large law firm immediately after law school (or after clerking for a federal judge, as the case may be) is the best way to keep your options open in advancing your career. In fact, it is not always the best idea to work for a big law firm immediately after graduation. While firm jobs are by far the highest-paying jobs in the short run, in the long run it is possible (with a little forethought) to put together a much more solid plan for career progression.

Law school career advisers are largely responsible for the second part of the big lie. Many students go off to law school with the idea that they will be able to use their legal

The big lie is simply the proposition that a legal education provides you with a golden ticket to achieve significantly more than you would have been able to without the degree.

The second part of the big lie is that going to work for a large law firm immediately after law school (or after clerking for a federal judge, as the case may be) is the best way to keep your options open in advancing your career.

education to achieve great things. They may see it as a ticket to start a meaningful public-interest career, gain success in business, or enter politics—and maybe even become president. Whatever the dream, law school career counselors somehow get it into the students' heads that going to work for a large law firm right after graduation is the best way to start down the path to achieving their goals. It often is not. Working for a big law firm can be a trap. The work is very demanding, and your free time—for personal recreation or to evaluate career opportunities— is extremely limited. During those years of working as a law firm associate you are likely going to be quite insulated, focusing on the deal or litigation matter to which you are assigned, watching the days and weeks and years go by without having made much headway toward the dream.

Now, granted, in a law firm you will make good money (though not as much as you would make in some professions, like investment banking). And you will get good training, particularly with regard to learning to pay attention to minute details and subtleties in documents. But working for a big law firm is not the most direct way to make a difference in public-interest law, nor is it the best way to start a business career. If you want to go into business, then I would recommend not spending those years working in a law firm. Instead, get a job in business, or in an investment bank, as soon as possible. If you want to make a difference in public-sector law or in a government agency, get a job that is more directly on point. Law school counselors and the recruiting system generally push law students toward working for the big firms, but, despite the high salaries, it can be in students' best interest to go for the jobs that are more directly associated with what they want to do.

WHAT SHOULD I DO *AFTER* LAW SCHOOL?

The question of whether you should go to a law firm is different from the question of whether law school career officials will push you to go to a firm. They will. Whether you should depends upon a great number of factors. However, let's limit those factors to just a few, which we can state here as questions. First, what do you want to accomplish with your career? Do you want to be a lawyer practicing in a big firm making a lot of money? Do you mind working long hours, and even longer hours as your seniority increases, on matters that may as often as not be boring and repetitious? Do you want to take the risk of doing something different that might advance your career in fantastic ways but deprive you of a six-figure income immediately after taking the bar? And, finally, do you need the law firm salary to pay off massive student loans?

Sometimes it is possible to predict the future, and sometimes it is not. If you join a large law firm you will get a fairly predictable experience. They will train you well in the practice of law, you will be well compensated for at least six years, and more than likely, after that they will tell you that you are not going to make partner, and they will help you find a nice in-house job with one of the firm's clients. If you take one of the alternative career routes, like going to work for a senator or becoming a federal prosecutor, the result is less certain. If your senator becomes president, you could become an under-secretary of something. If he retires, you could be out of a job. You could win some big cases, be promoted, and find yourself in a position to run for governor. The risk, depending on your tolerance for it, could be worth taking. On the other hand, if you crave a stable salary and a more certain five-year plan, then firm life might be for you.

First, however, let me give you a word of caution. I went to work for a large, prominent law firm immediately after completing my clerkship with a federal judge. That firm was in Washington, D.C., and it was a good experience for me. It was considered one of the top two firms in Washington and probably among the top ten firms in the United States, judged on the basis of reputation and ability to attract top law school graduates. There were many former Supreme Court law clerks in my class. Harvard and Yale law schools (as well as my own Columbia Law) were well represented. In all, I believe my first experience working for a large firm was about as good as it can possibly get. Nevertheless, in choosing to work for a big firm I gave up some opportunities that, in retrospect, I would have been better off pursuing in order to advance the long-term development of my legal career.

I will give you a concrete example of what I am talking about. Now— ten years out of law school—I work for the Securities and Exchange Commission in its Division of Enforcement. Working for the SEC is a great job. After about a year of service you get promoted from being a staff attorney to the position of senior counsel. In fact, no matter how much experience you have, unless you come in from private practice to the SEC as a senior officer, you will hold the title of staff attorney. I had nine years of legal experience, all at top law firms, before I came to the SEC. While my salary was pretty good, at least for doing government work, I was clearly starting at the bottom. Eight years ago, when I was finishing my clerkship with a federal judge, I received an offer to work for the Division of Enforcement. I would have earned about $40,000 a year verses the $80,000 that I was offered by a law firm.

However, if I had chosen to work in the Division of Enforcement those eight years ago, then eight years later I would almost certainly have achieved the title of branch chief and perhaps even assistant director. An assistant director makes about $160,000 a year—not a lot, but consider that today, an assistant director can generally go out on the open market for experienced securities attorneys and earn in excess of half a million dollars a year from a private law firm. This illustration shows that there may be reasons—particularly if you are able to put in place a compelling five- or even ten-year career plan—for biting the bullet and investing in a lower-paying government or other non-traditional job in the early part of your career.

"Straight out of law school, I would have sought a job with the Department of Justice."

Even very successful law firm partners often regret the fact that they went directly to a law firm after graduating rather than getting government experience early in their careers. I asked one friend of mine, who became a partner in a leading corporate firm and who by his mid-thirties was making about half a million dollars a year, what one thing he would do differently if he could start over in his career. He said, "Straight out of law school, I would have sought a job with the Department of Justice."

I should note that there are currently a large number of graduates of top law schools working at the SEC as junior staffers. In my group in Enforcement we had a graduate of Harvard, two graduates of Yale, and a Duke alum. Each of us had worked for law firms for from five to nine years, figured out that we were unlikely to make partner at the firm, and opted for a safer and hopefully more enjoyable experience prosecuting securities law violators with the SEC. Our bosses, however, were about our ages. They were, in order of seniority, a graduate of Fordham Law School and a graduate of Howard Law School. Neither of these schools is as competitive to gain admission to as Harvard, Columbia, and Duke. However, these supervisors—one an assistant director and the other a branch chief—came to the SEC soon after graduating from law school, perhaps with a year or two of private law firm experience. One had been at the commission for eight years and the other for over ten years—basically their entire careers. They did not have the academic credentials of the junior staffers, but they had much more experience and longevity, and a familiarity with the customs and practices of the commission. I point this out so that you will realize two things. First, even if you get into and graduate from a top law school, you can still end up working for someone from a lower-ranked law school if your career plan is not designed to keep you moving forward in terms of seniority. Second, you need to have a career plan that takes into account the low probability of making partner in a large law firm and which provides you with at least a backup plan that does not require you to start at the bottom of the heap relatively late in your career.

The fact that law firms are the employers of choice for graduates of top law schools may be a competitive disadvantage to such graduates in terms of their long-term career development.

Nevertheless, law firms are the employers of choice for the graduates of top law schools. You will get paid a lot of money for working at a large urban law firm. The average salary for a first-year lawyer right out of law school in New York City was over $125,000 for the class starting in 2005, with an expected annual bonus of at least an additional $10,000. In Washington, the average salary and bonus was a little bit less. Senior associates got paid even more. A sixth-year associate in New York can expect to make as much as $200,000 in base pay, with a discretionary bonus of up to $100,000. As attorneys get more senior, the bonus becomes more discretionary. At most firms, the bonus is used to tell fifth- and sixth-year associates whether they are welcome to stick around and contend for partner or if the firm would rather see them seek other career opportunities. This is the reason most firms publish a range of bonuses by class year at the same time the individual bonus awards are made. Money talks, and it is the clearest signal available to tell the senior associates where they stand in the firm's future.

When I was a sixth-year associate at a law firm, I made over $200,000 a year in salary and was eligible for an additional $100,000 annual bonus. That remains the year in which I made my highest salary as a practicing attorney. At the time, my personal expenses were not significant, and I was able to put about $50,000 a year into investments. Depending on your personal circumstances, it can be financially very nice to make a lot of money for a couple of years, as long as you take the opportunity to save a big chunk of it. If you keep your expenses low and resist buying a big house and expensive car, you can get a job that you will be able to enjoy—such as working at the SEC or becoming an Assistant U.S. Attorney, for example.

If you really want to put a lot of money away, look for law firms that are based in New York City, where the highest salaries are paid to associates, and find one that pays the associates in its regional offices the same base salary. Some large firms pay all associates the same regardless of the location of the office where they work. Other firms adjust for the local cost of living. Skadden, Arps, for example, had the tradition of paying all of its associates the same amount. The best salary in the world, adjusted for cost of living, was to work in Skadden, Arps's office in Wilmington, Delaware, and get paid a New York wage.[1] At that rate, you were pretty much at the top of the economic food chain in Wilmington.

HOW MUCH WOULD I GET PAID AS A LAW FIRM ASSOCIATE?

LAW FIRM PAY is a moving target, and in recent years it has been moving up quite rapidly. In the previous section we discussed what some senior associates get paid. However, all associates do not get paid the same. In general, associates at larger firms get paid more than associates at smaller firms. The NALP published a survey on April 1, 2005, of 573 law offices of various sizes. The survey found that first-year associates at firms with two to twenty-five lawyers earned a median salary of $67,500, while associates at firms with over five hundred lawyers earned a median salary of $125,000. Some of this difference is due to the fact that although large law firms are commonly located in large cities—New York and Los Angeles for example—some large firms are found in smaller cities such as Hartford and Indianapolis.[2] The following table illustrates NALP's findings.

Associate Year	Firm Size: Number of Lawyers					
	2–25	26–50	51–100	101–250	251–500	Over–501
First	$67,500	$80,000	$83,000	$88,000	$105,000	$125,000
Second	$75,000	$86,000	$86,000	$91,400	$108,000	$130,000
Third	$77,250	$83,000	$89,000	$93,600	$111,875	$135,000
Fourth	$88,000	$92,927	$94,000	$97,000	$118,300	$145,000
Fifth	$91,000	$83,000	$95,000	$101,000	$125,000	$153,000
Sixth	$94,000	$98,000	$97,510	$107,000	$131,250	$165,000
Seventh	$97,000	$98,000	$101,500	$111,625	$136,625	$175,000
Eighth	$109,000	$108,000	$105,554	$117,917	$144,333	$181,500

Source: NALP Salary Survey, April 1, 2005.

WHAT ARE SOME COMMON INTERVIEWING MISTAKES?

THERE ARE SO many possible pitfalls in being interviewed that it is impossible to anticipate them all. I have made many mistakes. I'll start by describing where I have gone wrong.

I remember when, as a first-year, I was interviewing for positions with law firms for my first-year summer. There were very few law firms interested in hiring first-year students. This is because the likelihood that a first-year would come back to the firm after graduating two years later was very small; most students would go to the firm they clerked for during their second-year summer. But I was able to obtain an interview with a leading New Jersey law firm based in Roseland, New Jersey. I am from New Jersey, so there was a plausible argument that I might be more inclined than most other Columbia law students to go work in the state rather than take a job in New York City.

My job was to convince them that I really wanted to come back and work in New Jersey. I knew this was the only way I could get a job offer. In this I did a pretty good job. However, I was still a naive young law student. When I was interviewing for one partner I thought I would be smart and mention what I thought of as a famous New Jersey Supreme Court case. It was a case I had studied in torts and was used to illustrate a major cause of action. I don't remember what the case was today, but that is the point of my illustration. At the time I knew the case name and its details. I somehow worked the case into the conversation in an effort to show I had learned something during my one year of law school. The partner I was interviewing with asked me to describe the case. Thinking it was a famous case that everyone would know, I said something along the lines of "Come on, you know that case." I didn't want to look foolish by repeating the facts of a case that everyone knew. Eventually I gave a truncated explanation of the facts, but it was a very awkward moment.

My point in telling this story is a broad one. It is to put yourself in the shoes of the interviewer. There was no way this corporate lawyer twenty years out of law school was going to know my little torts case. The fact that it had been a highlight of my class didn't mean that a practitioner would ever have heard of it. He was simply interested in learning how well I could describe some random case I had mentioned. I also should have known that by mentioning a specific case, I was opening the door to having the interviewer ask detailed questions about it. Don't introduce a subject unless you are absolutely confident about discussing it.

That point was driven home in another fiasco. I was interviewing at a major New York law firm toward the end of my time clerking for a federal judge after graduation. A senior associate reading my résumé noticed that I had published an article on the fiduciary duties of corporate directors to shareholders. He asked me what the article had recommended and I mentioned a couple of things, including a change in the Delaware Corporate Code. Then, of course, he asked what the provision was that I recommended changing and what the effect would be. Now, I clerked for two years and had written the article during my second year of law school, so it had been three years since I had written the piece with one of my classmates. I did not remember the specifics of our recommendation, and the point of the article was its analysis of the problem with the recommended solution merely an afterthought. Caught unprepared, I was unable to give a very good answer. That looks bad when you are the author of the article. So here is another example of why you should be prepared to speak about anything you introduce, including any items on your résumé, in exquisite detail.

Also, don't try to be funny. Law is a business and the interviewing process is a formal one. Stick to this rule no matter where you are in the interviewing process. During my clerkship, I had a couple of great interviews with the New York firm of Davis, Polk. When I was done with my last interview, I headed for the elevator and bumped into a good friend of one of my high school buddies. They had been roommates at Princeton. I knew him socially. It was a surprise, and after the stress of interviews, my reaction was to relax immediately and slip into an informal attitude. We were joking around near the elevator bank, laughing at some old inside joke, when one of the partners I had interviewed with walked by. He was busy and was rushing off to do something important. He looked at me and this associate yucking it up and did not seem amused. He had likely not written up his reflections on my interview yet for the hiring committee. I did not get an offer. I continue to think that this chance meeting with my friend's friend was a factor in that decision.

You will get lots of advice on what to wear for interviews. Men should wear dark suits—one and a quarter-inch cuffs, single breasted, with a white shirt and a conservative tie—while women should wear a conservative navy business suit and keep their hair up or above the shoulders. Anyone can give you this advice and it may change a little as business fashions evolve (though they do so slowly). However, I will tell you that I have seen students dressed well who did not get offers and students who dressed like fools who did get offers. More important were grades and an impression of seriousness. I guess the firms figure they can always teach you how to dress later on. In fact, considering that the partners would rather have a hungry associate willing to work ridiculous hours than a rich and idle one, it may be a plus if you are not dressed as if you were groomed from birth to go to Exeter.

HOW CAN I GUARANTEE THAT I WON'T GET A JOB OFFER?

WELL, OBVIOUSLY, THERE are a lot of ways to blow an interview. But what I want to tell you about is a way to have a great interview, top grades, everything, and still blow it. This is a true—and humiliating—story.

When I was in law school in New York, one of my suitemates was a former basketball player from Texas. He was brilliant—law review, top grades—and confident. Tall, good looking—he had it all. Seemingly, every law firm in New York wanted him. But he really wanted to return home to Texas.

After on-campus interviews in August he had a number of callbacks in Texas. Some were in Dallas and some in Houston, but he really wanted to work in Houston, closer to where he had family. He couldn't accept all of the interview invitations, so he selected a couple of the top firms and arranged to travel to Houston for the meetings. He would economize. On one trip he scheduled an interview on Thursday with one firm and an interview on Friday with another.

This trip would be his undoing. Both interviews went great—he was their perfect candidate. He had not grown up with money, rising instead from a small, dusty west Texas town to receive an academic scholarship, play basketball at big a eastern university, and then earn top honors at Columbia Law. Now, what he forgot to do was to mention to each of the firms that he was also interviewing with the other. Of course, he was not required to do this. But what he also forgot was to mention that each firm was reimbursing his travel expenses. Somehow, most likely in error, he had submitted for the same reimbursement from both firms for the same airline tickets, hotel, and meals.

But the law firms were not inclined to give him the benefit of the doubt. What amounted to a windfall of a few hundred dollars—not a lot of money given what was at stake—resulted in every firm in Houston refusing to offer him a position. These two top Houston firms learned that our guy had interviewed with each of them (perhaps he made too good an impression) and that both firms had reimbursed all of his travel expenses. One can imagine the conversation between the two firms that resulted in the discovery of the double payment. Both firms called him within a week demanding repayment. Needless to say, he did not receive an offer from either firm. What's more, all of the other Houston firms withdrew their interview offers. What you should learn from this is to be meticulous. Despite their reputations, lawyers are not supposed to be deceitful and dishonest. Duplicity in dealing with fellow lawyers is frowned upon, particularly when they are offering to take you into the fold. This extends to a great many things—including being truthful on your résumé. Law firms are increasingly researching the backgrounds of their potential hires. You need to be completely honest and open in your communications and dealings with them.

ARE THERE SHORTCUTS TO GETTING A JOB AT A LEADING LAW FIRM?

I HAVE HEARD of law students getting the advice that if they want to work for a particular leading law firm but are not qualified for a position as an associate attorney, they might be able to get their foot in the door by applying for a job as a paralegal. Barring very unusual circumstances, it is highly unlikely that a paralegal at a top firm will become an associate attorney at that firm.

Top law firms do hire individuals who have graduated from second- or third-tier law schools as paralegals. However, at top firms there is essentially no job mobility from paralegal to associate. It is a little bit like my experience as a lifeguard. I guarded on the New Jersey shore and on Nantucket for seven years during high school and college summers. The fourteen-year-old boys and girls we would take on as junior lifeguards rarely got jobs as lifeguards on the same beach. They would usually have to go to a pool or another beach if they wanted to guard when they got older. They were not going to get the respect of the other guards after spending a summer or two running around fetching us sodas. This is even more the case in law firms, where the social divide between the attorneys and everyone else—paralegals, secretaries, librarians—is immense.

There are, of course, the unusual circumstances that disprove the rule. If a lawyer who was employed as a paralegal at a top firm did something unusually beneficial for the firm, he might be elevated to associate. I have never seen this happen. However, there was one attorney at a firm I worked for who, as a junior associate, discovered a mistake that a senior partner had made. The mistake was such that the partner and the firm would likely have been sued by the client if the mistake had not been caught. This associate was not otherwise outstanding. His fellow associates considered him to be something of a dolt. However, the partner whose hide he saved made certain that he was elevated to the partnership in gratitude for the catch that he made. I imagine that sort of scenario could play out for a paralegal, but the person would need to be in the right place at the right time.

The other thing to keep in mind is that this advice applies mainly to large urban law firms like Skadden, Arps. Smaller firms may have much less rigid social structures. I could see a graduate of a lower-ranked law school getting a position as a paralegal in a small local firm, passing the bar, and working his way up to practicing law in the group. Indeed, this is the way the law used to be learned and taught—more on an apprentice basis—over a hundred years ago. It is how many of the founding fathers of this nation, and even Abraham Lincoln, learned the law. But I expect that most of the readers of this book will aspire to obtain positions with the larger, higher-paying urban law firms.

ANY ADVICE ON HOW TO WRITE A RÉSUMÉ OR HOW TO PREPARE FOR INTERVIEWS?

UNLIKE A LOT of career advice books, in this volume I do not spend a great deal of time teaching you how to prepare for interviews or how to write a résumé. Advice along these lines is pretty easy to come by. I am certain that your law school has an assistant dean whose job it is to make sure your résumé is in an acceptable format and that you are dressed appropriately for your interviews. That being said, I want to provide you with the basic interviewing tools. Appendix C contains a template that can be used for either a law student or a recent law school graduate's résumé. It is based on a time-tested model employed by The Wharton School at the

University of Pennsylvania and generally follows the "education first, then experience" format.

Writing a résumé is itself an art. There are many acceptable formats. However, generally, I advise that you keep your résumé to a single page. I still—even after several advanced degrees and a number of jobs—have a single-page résumé. In my job as counsel to an SEC commissioner, one of the things I did was to review candidates for both junior and senior appointments within the SEC. One candidate for a position as head of one of the divisions had a résumé that was more than ten pages long! Granted, he had been a university professor, had many publications, and had attended many academic seminars. But the guy listed the names of every research assistant he had ever had! Being comprehensive is fine, but it is a natural reaction for reviewers to look at including the kitchen sink on a résumé to be a sign of poor judgment. Exercising good judgment is more important than qualifications.

Law firm interviews may be changing as the industry itself is changing. In the past, they have generally been nonsubstantive. In most cases, the interviewer will ask you why you chose to go to law school and what you want to be when you grow up rather than the hard-core finance questions common in investment banking and consulting interviews. There was an assumption that having done well academically in law school classes was enough evidence that you could do the law firm work. As a result, the interview was more of a search for personality fit. The general advice to be yourself, know about the leading practice areas and recent successes of the firm you are interviewing with, and look your interviewer in the eye was therefore generally sufficient.

In the future, it may be that law firm interviews will get more substantive. Many of the more substantive questions will inevitably originate with material you put on your résumé. This is good because it means that by carefully managing your résumé writing process and making adequate preparation, you can orchestrate a potentially great interview. For example, if you have on your résumé that you assisted in drafting a Wells Submission in an SEC inquiry, you had better know not only that a Wells Submission is filed with the SEC staff in response to a Wells Notice, indicating that the staff believes the recipient has violated the securities laws, but also whether the alleged violation was scienter- or nonscienter-based (N.B. The U.S. Supreme Court has defined scienter as "a mental state embracing intent to deceive, manipulate, or defraud"), what the securities act code section was, what the general alleged violative conduct was, and, if you really want to impress your interviewer, which of the several SEC assistant enforcement directors the staff serving the Wells Notice was working under and what their reputation is among the private securities bar (unreasonable prosecutor style or reasonable fact-finder style). Moreover, if you wrote a law review article or note and list it on your résumé (as you should), you had better know that area of the law inside and out.

HOW SHOULD I DRESS FOR AN INTERVIEW?

You should wear a blue or dark gray, single-breasted, American-cut all-wool suit with a conservative, small pattern, and for men, a blue or red silk tie. That is the time-tested uniform. However, I happened upon a somewhat more detailed posting on a public message board that, though designed for investment banking interviewing, is equally applicable to law firm interviews:

"I work in an investment bank, and the key phrases regarding suits are high fabric quality, classic fit, and don't break the rules.

Fabric? Wool, nothing else. No stretch. Almost exclusively navy. Solid or patterned (including stripes) are fine. But the pattern must be subtle. From ten feet away, it must look solid. I personally like subtle herringbone wool. Navy and charcoal are basically your only options. Black is wrong. Pinstripes should be invisible from ten feet away. This isn't the '80s.

Classic fit? Versace is out, for one thing. Trousers should be loose, not fashion-tight. The key is in the details. The trousers should be cuffed and the right length, the jacket should be American style, preferably. single-breasted only, two or three buttons. Think Armani, HF, Ferragamo, Brooks, Zegna, Cerruti, Kiton, Brioni, Loro, Hugo, Donna Karan, Canali, etc. Don't think

Prada, Gucci, Valentino, Versace, Calvin, etc. You see what I'm getting at?

Rules not to break: No double-breasting. No big stripes. No weird material. No light colors. Shirts should be white, blue, gray, or any combination thereof. No oxford collars. Pinpoint or spread only. Remember to put in the stays. Ties should be conservative, but use judgment. Make a knot that fits the shirt. Use a four-in-hand for pinpoint, and a half windsor for spread (use judgment with this, too). I personally like Armani, Dunhill, Burberry, and Calvin Klein ties the most. Belt matches shoes. That means oxblood with oxblood and chocolate with chocolate, shiny with shiny and matte with matte. I'm talking MATCH. Socks should be black or navy, and knee high. Brown belts with navy suits, black belts with black suits. If you're going for an interview, keep your jacket on, and unbutton your buttons only when you sit down. When you cross your legs, hike up the trouser leg so it doesn't stretch.

THE SAFEST POSSIBLE OUTFIT (nothing can go wrong here):
- Solid navy suit, single breasted, 100% worsted wool, single-vented, cuffed and pleated trousers, 3" lapels, 2-button.
- Oxblood leather Ferragamo-type shoes, lace-up, half-inch heel.
- Dark navy dress socks
- White cotton dress shirt, button cuffs (not french), pinpoint collar.
- EITHER solid light blue silk tie with slight iridescence, OR conservative patterned red tie (diamonds, grid, paisley), four-in-hand knot
- Oxblood belt: gold buckle if the tie is red, silver buckle if the tie is light blue.

That's the safest outfit (the money market account kind of risk). If you want to take more risks:

FIXED INCOME kind of risk: Light blue dress shirt: use a dark navy tie with subtly silver or gray patterns

EQUITIES kind of risk: charcoal suit
- blue dress shirt with a navy or gold tie
- white dress shirt with brown, dark red, or navy tie

WARNING: Outfits whose colors are too warm can subtly convey the color red, which can represent poor market performance. This doesn't ALWAYS happen, and the red tie is such a staple that it has no meaning in itself, but be aware of outfits that are too warm. Navy is neutral and elegant and management always wears it.[3]

11. WORKING FOR LAW FIRMS

SHOULD I WORK FOR A LAW FIRM?

LAW FIRMS PAY well. You can reasonably expect to work at a law firm for about seven years after you graduate from law school. Then you will either be fired or you will be made a partner or —increasingly common— a counsel or a junior partner. What happens to you at the end of seven years will depend on three primary factors: 1. the policies of the firm, 2. the practice area you specialized in, and 3. economic forces beyond your control. If you have become an expert in an area of law that is in demand at the time you are up for elevation to counsel or partner, you will likely be asked to stay. If you are at a firm that nurtures its associates for eventual partnership and does not favor hiring experienced partners laterally from outside the firm, you will also have a better shot. But if you are in a general area of practice that does not give you unique knowledge— which will be the case if you are a general corporate associate or even a general litigation associate—you will as likely as not be asked to seek out other career opportunities.

You need to know what you are getting into before you join a law firm. It seems exciting to join a firm when you are in the heat of interview season and they are taking you to the top restaurants in town and telling you what a great practice they have. But keep in mind that this is a business, and working for a leading firm has its good aspects (including the high salary and top-notch training) and its negative ones (including the pressure to make partner when in the end you may not, and the lost opportunity cost of not building a career in, say, a government agency).

For most graduates of top law schools the answer has always been to join a large urban law firm directly out of law school. This is what almost all graduates of Harvard, Columbia, Yale, Stanford, and Chicago do and have done for generations. That is, law schools and the leading legal periodicals, like *The American Lawyer* and NALP (the Association for Legal Career Professionals) have an institutional practice of "ranking" law firms. Some are the "best place for associates to work," some are the "top corporate firm in X city." Top law students are drawn in by this and tend to want jobs at top-ranked firms. It is not surprising that outstanding law students are attracted to the idea of joining a first-tier firm. It is a pattern they are used to, given how hard they worked to get into a top-ranked colleges and then into a top-ranked law school. Going after a top-ranked law firm is just a natural extension of that competitive urge.

But you need to consider what you are giving up. The enormous amount of time you will spend working for that big salary will not be a significant consideration for most of the younger law students/attorneys who do not have families yet and who are gung-ho about jumping into the most challenging legal practice they can find. These young people want to prove themselves and think they will not mind the long hours. But for those of us who are a bit older, and for the rest of you after those seven years of practicing have gone by and you are looking back on them, we will realize that spending sixteen hours a day has extracted its price in the form of lost relationships and missed opportunities to spend time with children and family. That is, you will find that you have lost an important part of your life during those years. Nevertheless, you will not, as a twenty-five-year-old law school graduate, buy into the quality-of-life argument at this point in your career.

Therefore, let me remind you of another cost of spending your first seven years in a law firm: the lost-opportunity argument. I won't spend a great deal of time on it now as I'll address it in more detail in other sections of this book. But keep in mind where you will be after seven years if (in the likely event) you are not asked to stick around your old firm. You will be joining a government agency or a smaller law firm as a seasoned attorney but new to that practice. In government, you will end up making less money and having less seniority than if you had joined the government soon after graduating from law school. (Maybe not right out of law school, but perhaps a year after working for a law firm in order to take advantage of the government's effort to match private-sector salaries.) At that point in your career, you may find yourself joining a government agency to get real legal experience (litigation experience at the DOJ or securities law experience at the SEC), whereas if you had gone to those agencies earlier, you would have a fancy title by now and be looking to join a firm as a business-generating partner. So, my advice is, invest those first few years carefully in order to yield the highest expected long-term gains.

WHICH LAW FIRM SHOULD I WORK FOR?

IF YOU ARE going to work for a law firm, you should have some idea of what you expect to get out of the experience. At the very least, you should have an idea of which practice area you want to enter. This does not have to be very specific. That is, it is probably enough that you want to be a securities attorney and not that you want to be a trademark litigation specialist. It should be enough that you know you want to be a corporate attorney but you need not know at this early stage in your career that you want to specialize in designing poison-pills as defenses against hostile acquisitions.

Here is why it is important to have some idea about which practice area you are interested in joining: not all law firms are good at all things. Some great corporate law firms do not have the best litigation practices. Some firms are great litigation houses and not very experienced in doing large corporate deals. Similarly, some cities are known for growing great corporate law firms, whereas other cities are simply not in the flow of great corporate deal work.

Top firms in Washington are a good example. The federal government has all of its agencies in the nation's capital. It should not be surprising, then, that Washington law firms tend to have some of the best regulatory practices in the country. If you want to be an FDA lawyer specializing in drug policy, this is a great place to find work. Just be sure that the firm you pick has some partners who are known in the field and, best of all, some senior former attorneys who worked at the FDA. But Washington is a bad place for other kinds of practices, and a case in point is that of corporate law. Large public corporations doing corporate deals (that is, mergers and acquisitions) rarely use a Washington firm as their main corporate counsel. For that they rely on a large New York firm or, perhaps, one in Chicago or Los Angeles. If a Washington firm is tapped, it will be to address a specific regulatory area of law, such as making sure that the deal complies with the antitrust provisions of the federal laws.

This does not mean that Washington law firms do not hire corporate attorneys. They do, and most of the leading Washington firms do have corporate practices. And, therein rests your problem as a law student. The Washington law firm partners will tell you that they have a great corporate law practice, when in reality 1. they don't, and 2. what they mean by a corporate practice is not what you probably mean. The corporate practice most Washington firms have is limited to regional corporate deals; it is not what a leading New York law firm means when it says it has a corporate practice. Leading New York firms, like Skadden, Arps or Wachtel, Lipton, have institutional machinery in place that allows them to reliably handle the mergers of multibillion-dollar international public corporations. These are the deals you read about on the front page of the *Wall Street Journal*. The infrastructure I mentioned includes, in addition to experience, a density of trained corporate associates sufficient to conduct the massive due diligence needed to complete these deals in a timely manner and the reputation to hold sway over corporate boards of directors.

Washington firms have no hope of replicating these advantages. They don't have the experience and they don't have the consistent flow of deals to justify training and maintaining the number of corporate associates needed to do big deals. While corporate directors and officers may rely on the Washington firms for their regulatory (and perhaps litigation) expertise, there is no way they are going to let a Washington firm handle a live-or-die major corporate acquisition. Know this when you interview for corporate positions in Washington, or in any secondary city like Charlotte, Miami, or San Diego. The corporate practice you are likely to do there will involve a smattering of private deals, large real estate transactions, and the rare small public-company merger if you are lucky. To put it another way, the small corporate deal that gets handed to a mid-level Skadden, Arps corporate attorney as an accommodation to a good client is the best corporate case of the year for a top Washington law firm.

You also need to take this analysis down to the law firm level. Some firms are good places to work in the corporate field and others are better places to gain litigation skills and experience. The reasons you want to go to work for a law firm with expertise in the area you are interested in are twofold: first, you will get better training from knowledgeable superiors at the firm with a specialty in your subject and, second, the market for legal talent will value you more if you got trained in the right shop. For example, you are going to be recognized as someone who probably knows a lot about corporate deals and has developed good habits and valuable expertise if you come from Skadden, Arps or Wachtel, Lipton. On the other hand, if you want to work for Williams & Connolly in Washington, you are going to be viewed by other lawyers as someone who probably knows a great deal about Supreme Court and general appellate litigation.

WHAT ARE THE BEST LAW FIRMS IN THE COUNTRY?

THERE ARE A number of different lists of top law firms. Vault, at www.vault.com, annually prepares a list of "The Top 100 Most Prestigious Firms." Vault's ranking is based on a survey in which law firm associates are asked, simply, what law firm is most prestigious to work for (the ranking methodology is describe in more detail on Vault's Web site). I find Vault's list pretty good, and generally consistent with my understanding of the most prestigious law forms to work for. Here is Vault's list for 2007:

1. Wachtel, Lipton, Rosen & Katz
2. Cravath, Swaine & Moore
3. Sullivan & Cromwell
4. Skadden, Arps, Slate, Meagher & Flom
5. Davis, Polk & Wardwell
6. Simpson, Thacher & Bartlett
7. Cleary, Gottlieb, Steen & Hamilton
8. Latham & Watkins
9. Weil, Gotshal & Manges
10. Kirkland & Ellis

I do not wholly agree with this list. For example, in my experience Cleary, Gottlieb and Simpson, Thacher are both considered to be better law firms than is Skadden, Arps. That is, top law students from Columbia would be more likely to accept an offer from these firms. In addition, some firms ranked lower on the list deserve to be in the top ten. What is important to keep in mind is that there are a large number of very well regarded law firms. This is a good thing since every year there is a large number of well-qualified law school graduates. Predictably, many of the most prestigious firms—Wachtel, Cravath; Sullivan & Cromwell; Davis, Polk; Skadden, Arps; Simpson, Thacher; Cleary, Gottlieb; and Weil, Gotshall among them—are based in New York City. Wachtel does not even have an office outside New York, and Latham is in Los Angeles. Kirkland & Ellis is based in Chicago, with offices in Los Angeles, New York, San Francisco, Washington, Hong Kong, London, and Munich. Most of these firms, like Kirkland & Ellis, maintain offices outside of their home city, but it is best to work in the home office, where you will have contact with the best talent and training and also the best chance for career advancement (that is, a better chance of making partner).

Also, keep in mind that these prestigious firms are not necessarily the best places to work. Other surveys, including ones conducted by *The American Lawyer* and other publications, regularly rank firms by their treatment of associates. Therefore, while in the very short term it may help your career to work for the most prestigious firm in town, in the longer term you might want to consider whether the environment in that firm will let you continue to work there for multiple years.

ARE BIG LAW FIRMS REALLY THAT DIFFERENT FROM EACH OTHER?

LARGE URBAN LAW firms like to think they are different from each other, and they make a great effort to distinguish themselves from their peers. They do this especially in the two primary areas where they compete against each other: in attracting young associates and in attracting (and retaining) clients. In reality, most large law firms are pretty much the same. This is not surprising since they are governed by the same laws of existence. For example, they all depend on the same economic model[1], they all recruit from the same pool of graduates from top law schools, they all practice in the same areas of law (with some variation in emphasis), and they all provide basically the same services to clients. And yet, they have to distinguish themselves on some basis. Law firms have chosen to do this in different ways.

The Washington firm of Wilmer, Cutler & Pickering used to advertise to prospective associates that it was a "law firm for lawyers," the implication being that when law firms themselves need the very best representation, they turn to Wilmer. Other firms have tried other hooks. Some claim they offer a quality of life for associates that is better than at other firms. This is deceptive, as the realities of billing by the hour do not allow for a great deal of slack before partner salaries take a big hit. Other firms claim they are the best in a particular legal concentration. Prospective associates and clients can verify this by reviewing attorney biographies, so it is usually based in truth. However, this can change over time as lawyers come and go. In only a few cases do major law firms have a real lock on a particular area of expertise.

HOW CAN I EXPECT A LAW FIRM TO TREAT ME IN THE LONG RUN?

THIS IS AN important question, not one that prelaw college students, law students, or even recent law school graduates think about. Their perspective is much too short term. They tend to be focused on what is going to happen to them in the next, say, two or three years. I urge you to keep in mind that it is critical to do long-term planning and, in particular, to try to project how the decisions you make today will affect you many years into the future.

In the short term, law firms treat prospective associates and even young associates very well. While the level of the activity fluctuates along with the economic climate, law firms generally wine and dine prospective hires and make some effort to provide young associates with a variety of interesting work. This behavior is the product of the very competitive market for top law students and only slightly less true for junior associates. Remember, a law firm that can lure away a second-year associate ideally has acquired the asset (the young lawyer) after he has been trained and before his peak earning years for the firm (he is billing lots of hours and his salary is still relatively low).

In the long term, the treatment of young attorneys by their firms is quite different. This is chiefly because most firms still maintain an up-or-out culture that requires attorneys either to be admitted to the firm as partners or find other employment. Thus, as the years progress and you become a third-, fourth-, fifth,- and sixth-year associate, you will experience increasing pressure to distinguish yourself in front of partners (perhaps at the expense of your peers) and demonstrate that you are on the partnership track. Lunchtime conversation will increasingly center on who among the seventh-year associates is going to make partner, and your dreams will become nightmares about your own failure to be selected (just as once in law school you likely dreamed of entering a final examination and finding yourself totally unprepared).

Now, it is true that some firms have tried to break the up-or-out cycle by instituting permanent positions for lawyers other than partner. At some firms, the positions are called junior partner or nonequity partner, and at other firms they are counsel or special counsel. All of these titles mean essentially the same thing. The firm's partners did not feel the need to make you a partner (perhaps you are in such a specialized field that they don't believe you will be able to find a job elsewhere anyway, so they are at no risk of losing you), but they didn't want you to leave the firm, since your revenue in billings exceeds your salary and the administrative costs of employing you. However, this type of arrangement works only in a regulatory environment or a highly specialized field of substantive law. For the two practice areas in which most law firm associates are employed—general litigation and corporate transactional work— the model of a single senior partner who interfaces with the client and makes the big decisions, supported by a revolving team of young associates who do the bulk of the editing and due diligence work, remains the most economically feasible one.

The result is that the pyramid structure, in which there are a few elite partners and a large body of junior associates, is here to stay at large urban law firms. Moreover, law firm partners sincerely believe in this system—despite the lip service they give to wanting to make their firms places where young associates can plan to hang their hats for the long term. There are some compelling psychological reasons for this. First and foremost, individuals who managed to become partners in big law firms believe that the system works in selecting the best and brightest attorneys and that it weeds out inferior associates. After all, they were selected by the system. They do not recognize that the road to becoming a partner is an arbitrary process in which politicking, personal relationships, economic trends, and luck all play a role. On average, the brightest individuals leave law firms well before they are considered for partnership because they realize that the economic model of firms is one that requires increasingly long hours of commitment (partners often bill more hours than the associates who work for them) and only middling economic rewards (investment bankers and entrepreneurs make much more money). Nevertheless, suggesting as much to a law firm partner is tantamount to heresy, as this undermines his entire worldview and threatens his large but fragile ego.

A second reason law firm partners believe in the up-or-out system[2] is a bit more practical. Many partners believe that keeping large numbers of mid-level associates would prevent them from hiring the firm's share of the best and brightest law school third years. This would be unfair to the graduating lawyers, who feel it is their right to work for top firms, and would deny the firm the opportunity to select from the next generation of lawyers and weed out the few that have the mettle to become senior partners. The result is that up-or-out is largely here to stay.

WHAT PRACTICE AREA SHOULD I WORK IN?

LOOKING BACK ON what I knew about law firms when I was a law student at Columbia, even in my third year, I am amazed by how inaccurate my conception of law firm practice was and how little I understood about the division of labor within the different practice areas. I barely knew the difference between a litigation practice and a corporate practice—all the clients were corporations, after all—and that lack of knowledge was a severe handicap in applying for law firm jobs and deciding what area of law to focus on for my career.

For example, I remember that at the start of my third year I interviewed with the prestigious New York law firm of Cravath, Swain & Moore. (I had received a job offer from my second-year summer employer but did not want to go back to that firm, which was located in Delaware.) After my on-campus interview, during which some time was spent discussing a corporate law article I had written for publication, I was invited back for a second round of interviews at Cravath's imposing office in midtown Manhattan. I was surprised to have been invited back because, although my grades at Columbia were good, they were not the perfect grades that I had been led to believe Cravath expected of its law school hires. As chance would have it, I had also recently interviewed with several federal judges, one of whom sat in Miami and had led me to believe I would likely receive an offer. Knowing that federal clerkships are prestigious, I focused on my interest in litigation (which I was not necessarily interested in because I knew next to nothing about it) as a way of segueing into a discussion of my clerkship potential.

The thing I did not know was that every attorney I interviewed with—including two of Cravath's most senior partners—was a corporate lawyer. Had I done my research, I would have read in the legal industry press or learned from Columbia's career counselors that Cravath was desperate to hire a large number of corporate associates for what it expected was going to be a boom year for corporate M&A work. Not surprisingly, I did not receive an offer. Because of Cravath's tradition of granting offers by the end of the day in which you interview, I knew by the time I left their offices at 3:00 PM that I did not have an offer. Thus, not having the information about a firm's practice areas and relative hiring needs was a crucial mistake. Let this serve as a lesson to exhaustively research any employer in which you have a serious interest.

But let's talk for a minute about the real difference among different law firm practice groups. First, you might ask, what are the different practice groups? There are a large number of potential practices, including bankruptcy, intellectual property, tax, securities law. However, most large firms have two general practice areas under which most of the other practices fall as subspecialties: litigation and corporate law. Most regular law students (excluding the holders of advanced science degrees who are destined to become patent lawyers) will need to choose early in their careers—and probably while they are still in law school—which of these two practice areas to join.

Most law students assume that corporate lawyers are the ones who have the most business-oriented practices. For this reason, law students interested in concepts such as building businesses and making decisions that can make or lose money for companies gravitate toward corporate law. I and a number of my close friends, all of whom were interested in economics in general and business in particular, went into corporate law because we thought it would put us in the position of doing work that would be closely related to the operations of companies. We thought corporate law would help train us to make good decisions concerning issues of importance to companies in areas affecting their actual operations. We could not have been more wrong.

If you want to take a leading role in decision making, a legal career, at least as a corporate lawyer, may not be where your interest lies. As a corporate lawyer, your role will be to take the decisions made by your clients—the business people—and ensure that these decisions are well documented. One major difference between corporate and litigation attorneys that is often overlooked is that litigators actually have more decision-making authority than corporate attorneys. Clients are not experts on litigation strategy, on civil procedure, or on what facts presented at trial will lead to the most effective appellate strategy. They will therefore defer to their experienced litigation counsel in the waging of legal battles. Corporate counsel, in contrast, while officially "doing deals" for their clients, are actually papering the deals already done by the business guys. It can be very frustrating if this is not what you signed up for as a young attorney.

The downside of being a litigator is that you are always seeing your clients at their worst, and that can be depressing. Litigators usually come into the picture when the business deal has gone bad, or when the client's product has harmed someone. Business people get to see the highs and lows of the business cycle. They are on board when the venture posts record profits and when all the partners are fat and happy. Corporate attorneys are along for this ride as well, though they didn't make the actual business decisions that led to profit for the client. Neither corporate nor litigation counsel get to feel they are part of the process of building a business, which for business people can offer a significant psychological reward. Litigators, are even more removed than corporate counsel from the business-building process.

WHAT SHOULD I KNOW ABOUT STARTING SALARIES AT LAW FIRMS?

WHEN CHOOSING WHICH practice you will join first, you must look beyond the starting salary.

Using first-year compensation as a primary driver for selecting a law firm is problematic for several reasons. First, even if you are really motivated only by money, first-year salary alone does not paint a complete picture. You need to dig further and consider the firm's annual pay increases, or "steps," that attorneys earn as they gain seniority. Assuming you are planning to stay with the firm for a few years, you should also take the time to research the firm's history of awarding bonuses. One thing you may notice is that most law firms in a given city will offer the same starting salary to first-year associates. This is because firms compete directly with each other for recent law school graduates. However, after the first year both base compensation and bonuses can diverge among firms. This makes sense if you consider that after associates join a firm they are essentially locked in. You should be able to get information about how well a law firm compensates its mid-level and senior associates through the NALP and online services like Vault.com.

A second reason for looking beyond salary is that there is more to succeeding at the law—and life—than just your salary. Different law firms have very different cultures. An attorney who succeeds at one firm might have failed at another. This lack of consistency is very hard for law students to grasp. Many students base their decision of which offer to accept on factors such as compensation and firm prestige. However, there are many other factors that should be taken into account. For example, does the firm have a strong practice in the area in which you have an interest? Are there particular lawyers at the firm whom you could consider valuable mentors? Does the firm have a history of promoting partners from the associate ranks or does it bring in partners from outside the firm? What percentage of associates entering in any given class are eventually made partner? Is the firm friendly to female attorneys? Are there female partners there who could serve as mentors? Does the firm offer schedule flexibility for working mothers? These kinds of considerations should play a large part in your deciding which firm to join.

WHAT SHOULD I KNOW ABOUT BONUSES?

LAW FIRMS CAN calculate bonuses in three ways: based on meeting goals or targets, based on discretion, and based on class year. Historically, larger firms awarded bonuses based on associates' meeting target goals; smaller firms awarded them based on discretion or class year. More recently, law firms of all sizes have been moving away from class year-based bonuses and even discretionary bonuses and toward target-based bonuses.

Class year-based bonuses were common several decades ago and reflect a more genteel time in the practice of law when competition between associates took second place to the theory that all associates should be working together for the good of the firm. In recent years, such bonuses have become quite rare.

Let me explain each of the three ways of calculating bonuses. Law firms categorize their associates by "class year," which is usually their year of law school graduation. (It can be later if the individual associate has, for example, clerked with a judge for more than one year, worked in the government for a period of time, or transferred to the firm laterally from another firm. In those cases, the associate may get "left back" to the year after graduation.) In any event, bonuses for associates are keyed to this class-year system regardless of how the firm actually calculates the annual bonus.

It used to be that many of the top firms offered the same bonus to associates of the same class year. For example, first-year associates would get $5,000 and second year associates $7,500. This system was favored because it was considered effective in reducing competition among associates and fostering a cooperative outlook to completing the firm's business. However, in more recent years the trend has been toward paying "discretionary" bonuses to associates based on either partner reviews, hours billed over the previous year, or perhaps a combination.[3] This system became favored because it fostered competition among associates and was considered to be fairer to those associates who, early in their careers, showed particular promise. It also let associates know early on whether they were on the partnership track.

Firms that employ discretionary bonuses often announce the range of bonuses granted to each class year. The firm may send around a letter from the managing partner to all associates announcing, for example, that fifth-year associates received a bonus between $2,000 and $20,000 and so forth for all classes, and thanking everyone for their hard work. If you are a third-year and you did not get close to a $20,000 bonus, you had better start thinking of other career options. This sense of urgency should increase if you are getting less than the top bonus and you are approaching your seventh or eighth year as an associate, since that is generally the time law firms make their final decisions about who is going to make partner. In fact, law firms are notoriously bad at providing timely feedback on associate performance. The firms are afraid of scaring away good associates who they do not view as being on the partnership track. The associates are still profitable for the firm, after all, even if they are not deserving of a piece of the partnership pie. Thus, sometimes, the annual discretionary bonus is the best way to determine your prospects.

It is difficult to determine a first-year associate's performance. In the first year there is a good deal of training and the learning curve is steep. Therefore, most firms will award a class-based bonus for the first year and then adopt the discretionary bonus for later years. Other firms will have a combined class-based/discretionary bonus system. My own view is that money is not the best way to provide an incentive for outstanding work performance, and therefore I am not a fan of discretionary bonuses.[4] Moreover, an associate making a six-figure salary has enough money to live on and, in fact, to live quite well. Making associates compete against each other for money does not, in my opinion, improve morale or further the firm's mission, which should be to provide the highest-quality legal services to clients. This goal is, in my view, most readily met when lawyers work together as a team. Nevertheless, many firms now embrace the discretionary bonus model and use it as a carrot to encourage more billable hours and, perhaps, better performance.

Some firms will take issue with my negative characterization of discretionary bonuses. These firms have created interesting variations. For example, they may employ a bonus system in which associates get an additional bonus if they hit, say, 2,000 billable hours in a year. The claim is that this allows associates to choose what lifestyle they want. If associates want to spend more time with their families, they can choose to bill only 1,800 hours (still quite a lot since it requires working many more hours than that) and get a $5,000 bonus, instead of billing 2,000 hours for a $10,000 bonus. I know of at least one firm that has adopted this kind of structure as part of its bonus system. It sounds good in theory, but everyone knows that if you are not billing 2,000 hours, you are not on the partnership track.

Over the last decade, law firms have been shifting away from lockstep bonuses and toward those that take into account billing targets, or those that are discretionary, based on partner reviews. Firms became more likely over the period to use "meeting goals or targets" and "discretion" as means of determining bonus eligibility, with larger firms increasingly more likely than smaller firms to use these criteria.

HOW HAVE LAW FIRM SALARIES CHANGED OVER TIME?

From 1950 to 1965, associates at leading law firms were paid very little. The most senior partners at major firms—those emeritus hangers-on who are now past eighty and will soon no longer be around to remind us of our history—will tell you about how they made $7,500 out of law school and were happy to get it. Even adjusting for the time value of money, which is $40,000 in current dollars, it is not a lot compared with what law firms are paying their junior hires today. In those early days, it was recognized that recently minted lawyers knew very little of practical value. Their first years on the job were their apprenticeship, during which they would learn the tools that would later make them valuable members of the team.

Changes in the way law is practiced in large firms and time is billed have altered the roll of junior associates, and completely transformed their pay packages. The pyramid structure of most major firms, in which a small number of partners direct the work of a large number of associates, who are billed out at rates exceeding $250 an hour to do tasks that are often clerical in nature, means that large firms have an ever-increasing appetite for young and inexperienced—but smart and well-credentialed—attorneys. In just the last decade the increasing dominance of the highly leveraged firm structure has contributed to an ever-increasing demand for young attorneys, which has translated into rising associate salaries.

Some specific data points will help illustrate where salaries have come from and where they are likely heading. When I graduated from law school in 1994, the top firms in New York and Los Angeles were paying about $85,000 a year, with the prospect of a small bonus if all went well. By 2006, first-year associates were getting about $135,000 as base compensation, with bonuses of $20,000 or more not out of the question.[5]

Salaries have not risen at a completely steady rate over those twelve years. In fact, they climbed steadily between 1994 and 1999 at leading corporate law firms as they fought to keep their associates from jumping ship to join investment banks and Internet start-ups. This was done mainly by hiking up the bonuses offered to junior and mid-level associates. When I was a fifth-year associate in 1999, for example, I would have received a bonus of an even $100,000 on top of my $206,000 base salary had I not left to join an Internet startup. However, from 2000 through 2002, associate salaries were relatively flat, as were bonuses, as the economy languished.[6] Then, starting in 2003, the economy began to rebound, and associate salaries continued their upward march.

It is interesting to observe a legal market when law firms are in the process of increasing associate salaries. Law firms from any given city that are recruiting on campus all pay roughly the same salary (although the salaries paid by different firms to their more senior associates may differ). The main competitors law firms face in hiring new associates are each other. If a leading firm in a given market raises its salaries, the peer firms in that market will invariably follow suit. When business is booming, the demand at leading firms for young associates increases, competition among firms intensifies, and salaries rise.

One important point is that these salaries—recently exceeding $135,000 for first-year associates—are not representative of the broad legal market but rather are characteristic of leading law firms in major metropolitan areas. Graduates of top-ten law schools and the highest achievers at secondary law schools (those on law review, for example) can hope to achieve starting salaries in this vicinity. However, lawyers at smaller firms and, certainly, in the government sector must expect much lower compensation. For a chart showing the divergence between salaries at large firms and smaller ones, see Appendix E, which also shows that the salaries at large firms increased more rapidly from 1996 to 2001 than they did at smaller firms. This trend seems to be continuing. In 2007, leading New York law firm Simpson, Thacher increased first year associate base salaries to $160,000 (and second year to $170,000), a $15,000 bump over 2006. This far outpaces any increases among smaller firms.

Another thing to keep in mind is that these jobs at large corporate law firms entail a very large number of billable hours, and an even larger number of nonbillable ones. Let's say a firm requires that an associate bill 2,500 hours a year. This is not uncommon for large firms. In order to bill 2,500 hours you might need to work 3,000. A salary of $135,000 divided by 3,000 hours works out to $45 an hour. And then you have to take out a healthy amount for taxes, FICA, medical insurance, and so on. On an hourly basis, you could probably do about as well doing a union construction job. Some days—probably as you are sitting at your desk late at night—that will seem like an attractive option. However, consider that, unlike construction, lawyer salaries go up considerably each year. By the time you are a fifth-year, you could easily be making more than $200,000 a year. If you just want to make money, working in a big firm is a pretty reliable way to do so.

Of course, not everyone is interested only in making money. Many law students want to make a difference in the world and would love to be a public defender or a small-town lawyer working for real people rather than corporations. The reality, though, is that graduates of top law schools—and even second-tier firms—can come out of their pricey educations with a great deal of debt. It is not uncommon to have over $150,000 in student loans after spending three years in law school, even with summer associate salaries helping to reduce the burden. This means that, as a practical matter, even those law students who feel drawn to public-interest work find that they can not turn away from the hefty salaries paid by large firms.

COMPETITION ON BONUSES AMONG FIRMS

LEADING LAW FIRMS are very competitive with each other for the "best" associates. They will watch each other very carefully to see how much they are paying young associates. They also watch each other regarding bonuses. In New York City it is often said that the leading law firms will watch and copy the corporate leader Cravath, Swain & Moore's bonus decisions. Sometimes these amounts can be quite significant (though not as significant as they are in the investment banking world, where annual bonuses can easily exceed base salary). The highest bonus I ever received was in 1999, when everyone in my class year was given $100,000.

Bonuses are closely tied to the economic performance of firms. For a while, in the late 1990s, it seemed that firm prospects and bonuses could go nowhere but up. That changed after 2000, when the economy in general and corporate law firms in particular saw a slide-off in activity. In November 2002, Cravath announced that it was lowering its bonus range to between $15,000 and $25,000, down from the $25,000 to $50,000 it was paying in 2001. Cravath stated, "The serious downturn in the national economy and the environment for business transactions that began in 2001 has continued unabated throughout 2002. The impact of that downturn has been felt in the legal community and by our clients." Other firms, including Cleary, Gottlieb, Steen & Hamilton, matched the Cravath move.

Bonuses are closely tied to the economic performance of firms.

One firm, however, is in a league by itself. The New York firm Wachtel, Lipton, Rosen & Katz traditionally pays far higher bonuses than does any other New York firm. In 2002, Wachtel paid bonuses starting at $50,000 and reaching as high as $170,000 for senior associates. Other firms make public statements that they will match any other leading firm's bonus—except for that of Wachtel. For example, the partners of the leading corporate firm of Sullivan & Cromwell announced early in 2002 that the annual bonuses would be adjusted if necessary to match that of any other firm. This kind of move is designed to prevent other firms from making a preemptive strike and announcing slightly higher bonuses after a leader like Sullivan announces their bonus structure.

Bonuses are a serious issue for law firms. They can have a direct impact on how desirable the firm is considered by law students as a place to work. The rankings change each year, though the same ten firms generally dominate the top five slots, and the top law students always want to go to the top firms. With multiple offers in their pockets, the members of Columbia and Harvard law review have their selection of leading firms. In 2001, a bonus scandal rocked the rankings of top New York law firms. In October of that year, a memo from partners at Davis, Polk & Wardwell stated that there would be no bonuses that year. While the firm later reversed that decision, the uncertainty over whether Davis Polk would pay 2001 bonuses appears to have been a primary reason the firm dropped from number four to number five in the rankings of top law firms. In the world of the top firms, this is a serious consideration.

Bonuses are sometimes given to associates according to the number of hours billed. Such a structure is seldom received well by associates. In October 2001, a memo to associates at the international firm of Clifford, Chance advised that the London-based firm was tying bonuses to a requirement of 2,200 client hours plus an additional 220 other hours billed. In 2003, Piper, Rudnick announced it would give out bonuses in its New York ranging from $10,000 for first-years to $45,000 for senior associates, with the highest bonuses paid to associates who billed between 2,100 and 2,400 hours in the past year. It is better to announce these guidelines at the start of the year, so that associates can work toward them. Even so, the reaction by associates is often negative. For one thing, pegging compensation to hours billed encourages associates to bill unnecessary hours to client accounts. The result is that some firms have backed away from bonuses tied to hours billed. Clifford, Chance, for example, later dropped the 2,420-total-hours guideline and paid bonuses starting at a flat $17,500 for first-year associates.

WHAT CITY SHOULD I WORK IN?

WHAT GEOGRAPHIC REGION you choose to work in after you graduate from law school will depend on a variety of factors, not the least of which may be personal considerations such as proximity to family and perhaps friends. Setting those intangible factors aside, however, the place you hang your shingle after you graduate is a strategic decision that will significantly shape your blooming career.

Let's assume, as a start, that you are a graduate of one of the twenty or so top ten American law schools and have received employment offers from equally well-regarded law firms in various cities, including New York, Washington, San Francisco, and your home city of Charlotte, North Carolina. While you will get paid more if you take the job in New York than you will in Charlotte, you realize that the cost of living difference means that, by your calculation, your buying power will be roughly equivalent in each of the markets you are considering, at least initially.

SHOULD I AVOID JOINING A SATELLITE OFFICE OF A NATIONAL FIRM?

GENERALLY, YES, YOU ought to avoid working at a satellite office of a major firm, at least in the case of the first job you accept after you graduate from law school. I'll explain why in the next few paragraphs. First, though, it's important to understand what is meant by satellite office. Most of the leading law firms—with some notable exceptions—have offices in more than one city.[7]

The standard model is for there to be a home office, which is generally the office with the largest number of practicing attorneys and is usually located in the city where the firm was originally founded. Of course, there are some exceptions to this pattern of expansion where the original office retains its dominant stature, such as in the case of the old Philadelphia law firm of Morgan Lewis & Bockius.

Morgan Lewis began as a two-lawyer firm back in 1873 and for many years was known primarily as a regional Philadelphia law firm. However, in recent decades the firm has experienced a steady and exponential growth in size to the extent that, by early 2004, it had more than 1,100 attorneys operating in seventeen offices worldwide. Much of the growth of Morgan Lewis was due to the success of two of its satellite offices, New York and Washington. These two offices actually grew to have more attorneys than the firm's original Philadelphia office. Morgan Lewis's New York office was founded in 1972, and by early 2004 had more than 300 lawyers representing traditional New York corporate and securities law clients, including investment banks, commercial banks, broker dealers, and a wide range of large corporations. The Washington office was founded more than fifty years ago and had also by early 2004 grown to more than 300 attorneys. They were generally focused on traditional Washington business including regulatory work in the energy and tax arenas and in the fields of labor, employment and antitrust law. In contrast, by early 2004, the Philadelphia office had somewhat less than 300 lawyers and describes itself, on its Web site, as being composed of attorneys serving "diverse businesses and individuals whose interests are focused in the region as well as national and international clients." As you can see, each of the firm's three major offices developed regionally appropriate practices that likely do not tend to compete with the businesses of the other offices, and in fact are likely complementary in many cases where, for example, a business client in New York is referred to a Washington lawyer for regulatory advice.

SHOULD I GO WORK FOR MY FIRM'S FOREIGN OFFICE?

PARTICULARLY IF YOU are young and single, or young and have an adventurous spouse, spending a couple of years at your firm's foreign office can be a tremendous growth experience and one that can lead to promotion within the firm. I have worked for several law firms, each of which had foreign offices. I have known associates who worked in offices in Moscow, London, and Hong Kong, and all have said that they would not trade the experience. I have never worked in a firm's foreign office, although I made international trips and lived in England for several months. I also have spent considerable time in Asia. I can tell you that you will likely experience a certain degree of culture shock during the first months of your overseas stay, and then again when you return to the United States. This is due, as I understand it, to the absence of the little things you take for granted in your everyday life. This causes unconscious emotional stress that can wear you down. Culture shock passes, however, and having this experience will add significantly to your understanding of international business and the global practice of law.

One thing you might want to look into before taking up a foreign tour of duty is the working standards at the foreign office. Your expectations may differ from reality. One of my friends, for example, went to Cleary, Gottlieb's London office expecting to take weekend trips to different European cities and see the world. He ended up working nearly every weekend and late into the night on complex financial transactions. The London office was very busy, and he had been asked to go there to work rather than to take a vacation. In fact, he worked even harder than he had at the already hard-charging New York office. Let this be a lesson to fully research the move before you jump and are disappointed.

WHAT IS A WHITE SHOE LAW FIRM?

YOU WILL HEAR the phrase white shoe law firm, particularly when interview time approaches, and much more after graduation. White shoe firms were the major New York City law firms that represented leading institutional clients like JP Morgan from the 1920s through the 1970's and were controlled by predominantly Protestant partners from elite backgrounds who went to Andover or Exeter for high school, Princeton for college, and Yale or Harvard for law school. In my opinion these firms are largely extinct or, more accurately, have evolved into something other than the true white shoe environments that they once most certainly were.

You may still be wondering what the specific term *white shoe* actually means. It means, literally, that the partners and associates employed there wore white shoes on weekends when they were playing tennis at their exclusive clubs outside of the city. It implies that these same associates and partners had time to go to their exclusive clubs on weekends.

When I say that the white shoe firm is extinct, I don't mean that the firms themselves are gone. They are still there: Cravath, Swain & Moore and Davis, Polk & Wardwell are two of them. But the people have changed and so have the social habits. Competition from upstart firms like Wachtel, Lipton, Rosen & Katz have forced these firms to take on a more aggressive, businesslike approach that has partners and associates working over many weekends. Nevertheless, particularly with the older partners, one can perhaps still glimpse the lapsed gentility that these firms once represented within the highest levels of the legal community.

I HAVE SOME FAMILY MONEY. SHOULD I TRY TO HIDE THIS FACT FROM PEOPLE AT MY FIRM?

MONEY IS A delicate subject at many law firms. You have to consider your audience. Lawyers are, by and large, self-made men and women. Many did not have a lot of money growing up. In fact, people with a lot of family money rarely go into law as a profession. Law is hard work and the hours are bad, though the career promises a good and fairly stable salary. Wealthy people may tend more toward going into business positions. Lawyers can also be very competitive. They view salary as a badge of success perhaps more than most people do, and certainly more than do people who grew up with money. Thus, in the end, I don't think you are going to do yourself any favors by advertising as a young associate that you have money. In fact, unless there are unusual circumstances, I would suggest that you hide it. For one thing, if you are perceived as being wealthy, then your superiors may be less likely to recommend you for a big bonus.

An exception may be if you are extremely wealthy. If you are a Rockefeller or a Ford, you are going to have some difficulty hiding the fact. Moreover, it may not be as much of a detriment as if you were only moderately wealthy. This is because, at some point, partners are going to stop viewing you as an associate and start viewing you as a potential client. One of the associates who started working with me came from a family that controlled a large public biotechnology company in the Washington area. He was treated extremely well by the firm and was viewed in a special light because of his family. It was a bit of an unusual circumstance because both his family's company and the family itself were already clients of the firm. Even in this case, however, in which the family was extremely wealthy, this individual gained personal points with the other attorneys by taking care never to flaunt his money. Things change somewhat when you become a partner, as it seems to be more palatable to the other partners that one of their own has significant personal wealth. In fact, they seem to take some stock in the fact that they belong to an elite club that includes among its member a particularly wealthy person. For example, at one firm where I worked, there were a couple of senior partners who had large personal estates. One was the son of a wealthy business family who had inherited great wealth and a massive mansion in Georgetown. The other was a self-made businessman who had bought up large real estate holdings in Washington and lived in a former embassy that he had converted to his personal home. These people talked freely of their wealth—more so in the case of the self-made man than in the case of the one who had inherited his fortune. In any event, both partners held positions of leadership (and apparent respect) within the partnership.

12. THE POLITICS AND PITFALLS OF LAW FIRM LIFE

WHAT CAN I DO TO BE CONSIDERED A SUCCESSFUL FIRST-YEAR ASSOCIATE?

THE KEY TO being a successful first-year associate is much the same in the long run as that of a successful summer associate or a successful law firm associate—you must consistently exceed expectations. And expectations will be high. Doing a good job is not enough. Getting a memo done on time is not going to get you noticed. What you need to do is turn in a perfect memo overnight when the partner expected it would take you two days to get a draft done.

Your reputation is formed in the firm during your first year. Partners talk to each other. They discuss which associates are good and which are not. The good ones have significantly exceeded the partners' already high expectations. They have stories that illustrate why a particular associate is so prized: "He researched and drafted a perfect memo the next day when I thought there was no way he could even get it done within two." Exceeding expectations early in your career will build your reputation so that in later years, the good work you do will be considered great.

If you start out slow, as some associates do, you will not have the benefit of the doubt later on. If you screw up once or twice for a partner, that is how you will be perceived. You will never be trusted completely. Later, when you do truly great work, it will not be appreciated—at best it will be considered good. You may think of ways to recover, but it is difficult to accomplish in practice. The best thing you will be able to do is to diversify and work for other partners. So, as a first-year, the first impressions you make are going to have a great deal of weight.

HOW IMPORTANT ARE BILLABLE HOURS?

BILLABLE HOURS ARE very important to law firms. They are its lifeblood, on which all revenues are based, and which pays your salary and that of your secretary. Without them you would not have a job. Partners are very focused on billable hours and, though it is a pain for associates to keep track of them so meticulously, it is important that you understand how important they are to the business of the firm.

Everyone complains about billable hours. Associates hate tracking their time in five minute intervals. Firm management claims that billable hours are not the primary gauge of success for associates at the firm. Maybe there are other means of measuring performance, but hours remain a key factor in determining the amount of bonuses paid to associates and whether lawyers are offered promotions. This focus on billable hours is strong for associates but even more critical for partners. It is often said—and I have seen the billing records to prove it—that partners actually bill more hours than associates. It is just that partners do not complain about it.

HOW MANY BILLABLE HOURS SHOULD I AIM FOR?

UNDERSTAND THAT IT takes more than an hour to bill an hour. A billable hour is necessarily a subset of your total time working, since it is, by definition, the time actually spent doing work for a client. You, being a human being, need to eat and go to the bathroom. There will also be meetings, and times when you are simply not productive. Time spent on pro bono projects may or may not be considered billable by your firm and, even where pro bono is considered billable the firm will likely frown on a particularly large amount of time spent on non-revenue generating activity. From the perspective of the associate, the term *billable* means whether or not they get credit for working those hours for purposes of calculating their annual bonus.

So, how much time should you try to bill? It depends on where your firm is located and on the firm's culture. New York firms tend to expect a high number of billable hours. Top-ranked firms also tend to expect higher billings from associates. Some firms, like Wachtel, Lipton in New York, are reputed to take extraordinary measures to help associates maximize their ration of billable hours to time at work. These methods may including delivering lunch to associates' offices (not so common) and arranging for car services to bring them home late at night (quite common). Firms in Seattle or Denver generally have lower billing expectations.

Let's analyze the numbers. How much time could you bill in theory? If you worked ten hours a day, six days a week, for fifty weeks a year and billed every single minute of that time, you would be billing 3,000 hours. This is nearly impossible to do. The one way I have known a very few associates to bill in the 3,000-hour range is when they were involved in a protracted case that required them to travel a great deal and the client allowed the firm to bill for their travel time (in which case they had many days with 14-plus hours billed). A more reasonable target for a top firm in an urban setting is 2,000 billed hours, which works out to about 170 hours a month. At most firms you should be fine as long as you are billing at least 1,800 hours a year. Anything less than 1,600 hours and you may have a problem. Each firm has a minimum threshold below which associates' billings do not adequately cover the cost of their salary, support staff, and office rent.

Most firms will know where this cutoff is. Those that don't are mismanaged. As a general rule, firms tend to think of billable hours this way. An associate's billings—like the firm's earnings overall—should be able to be divided into three tranches of equal size: one to cover salary, one to cover overhead (including secretary and rent), and one to go to the partnership as profit. Mess with these economics and an associate's future with the firm is in jeopardy. In fact, there is a degree of flexibility in this rule as it relates to associate billings. Young associates, and particularly first-years, are not expected to make a positive contribution to the partnership, although they should cover their own room and board. As a result, mid-level and senior associates are expected to make a larger contribution to the partnership pie. As an associate, you would be well advised to learn what numbers the partnership has in mind.

WHAT IS THE "FOUR-LEGGED, TWO-HEADED PARTNER"?

THE FOUR-LEGGED, two-headed partner is a term some firms use in for a senior partner who has a very close working relationship with a slightly less senior attorney, who may be either a senior associate or a junior partner. This more junior attorney will work just about exclusively for the senior partner. The senior partner will be well respected and considered powerful. The more junior attorney will be totally reliant on the senior partner for his or her career. The junior person will be very protective of his or her position under the senior partner, who will generally be a terrible manager and often quite overbearing. Junior associates will want to avoid working on projects originated by this senior partner but usually, because the work is profitable for the law firm, will be required to rotate into this group periodically.

I have heard of such systems where the required penance was in the range of six months and others where it was as long as three years. Working for such a team is thankless because the more senior associate will never be supplanted from his or her position directly under the senior partner—nor would anyone want to take said position—and yet the arrangement is pervasive because it benefits the firm and is condoned by the senior partner. It is a symbiotic relationship that benefits everyone but the junior associates stuck at the bottom of this pyramid. The senior partner is happy because his work gets done, the more junior senior attorney is happy because he or she has a job as long as she keeps the senior partner happy, and the firm is happy because more money comes in than is paid out in salaries and expenses. The junior associates count the days until their time is served.

Now that you know what the four-legged, two-headed partner is, you may think of ways to avoid getting stuck at the bottom of such a group.

Good luck to you. All I can say is, if the time of rotation is short enough, do as good a job as you can and move on. You will get credit from the rest of the firm for having made your contribution. By not complaining. you will earn deserved credit from what is likely a sympathetic audience. (I would guess that a good number of the junior partners had to do their time as well.) On the other hand, if you find you are about to get stuck at the bottom of one of these pyramids on a more permanent and exclusive basis, I would consider taking action to extricate yourself. Ask around for the best way to do this. It may mean expressing a strong interest in the practice of an equally or more powerful senior partner. Usually something less extreme than finding another law firm can do the trick.

DO ASSOCIATES USE FLIRTING AS A MEANS OF CAREER ADVANCEMENT?

SOMETIMES, YES. A study conducted by Tulane University researchers found that 49 percent of MBA graduates polled admitted they had attempted to advance in their careers by occasionally engaging in sexual behavior that included wearing revealing clothing and sending flirty e-mails.[1] However, the same study apparently found that such flirting did not work—that is, women who dressed provocatively and rubbed men's shoulders were found to get fewer promotions. This, obviously, suggests that flirting may not be a good idea.

Let's talk about flirting in the legal environment specifically. In government, at least, I can tell you that flirting either by a man or a woman would be very poorly received. Believe it or not, government is an environment where, at the staff level, any form of favoritism between managers and their reports is strongly discouraged. A manager hiring for a position under her cannot even go to the junior staff she thinks would be appropriate and suggest to them that she thinks they should apply (at least this is the case within the SEC). Flirting as a strategy for promotion would be so far beyond the pale that it is almost unimaginable, at least today. I understand that, in years past, there were some divisions of the SEC where there was some inappropriate behavior, but that was in a branch office that has since been closed down and in any event, it took place over a decade ago.

Forty-nine percent of MBA graduates polled admitted they had attempted to advance in their careers by occasionally engaging in sexual behavior that included wearing revealing clothing and sending flirty e-mails.

In law firms, things are a bit looser. In each of the three major firms I've worked for, I have heard stories about some kind of illicit relationship between the male partners and the female associates, which resulted in at least one case in the divorce of the partner to his longtime wife and his marriage to the younger associate. But that is not what we are talking about here. We are talking about more innocent flirting. I have seen this kind of flirting work on one occasion in which an attractive young attorney flirted with an older partner. It was pretty obvious that she was flirting, and the two of them did lots of travel together. The rumors were rampant that the two were having an affair. I don't believe they were but, rather, I think he enjoyed her company and that she did good work for him. But she did flirt with him and it apparently did not hurt her career (she was eventually made a partner in the firm).

I have also seen women in law firms try to flirt, with disastrous consequences. A female summer associate in a firm in which I was spending a summer during law school made it a habit of wearing revealing outfits (which we all found kind of strange because her husband was a minister). She did this on a regular basis and maybe it would not have doomed her chances of getting an offer except that, on a golf outing she wore a white T-shirt and no bra. She also had had a bit too much to drink and started hugging some of the male lawyers—albeit in a "friendly" way. There were a handful of the lawyers' wives there. You can just imagine the talks between the wives and their husbands later on. It was all quite surreal, and needless to say, she did not get a partnership offer.

WHAT ARE SOME OF THE BIG MISTAKES ASSOCIATES MAKE AT LAW FIRMS?

THERE IS AN expression commonly employed in law firms: showing your warts. Everyone has warts. They are the stupid mistakes you inevitably make as a young, inexperienced lawyer. I made them, you will make them, everyone does. The secret to being a successful associate is, first, to recover from them quickly and, second, to learn from your mistakes and not make the same one twice.

Generally, a good rule is always to look good in front of the partners. As any Hollywood PR firm will tell you, image is everything. You need to dress well, speak well, be serious about your job, and always hand in excellent work on or before the deadline. Avoid some common mistakes young associates have made. Make sure any written work you give to a partner is perfect or as near to perfect as possible. Keep in mind that, once you hand in an assignment, you cannot take it back. One fault I had as a first year associate was that, once I gave a partner a memo, I could not help but continue to edit the work and try to find better legal citations. I would continue to look for cases that contradicted my conclusions. I did not realize that there are so many cases out there that it is always possible to find some case that could be interpreted as countervailing. Going to the partner with an alternative theory after you already gave him a memo makes you look incompetent

WILL BEING ACTIVE ON THE ASSOCIATES' COMMITTEE GET ME NOTICED BY PARTNERS AS BEING PARTNERSHIP MATERIAL?

THE ANSWER IS yes and no and depends on what sort of activity you are involved in. I had a friend at the firm I worked for in Washington who reduced his chances of making partner by being active on the Associates' Committee because he was too outspoken in seeking improved pay and working conditions for associates. Rather than receive respect for being a strong and effective advocate, he was viewed by some partners as a troublemaker. Partners do not want to make troublemakers partners in their firm. They have enough trouble dealing with the people they did not think were troublemakers but who, once they were made senior partners, became strong advocates for their own personal interests.

Being a first-year associate in a law firm can be very confusing. The rules are different than they were in college and law school. This can result in associates' doing things that they have been rewarded for doing during the last seven years—four of college and three of law school—that are just fatal in the law firm environment.

When I was a first-year associate, we had an Associates' Committee that had been set up some years before to provide a mechanism for associates to make recommendations to the partnership. Most of us were busy focused on trying to do a decent enough job on our legal work to take much interest in this committee. However, one of my friends in my class—a very sharp young attorney who had just graduated from Harvard Law School—had been an active student advocate during college and had participated enthusiastically in student government while in law school. He obviously viewed the Associates' Committee through the prism of his experience as a campus leader.

What my friend did was to take this nearly dormant committee and transform it into a forum for some rather substantive requests. Now, in college there is no penalty—and likely some reward in terms of renown and respect—for acting as the advocate for your peers. But law firms are a different animal altogether. Law firms are run for profit and, while they give something more than mere lip service to the desire to make associates happy (they really do want associates to be happy so long as it improves productivity), they need to see some benefit in return for any expenditures. In addition, you are graduating from college in four years (who really cares if you piss off the dean?) whereas with law firms, those same people will be deciding whether you make partner in a few years.

My old buddy took a number of grievances the associates had been griping about for years and brought them to the forefront. He demanded greater performance feedback, upgrades to the software system that was causing computers to crash on a regular basis, and changes to the menu in the firm's cafeteria. These were all legitimate requests—but they were made in an aggressive way. Five years later, he did not make partner.

What I do know, however, is that he was viewed by the partners and the associates as a very aggressive individual when it came to articulating his belief in the rights of the associates. I suspect he believed this would put him in good standing with the partners—who would interpret his conduct as that of a strong advocate that they would like to have on their side. This belief was immature and did not take into account the perspective of the partnership, in particular, the older partners, who have a lot of influence over who is made a new partner. In partnerships, there is always a good deal of wrangling: over who gets to use the best associates, who gets the biggest firm draw, and who gets credit for new clients coming in, for example.

There is also the inevitable fact that some partners turn out to be troublemakers after they are made partner, and after which it is too late to get rid of them. I suspect it is likely that many partners viewed my friend as a risk on both fronts. My lesson for you is to think carefully before branding yourself as an advocate or complainer. The law firm environment is fundamentally different from the academic one. Your reputation, once formed, will stick with you when promotion decisions are made.

SHOULD I TEACH AS AN ADJUNCT LAW PROFESSOR?

I TAUGHT AS an adjunct law professor at the University of Miami School of Law (in Miami, Florida), and some years later, assisted a law firm partner I was working with while he taught a class as an adjunct at Georgetown University Law Center. In fact, teaching as an adjunct is quite popular among law firm practitioners in Washington, a city in which there exist a number of top law firms and an impressive collection of receptive— and good—law schools. For law schools themselves the proposition of hiring adjuncts is a no-brainer. Practicing attorneys are a great resource: they know their particular practice area well, are up-to-date on the most compelling issues, and can provide a real-world practice perspective that career academics lack.

I enjoyed teaching and I was good at it. My students voted me one of the best professors they had and asked the administration to hire me as a full-time professor (I could not do this, as I was about to join a firm in Washington). I mention this because I believe that enjoying teaching (or any activity, for that matter) and being good at it are related. That is, not everyone is going to be a good teacher. It takes a great deal of dedication and patience, as well as knowledge and intelligence. Patience is perhaps the most important attribute. Law students don't know very much. They have to be taught—and taught again—the fundamentals. Practicing lawyers, particularly partners who have spent years focused on one area of law (likely the one they are teaching), forget this too easily. If the teacher is not extremely patient, it can be a painful experience for everyone.

Your experience as a teacher, whether you end up enjoying it or not, will directly reflect your own perspective. When I taught my class at Miami, I was less than two years out of Columbia Law. I remembered not knowing what a corporation was, or the Uniform Commercial Code. I was learning alongside my students and we all enjoyed the ride a great deal. But when I assisted a senior partner from my firm in teaching a class at Georgetown Law, the experience was different. He had no patience, and it showed. He made the class far too difficult and graded students harshly. The students hated him (quite a few dropped the class) and the objective—teaching students as much useful information about law practice as they could absorb—was far from met. It was another lesson, that working for a senior partner with no patience can be a hard way to earn a buck, that was likely communicated more effectively.

SHOULD I PUBLISH SCHOLARLY WORK?

THERE ARE TWO kinds of legal research you can publish: as a law student you can write a "note" and as a legal professional you can publish an "article". Publishing a law review or journal note while you are in law school is always a good idea. It will likely be completed and either published or ready for publishing in time for inclusion on your résumé. Law firms like to see this kind of intellectual initiative; it is consistent with their formula for picking new associates who are likely to succeed in the academically rigorous law firm environment. Publishing a law review or journal article after you graduate may not yield as immediate a positive result, but it can have more long-term benefits for your career, including attracting clients. The subject matter of professional articles is of much greater value to you than that of the student-written note, whose subject matter was less important than the fact that you wrote it and it was good enough to get published.

Before I explain my stance on professional articles, let me tell you about my own experience publishing work in the academic literature. I have published three articles, two in the *Columbia Business Law Review* and one in the *Securities Regulation Law Journal*.[2] These are both well-regarded journals. In fact, the *Securities Regulation Law Journal* is probably the most acclaimed publication for the securities law profession. I cowrote one of the *Columbia Business Law Review* pieces with a classmate while we were still in school, yet it was published as an article rather than a note as a result of its high quality and because we had both graduated before it went to press.

Writing with a coauthor has its pluses and minuses. In addition to that

CBLR piece, I also had a coauthor for the *SRLJ* article. I was the sole author of the final *CBLR* article. Writing with a co-author, particularly one who has knowledge of the field in which you are writing, can result in a much more polished finished product. For one thing, you have someone to tell you when your research is going in the wrong direction and your writing is no good. For another, it is a way to share what can be a very significant amount of researching, writing, and editing work. On the other hand, writing with someone else can result in unevenness in the finished product. The sections you write may not flow easily into the sections he wrote. It can also result in frustration as, inevitably, both writers feel as though they have made the better part of the contribution and that the other writer is somewhat of a slacker. It is a rare friendship that is as strong after a joint writing experience as it was before, though sometimes great and enduring collaborations are formed.

As I have mentioned, writing as a seasoned attorney makes the subject matter of your research more critical. You are no longer writing in order to secure a job. Rather, you are either writing for yourself or in order to impress prospective clients that you are the lawyer for the job. For that reason it makes sense to write in an area in which you are practicing, or in which you hope to practice. It should also be an area in which you are interested. I wrote up my research in the area of corporate and securities law. This was highly practical, as both are areas in which a great deal of time and money is spent in the legal market. Nevertheless, writing the pieces has not resulted in great recognition or even directly led to clients or better jobs. The most direct recognition I have received are a couple of calls from former colleagues commenting on having run across my work, and once, during an insider trading investigation I was conducting for the SEC, from the general counsel at a major investment bank who was concerned that I might be calling about a more serious corporate governance issue (she had read my work on corporate governance and assumed I was the SEC's resident expert in the field).

My published work has received some rather nice recognition within the academic community. Many law review articles have cited my work.[3] And I believe it is true that having publications on my résumé as a more senior attorney has added a certain gravitas to my profile, but this has consistently failed to get me certain senior-level jobs for which they would suggest I am qualified. For example, I interviewed for but failed to secure the position of Chief of Mergers and Acquisitions at the Division of Corporation Finance at the Securities and Exchange Commission. My two publications in the Columbia Law Review dealt with M&A, and I had some experience, albeit limited, in both negotiated and hostile takeover transactions. I mention this only so that you may have a realistic sense of what publishing can and cannot do for you.

When you do decide to publish, keep in mind that you have the option of writing either a full-length law review article, as I have consistently done, or a short piece for a local professional legal periodical, as some of my former colleagues have done. There is a very big difference between the two. A full-length law review article will be as much as a hundred pages long, and no less than fifty, and will have between one hundred fifty and three hundred citations. A short piece for a local professional legal periodical will be a couple of pages long and have about a dozen citations. Whereas the article will tackle a serious legal issue—a split between the Circuit Courts of Appeal, say, or a proposed change to the Delaware Corporate Code—a short piece for a local legal periodical will generally address a new trend in the law that is of general interest to potential clients. This might be a change in the tax law that rich clients should be aware of, or a new kind of transaction that corporate clients should consider entering into. The marketing powers of an article versus a short topical piece differ significantly. Short pieces lend themselves better to attracting paying clients in the short term, particularly less sophisticated or more business-oriented clients. They appear in publications that are often read more by business people than by lawyers. These may include publications specific to a relevant industry, such as a real estate newsletter in the case of a piece about a tax law change effecting real estate transactions, a publication for CFOs, or another business journal in the case of a piece concerning a new type of corporate transaction recently blessed by the Delaware Court of Chancery. Short pieces can also be printed on card stock and handed out to clients visiting the firm's offices, or placed in convenient holders in the lobby.

Articles, on the other hand, are written for other lawyers. They may yield long-term recognition by legal peers and perhaps result in some business from an academic-minded corporate general counsel who reads the serious law reviews. But the business benefits will be indirect and will take much longer to gestate. In fact, I have had several people ask me whether, in writing my law review articles, I was preparing for a position as a law professor. This would never happen as the result of publishing a short piece. So, as you see, the perceptions are quite different.

WHAT SHOULD I DO IF A PARTNER ASKS ME TO WRITE A LAW REVIEW PIECE AND NAME HIM AS THE AUTHOR?

I HAVE HAD the privilege of working with partners who have treated me as a true equal, and the displeasure of working for partners who treated me as a tool that they could use and throw away. Curiously, the former were great men, widely recognized in their field as top talent, with significant achievements behind them. The later were small men, desperate to prove themselves within their own firms.

When I was a new associate, I had the chance to work with a partner who had recently joined the firm. He had been the director of the Division of Market Regulation at the SEC, where he had been charged with regulating the trading markets, including multibillion-dollar broker-dealers and stock exchanges. He encouraged me to write an article on a subject that he was personally interested in, but when I finished it, he refused to put his name on it, saying that I had done most of the work and that publishing the article would do more for my career than for his.

When I was at another firm a few years later, I worked for two partners who asked me to write a short article on a new twist on a certain type of corporate transaction of interest to smaller public firms. They were partners operating in the boondocks, stuck in the Washington office of a mid-tier regional firm whose head office and most of the firm's power was in Boston. Their client firms were small and their practices indistinguishable from those of a thousand other corporate attorneys. When I finished the piece, they put their names on it and removed mine. Without telling me, they published it under their joint byline in a small local periodical read by local businessmen.

Keep these two examples in your mind when a partner asks you to write a law review piece. Clarify from the start whether the partner intends for you to publish it under your name or write it for his eventual attribution. In either case, you will want to write the piece. After all, doing this kind of work is what the firm is paying you for. If you write a good article, and the partner who puts his name on it gets good press as a result, he will think well of you. Very likely he will ask you to write another article for him, at which time you should press more firmly for joint recognition. The only real downside is if writing articles becomes so much of your job description that your billable hours decline. In the world of law firms, the ultimate gauge of performance will always be the billable hour. But, aside from this, and though it can be frustrating to write something publishable and not get external credit for it, in the long term it can be an opportunity to build a good reputation within your firm.

13. MAKING PARTNER

HOW DO LAW FIRM PARTNERS DECIDE WHOM TO NAME AS NEW PARTNERS?

IT IS IMPORTANT that you understand the way partners think about the partner-making process. There are strong emotional and economic forces at work that you should be aware of early in your firm career if you are going to have a chance of making partner.

Understand the partnership decision from the perspective of partners. Every firm has partners that the rest of the members regret having made partners. These are people who were obviously impressive enough as associates to be considered for partnership but who did not live up to the expectation after being elevated to partner. In the old days it was difficult, if not impossible, to get rid of a partner who did not work out. Being made partner was something like getting academic tenure. You could basically not be fired except for illegal or immoral conduct. This has changed, with lawyers first promoted to provisional positions as non-equity partners, but it is still true that it is extremely difficult to reverse a decision to elevate someone to partner. It is considered much better not to promote the individual in the first place.

I recall that at the Washington firm where I worked during the 1990s, there was a partner whom the other partners regretted having made partner. His infraction was that he did not work hard enough and had too much fun in his free time. This man really did not work very hard during the week and, worse, left early each Friday afternoon in order to drive to Annapolis, where he kept a 45-foot sailboat. His practice was to sail all weekend and come back to the office late the following Monday.

At that time, salaries for partners were largely decided on in lockstep, meaning that all partners were paid about the same amount based on the year they were made partner. (Incidentally, most firms have now moved away from the lockstep pay method for partners and now more directly compensate them for their direct contributions to the firm's bottom line in terms of new clients and billable hours.) All this partner wanted to talk about at meetings was what he was going to name his next boat. The other partners were largely workaholics who spent nights and weekends at the office, and they had clearly grown to hate this guy. But they could not get rid of him. What he had done, apparently, was to work his ass off for eight years as an associate and then, a few years after having been made partner, slowly adjusted down his schedule to the point where he was now significantly underperforming.

The partners in this case were not going to make the same mistake again. They were not going to let another associate hoodwink them into believing that he was going to work hard after being named a partner and then take a permanent vacation while sucking up firm money. After all, this guy got paid over a million dollars a year to work what they felt was part time. Their reaction was to overcompensate. Any character traits linked to this guy would be death to an associate's partnership aspirations. Even a general interest in sailing would draw a frown. And, while normally it might be a good idea to develop personal relationships with individual partners, here it was not. Buddying up to this partner by accepting an invitation to join him for a weekend of sailing would not be viewed as a good sign by the rest of the partners. Partnership decisions are made by majority vote. His one vote would be far outweighed by the others.

HOW CAN I INCREASE MY CHANCES OF MAKING PARTNER?

1. Realize that it is okay to admit to ignorance when a partner asks you a question. There are very few times when a question must be answered immediately. It is far better to admit ignorance than to have to come back later and correct your mistaken reply.
2. Set reasonable expectations and practical deadlines when asked by partners to perform a task, and then work to exceed them.
3. Don't be afraid to turn down work. You do not always have to say yes to partners. Partners will forget that you turned them down, but they will not forget if you turn in work product that is below their expectations.
4. Never say you are bored, angry, or tired when on the job. Find something interesting to do, go to the gym to work out your aggressions, or get some more sleep. Projecting a positive aura will be noticed.
5. Make the firm's clients happy.

It is important that you be serious about the practice of law. This is critical both for your success as an associate and to increase your chances of making partner. It is very tempting, amid the pressures of working for a large law firm, to blow off steam by joking around with your fellow associates. I had a lot of fun joking around with my fellow associates during seemingly endless hours of working on due diligence projects when I was a young attorney. We would joke around during our nightly dinner breaks over ordered-in Chinese food and also during long days of document reviews. We told jokes, played pranks, and generally tried to have as much fun as we could while still doing our jobs. Sometimes we would try and get the junior partners to joke around with us, but they rarely did.

The thing was, the partners did not tend to joke around because they were directly responsible for the outcome of our work. They were under a great deal of pressure to keep each individual client happy while balancing the demands of multiple clients. From their perspective, a great deal (of money and reputation) was at stake both for the client and for the firm. Looking back on it, I am sure they were dismayed by what appeared to be the lack of seriousness we displayed. But we did not think of it that way at the time. As a result, it is good policy not to joke around at the office, or if you do, take pains not to let the partners catch you at it. Blow off steam away from the office and maintain a businesslike demeanor anytime you are in the firm's offices or conducting firm business.

Partners may tell you that there are no dumb questions, but they don't always mean it. The truth is that much of what you are asked to do in practice will be counterintuitive—that is, you cannot use pure reasoning to figure out what you should do, even in some simple cases. I am reminded of the time when I was a young associate involved in my first major litigation matter and sent out all of our pleadings through a process server. I had been instructed to serve the initial complaint in this manner, but the rest should have been sent by Federal Express. It was a stupid mistake that cost the firm money (they did not bill the client for the error).

My recommendation with regard to dumb questions is twofold. Ask the dumb questions early, and—for the really dumb questions—ask the most junior person you can find so that you can present yourself as more knowledgeable to the senior people who will be evaluating your performance. This will allow you to save the slightly less dumb questions for the partner or senior associate. After all, you do have a limit on how many times a day you can come to them with questions. Another thing you might want to consider—and I realize it is easier said than done—is to develop a relationship with one senior with whom you develop a mentoring relationship. That might be a person to whom you can go with some of the dumb questions on a regular basis.

You should also prepare for cases in advance. If you are embarking on the defense of a leverage buyout, find others in the firm who have done one before and ask them to go through the process and highlight the likely pitfalls. Take notes and learn from their experience. If you are given a small M&A transaction to do on your own, gather all of the deal documents from a similar deal and spend some time with the attorneys who worked on that deal to learn how they all fit together. In this way you will have a good chance of exceeding the expectations of the assigning partner. And that is what you need to do if you are going to be considered a partnership prospect: exceed expectations consistently. You want the partner to go away wondering how you know this stuff so well.

WHAT KINDS OF PEOPLE MAKE PARTNER; CAN THEY BE CLASSIFIED INTO DIFFERENT GROUPS?

PEOPLE WHO JOIN law firms are a diverse group, but it often seems that only a few kinds become partners. Some leave of their own accord, some are effectively fired, and the ones who remain are inexorably shaped by the experience of going through the law firm associate-to-partner experience. I have worked for three different leading law firms as an associate and for two additional firms as, respectively, a law clerk and a summer associate. Throughout this experience I have come to recognize several basic forms that partners commonly come in:

The Egotist: There is some of this person in every law firm partner. This person believes the hype that he made partner because he is a better person than all of the other associates who did not make it. He believes he should be worshipped because of his success within the firm. In the back of his mind, he may realize that success in the firm has nothing to do with success in life, but as a result, he holds even more closely to the belief that his position justifies his existence.

The Micromanager: This individual cannot delegate. He would be a failure in a corporate setting but gets away with it in a law firm because there is less accountability for performance efficiency. He must review everything that is done by the associates who work for him and, as often as not, redo it. This habit is a result of having done all the work as an associate while moving up through the ranks and an unwillingness to let go. He is worried that he will be blamed for a screwup by his underlings and will look bad in front of a client. He lives in a perpetual state of fear.

The Screamer: This is perhaps more common in New York than in some other cities. Some firms even go so far as to say they do not (any longer) tolerate screaming. But in some New York firms it remains an accepted character trait. These people scream at their secretaries, at their associates, and at their spouses on the telephone. If they make enough money for the firm, the firm tolerates it. These are angry people: angry at their clients, angry at their opponents, and angry at themselves (probably for being lawyers).

The Nut Job: There are several of these in every firm. Other attorneys are instructed to keep the summer associates away from these people until they come back as full-time associates and can't escape as easily. I have seen the Nut Job's insanity take several forms. One partner refused to have anything in his office except his desk, chair, and laptop computer—no paper and no guest chairs. Another partner refused to cut his fingernails, which were filthy. Another incessantly picked his nose in public. A third drank so much coffee that his body shook. Some of these quirks are mildly amusing, others are grossly antisocial.

The Isolationist: This person can also be, ironically, the micromanager. He hates to delegate but when he does, he has to give detailed instructions—usually in writing—about exactly how the work is to be done. Any variation from the way he would have done it is a mistake—even in highly subjective tasks. It is nearly impossible to satisfy this very unhappy person.

The Mentor: These are rare. When they exist in a law firm setting it is usually because they came from government and not through the associate ranks. I have known only one in my career and he was a very good man and a terrific lawyer (he was also something of a Nut Job but we should forgive him that). I knew this partner when he was just a year out of serving as the director of the Division of Market Regulation at SEC. As I've already mentioned, he encouraged me to write a law review article, helped me to write it, and then refused to put his name on it because he wanted to help my career. I hope this man has not changed with the last ten years of practice in a leading law firm. If you find a partner with this characteristic, you should nurture her or him as your mentor.

AS PART OF MY PARTNERSHIP STRATEGY, SHOULD I REALLY TRY TO WORK WITH A RANGE OF DIFFERENT PARTNERS OR JUST DO GREAT WORK FOR ONE PARTNER?

WHILE AN ARGUMENT can be made for putting all of your effort into doing great work for a single partner with whom you get along really well, almost always the better approach is to work with at least a limited range of different partners. For one thing, with a single partner you never know whether he or she will return your loyalty or stab you in the back when it comes time to elevate associates to partnership. In addition, you have no real insurance in the event it turns out that the area in which that one partner is practicing is determined by the firm not to be big enough for you both to serve as equity partners.

It is easy to get into the habit of returning to the same partner for assignments, particularly if you have done outstanding work for him or her. For one thing, the partner will likely reach out to you if you have exceeded his expectations in the past. For another, once you know what a partner likes and dislikes, it is easier to ride this learning curve to improved job performance. Indeed, partners appreciate and will reward loyalty, and being a partner's go-to guy can have its benefits, particularly when the partner is particularly well regarded in his area of expertise.

HOW IMPORTANT IS IT TO FIND A MENTOR AT A LAW FIRM AND HOW CAN I DO THIS?

FINDING A MENTOR is very important in a law firm. Law firms are high pressure places that are very competitive on a couple of levels. That is, there is pressure to perform well and to fit in to the overall firm culture. It is difficult to know what is expected of you as a new associate. It can also be very difficult to ask the dumb questions of the partner you are working for. Therefore, having a less formal relationship with someone who has experience working in the firm can be of enormous benefit.

Some firms operate formal mentoring programs. These can be good or bad. They are good because they make certain that someone is available to serve as your mentor. They are bad because they often force a round peg into a square hole, matching you with someone with whom you are either not personally compatible or who is an unwilling participant in a mandatory mentoring program. There is little that is less productive than a mentoring program in which the mentor is too busy billing hours to spare a few moments for his advisee.

DO I REALLY WANT TO MAKE PARTNER?

IF YOU HAVE gotten into a good college, achieved the grades to get into a good law school, and again met the grade to obtain a job at a leading law firm, then you have been well trained to gun for the next hurdle: partnership. Like your earlier milestones, making partner is a goal on which you can focus. You will dedicate all your energy and effort on this goal for at least seven years—perhaps longer, as partnership tracks are being extended by many leading firms. But you should at least question whether partnership is a goal worth achieving.

Not long ago, I was talking to an SEC colleague who had come to the commission from a position as a partner in a large Washington law firm about how different working in private practice is from being with the government. He told me how he decided to leave his partnership post. When his second child was about to be born, he called one of his partners to tell him that his wife was going into labor and that he was heading to the hospital. His partner's response was, "How long is that going to take?" This story is characteristic of the increasing pressures placed on partners as they rise to levels of responsibility in the firm. The expectations for high billable hours do not decline when you are elevated from associate to partner but, rather, they actually increase. The layer of protection between associates and clients is removed: the partner is directly responsible for delivering results. Moreover, partners need to negotiate with clients over bills, and perform the delicate balancing act of collecting money due while maintaining good client relations.

When law firm partners go on vacation with their families it is common that they remain glued to the cell phone or, now with mobile

Internet communications, married to their laptops and PDAs. Government attorneys, on the other hand, can usually walk away from work (at the end of the day or even for a week with the family) and not have to worry about the office. In-house counsel, because they are the boss of the law firm attorneys whom they hire to do the company's legal work, can usually delegate responsibilities to the outside counsel and walk away for an uninterrupted holiday (unless a big transaction is under way, of course). Now, it is true that government lawyers get paid a lot less than partners in private firms. Even in-house counsel, unless they work for very large corporations and are the lead general counsel, are unlikely to get paid what one can earn as a firm partner. Nevertheless, as you get older you will find that lifestyle choices become more relevant—what good is all that money if you don't have the time to enjoy it? You need to keep this in mind while you have got your nose to the grindstone trying like hell to make the partnership grade.

IT'S HARD TO MAKE PARTNER. IS THERE ANOTHER WAY TO ACHIEVE GREAT POWER AND WEALTH?

WHEN YOU ARE a law firm associate and all your peers are focused on making partner, when every lunch discussion revolves around that subject and the concomitant one of who has the highest billable hours, it seems that making partner is the only route to personal fulfillment. You feel that failure to be named a partner would be tantamount to death. However, it simply isn't so. I can tell you that making partner is not the most important thing you can do with your career as a lawyer, or in your life as a human being. In fact, some of the most gifted and imaginative attorneys I have known have rejected opportunities to become partners in law firms in order to accomplish other career goals. I believe those people are far happier today because of their decisions.

First of all, ask yourself what are the character traits of the perfect large-firm partner. The answer is, from an admittedly cynical perspective, that an ideal partner would be a detail-minded person who is not easily bored by repetitive work, who is willing to slavishly sacrifice his personal life for his clients, and who lacks the imagination to consider—and be tempted by—alternative means of making a living. Such a person—smart but highly risk averse—is going to do consistently good work for clients and generate a reliable stream of revenue for the firm over a long period of time. He will not yearn to leave the safety of the organized firm environment to pursue a new venture or opportunity. Such a person is going to take pleasure from belonging to the larger family of law partners. They are his peers and, perhaps, his only friends. However, in the end he may find that while he has contributed a great deal to the partnership, he has sacrificed his relationship with his family and the opportunity to do other things that could have brought much greater psychological and financial rewards.

The fact that there are better things to do with a legal career than become a partner is illustrated by the fact that some lawyers voluntarily leave their partnerships for other opportunities. I knew an associate at my first law firm who made partner and then quit within a year to join a venture capital firm. He might not have been offered that position had he not made partner, it is true, but in any event he chose not to spend the remainder of his career practicing law. Others have left without making partner even though they could have. I knew one associate who left the firm we were working for in Washington to become head of the U.S. Track and Field Association in Indianapolis. Craig Masback, with whom I worked my first corporate proxy contest, attended Princeton and Yale Law, was the second person after Roger Bannister to break the four-minute mile, and was very well liked by the partnership. He would almost certainly have made partner at Wilmer, Cutler & Pickering but gave it up for a position in a sport he loved.

Politics can also be a draw. One associate I worked with at a large Washington firm left voluntarily, though he was well on his way along the partnership track, in order to return to his hometown—a small hamlet in rural Pennsylvania—to run for local office. His objective was to eventually run for Congress, and he recognized the need to develop a grass-roots base of support in order to achieve that very specific objective. There are many other examples, but you get the picture.

WHAT IS THE EMOTIONAL EFFECT ON LAWYERS AND THEIR SPOUSES OF NOT MAKING PARTNER?

NOT MAKING PARTNER after having worked tirelessly for seven or more years with the sole objective of making partner can be devastating for young lawyers and their loved ones. Consider that the young men and women who get into good colleges, graduate from top law schools, and do well enough to land jobs at great law firms are not accustomed to failure. Consider, also, that law firms build up the partnership selection process as a judgment of whether the attorney is good enough or is partnership material and you can begin to understand how injured a young attorney can become who wants partnership, works for it, but does not get it.

I have known at least half a dozen couples whose marriages were destroyed when a lawyer-spouse (always, in my experience, the husband) did not make partner. That is, I have known couples—seemingly happy up until then—to have separated and then gotten divorced within months after a husband did not make partner. I have also known (and today know of) men who are delaying asking their longtime girlfriends to marry them until after the partnership selection committee meets (as it does in many firms each October). One might ask why it matters whether the guy makes partner if the couple is in love. The answer is both a practical and an emotional one. On one hand, making partner means a much higher compensation package as well as the feeling of belonging gained by being told, "You are one of us." In contrast, rejection from partnership means fiscal uncertainty, and certainly a much lower spending power, as the lawyer will often have a short period of time to pack up and find a new job. It also hurts to be told that you are not acceptable to the people for whom you have slaved for nearly a decade, and that rejection too easily translates into general depression that carries over to interpersonal relations between spouses.

That partnership rejection destroys marriages is the reality, and it is a shame. The truth is that the partnership selection process is inherently flawed. That is, after having excelled in college and law school sufficiently to gain a position at a top law

The partnership selection process has little to do with associates' capabilities as attorneys and nothing to do with their qualities as human beings.

firm, just about every associate is partnership material. They are all brilliant, hardworking, good men and women. The failure of a firm to elevate an individual to partnership is due to the simple fact that the firm does not need that many partners. Who makes it and who doesn't often depends upon office politics and dumb luck. The luck part commonly comes in the form of who was fortunate enough to get placed with a good senior mentor, or who entered a field of law that was particularly busy during the year when the partnership decision was made. But because law firm partners by definition made it through the selection process, they convey the message to associates that the partnership vote is a vote on the inherent goodness of the candidate. This message pervades the law firm culture and makes rejected candidates feel intensely inadequate. All law firm associates therefore need to understand that the partnership selection process is an artificial construct that has little to do with their capabilities as attorneys and nothing to do with their qualities as human beings.

WHAT IS THE SECRET OF LAW FIRM PARTNERS WHO HAVE HAD A PARTICULARLY SUCCESSFUL LEGAL CAREER?

THE FACT IS, while it remains true that it is very hard to make partner and making partner itself often depends on luck, some lawyers have had extremely successful careers as law firm partners. Consider Larry Sonsini, often described as Silicon Valley's most feared and sought-after lawyer and as a lawyer-rockstar. Sonsini is a name partner at the Palo Alto firm of Wilson, Sonsini, Goodrich & Rosati, who throughout his more than forty-year career has represented nearly all of the major technology firms emerging from Silicon Valley:semiconductor companies like LSI Logic, Cypress Semiconductor, and National Semiconductor; hardware companies like Silicon Graphics, Apple Computer, Sun Microsystems, and Seagate Technologies; software firms like Novell, WordPerfect, and Sybase; and Internet pioneers like Netscape, Google, and YouTube.[1]

Sonsini is credited with pioneering the idea of law firms investing directly in their clients' companies (for which he has taken a significant degree of criticism, particularly in recent years in light of the stock options backdating scandals affecting many of his clients). He also played a pivotal role in assisting in the formation of the companies that would give rise to the new information-based economy. The defining moment in Sonsini's career was likely his decision, upon graduating from Berkeley's Boalt Hall Law School in the 1960s, to work for a small firm in the Santa Clara Valley (not yet Silicon Valley) as the firm's first associate instead of than joining his classmates at large firms in New York or Los Angeles.

What is instructive about Sonsini's experience is that he did a couple of things that are strategically very smart for a young lawyer. First, he recognized an emergent need. Specifically, he saw that there were a large number of young companies in the Palo Alto area that were being formed based on technology being developed at Stanford University and Berkeley. In time, these companies would need to seek financing and, eventually, go public. Second, he was willing to take a risk by not following the path chosen by most of his fellow law school graduates. Going to a top firm in New York or Los Angeles would have brought him a higher initial salary, been more prestigious, and would probably have offered greater job security. But in order to pursue his long-term career vision, he was able to set these temptations aside and take the first step. Recognizing an opportunity takes imagination and vision, and executing a strategy to take advantage of the emergent opportunity takes self-confidence and, let's face it, a significant dose of bravery. Individuals with the fortune to have both characteristics, plus the necessary drive to succeed, are rare enough that few graduating law students deviate from the standard course of going to work for the largest and most prestigious firm that will hire them. However, look carefully at the examples of those few successful lawyers—like Sonsini and others—who have reinvented the profession and realized satisfying careers as a result.

14. ALTERNATIVES TO LAW FIRM LIFE

SHOULD I WORK FOR THE GOVERNMENT, AND WHAT ARE SOME DISADVANTAGES OF DOING SO?

WHILE THE GOVERNMENT offers a stable work environment and good benefits combined with usually a livable workload and sometimes a decent pay package, there are several significant disadvantages to working for the government. In general, the job can be limiting to your career, in contrast to a law firm where you can build general legal skills. This is particularly true if you are employed by a narrowly focused federal agency like the Food and Drug Administration rather than an agency with a broad scope like the Department of Justice.

You might want to obtain the broadest possible experience early in your career to build your general lawyerly skills. In addition, as you would anticipate, the pay is less and the bureaucracy is large, both of which can be frustrating. Some lawyers will be much less intelligent than others, as there will be a broader range of backgrounds in the government than at a private firm. Finally, support services (secretaries, paralegals, and copy assistants) are notably well below the level that would be expected at a private firm. If you move laterally from a firm, it can take some time to get used to doing many of the copying and mailing chores yourself.

More specifically, you need to keep in mind that the government is not run for profit, as a law firm is. This results in some rather significant differences in approach. The government does not place the same premium on productivity, nor does it particularly reward or teach leadership skills or encourage innovations that would help to improve the efficiency of the work process. This can be frustrating for lawyers who are intelligent and ambitious. I have encountered a surprising lack of interest among some government bureaucrats in adopting innovations that would improve efficiency. Rather, in some cases, I have observed more of a focus by some supervisors on what immediate actions they can take to bring themselves to the attention of more senior supervisors who may have the power to promote them.

I have also found that there is a great disparity in the management capabilities of low- and even mid-level supervisors in the government, even more so than in private law firms. All institutions composed of lawyers—including law firms—have the same problem: lawyers generally do not make very effective managers. This may result from years of working alone, or it may be that people who go to law school self-select for characteristics that do not lend themselves to being good managers. In any event, the problem is worse in government because there is no profit incentive. Moreover, it is more common in the government for political forces to cause incompetent people to be appointed to lead others. Conversely, highly qualified persons can be denied promotions to supervising roles for political reasons at a rate that is higher than average. This can be very disconcerting to the more competent and business-oriented attorneys.

WHAT FEDERAL AGENCIES CAN I WORK FOR AND WHAT SHOULD BE MY FIVE-YEAR PLAN IF I DO?

FIRST YOU NEED to consider why you want to work for the federal government. Is it so that you can gain valuable experience that will place you in high demand in the private sector? Or is it because you want a stable job that can last the remainder of your career? Is it because you want to pursue a specialty area of the regulatory law? Or is it because you want to have a job that lets you spend more time with your children? The answers to these questions will determine which government agency you should join.

As a general rule, government jobs pay lower salaries but allow for more flexible work schedules than private-sector jobs. Indeed, the drop in pay can be the reason some lawyers feel they cannot seriously consider joining the government. Even though they would love to take a break from the pressures of working in a law firm, they feel they can't support their lifestyles (particularly if they have families) on a government paycheck. However, not all government agencies use the same pay scale. The SEC, for example, pays its junior attorneys a good deal more than many other government employers, including the U.S. Department of Justice, which is the largest federal employer of attorneys.

One reason for the SEC's higher pay scale is the demand for experienced securities lawyers in the private marketplace. The turnover rate at the SEC has been running at about 14 percent each year since 1994. At one point in the late 1990s, the need for new attorneys was so great that officials reportedly began cold-calling law firms looking for lawyers.[1] Other federal agencies have experienced similar patterns of attorney attrition. Federal Communications Commission lawyers, for example, who specialize in telecommunications law, left at a rate of 12 percent throughout the 1990s.[2]

WHAT IS IT LIKE TO WORK AT A PRESTIGIOUS FEDERAL AGENCY LIKE THE UNITED STATES SECURITIES AND EXCHANGE COMMISSION?

THE SEC IS a great place to work. It is a wonderful feeling to practice law in a generally relaxed atmosphere with very intelligent, dedicated attorneys working hand-in-hand with experienced accountants and economists toward making the U.S. securities markets safer for individual investors. You are the good guy. You earn a decent salary for a reasonable amount of work doing something that is generally considered worth doing. You are not defending bad guys or working for rich clients who earn more than you ever will, and you have a great deal of control over your time and what kind of work you take on. There is no limit to what you can achieve professionally. You can either spend the rest of your career making around $140,000 as a long-term SEC staff member or you can go for the big promotions and, after perhaps eight to ten years, having risen to associate or assistant director, leave for a partnership in a major securities law firm and earn over a million dollars a year.

The SEC regulates the country's financial markets. Any company that is either listed on a national securities exchange, such as the New York Stock Exchange or NASDAQ, or any company that issues securities privately but is not exempt from registration under the federal securities laws is subject to the commission's oversight. I worked in the Division of Enforcement, as well as for one of the commissioners appointed by the president to oversee the SEC.

The other divisions making up the SEC are Corporate Finance, which among other things reviews the periodic disclosure filings made by public companies; Market Regulation, which regulates brokerage firms; and Investment Management, which oversees mutual funds. There are also other units within the SEC, including the Office of the General Counsel and the Office of Compliance, Inspections and Examinations (OCIE). The Office of the General Counsel acts as legal counsel to the commission itself. OCIE conducts in-depth, on-site inspections of regulated entities such as brokerage firms and stock transfer agents

The Division of Enforcement investigates instances in which securities laws may have been broken. If we find that the laws have been broken, we may bring suit against the violators. Our lawsuits are civil, which means we can only sue for money damages or seek an order from a federal judge barring individuals from serving as officers and directors of public companies. There are also instances in which we can request an administrative proceeding, which may result in the party under investigation being barred from participating in the securities industry more generally. However, Division of Enforcement attorneys can also work hand-in-hand with the FBI and the Department of Justice in bringing a criminal case.

Recent high-profile criminal cases such as those against Martha Stewart, and Bernie Ebbers of MCI-WorldCom, have made both our division and the commission an attractive place for young attorneys interested in securities law to work. But even before these cases, the SEC's Division of Enforcement was generally considered a valuable place to learn a great deal about the securities laws and to pick up strong litigation skills.

ARE SOME PEOPLE BETTER SUITED TO WORKING IN THE GOVERNMENT THAN OTHERS?

THIS QUESTION CAN be interpreted in two ways. First, it can be read as whether a certain personality type is happier working for the government. Second, it can be one of whether a particular life or career experience leads one to embrace the government lifestyle more heartily. I am going to focus on the easier question—that is, what impact certain career or life experiences can have on whether one finds pleasure working in for the government. Basic personality traits may also pay a role in determining whether one would be happier working in the government versus private industry, but that is a more difficult question to answer.

Working for the government gives you a very secure feeling. After one year of experience you essentially have life tenure and cannot be fired. Since most positions (including those of staff attorneys at the SEC) are unionized, it is very hard for management to remove you from your job unless there has been a clear ethical lapse on your part. Unlike at private law firms, there is no pressure to drum up business. There are no billable hours. There is no risk that the firm is going to go out of business or not have enough money coming in to pay salaries or bonuses; taxpayer dollars take care of that. Schedules are generally quite flexible. No one holds it against you if you miss an afternoon to attend a parent-teacher conference or expects you to be in the office over the weekend. There is no up-or-out rule requiring you to advance in the organization or else leave the agency. And, to cap it off, for most positions there is the possibility of working a flexible schedule which can result in your taking off one day of work every two weeks (usually every other Monday or Friday so that you have a three-day weekend).

These are very livable working conditions and contrast sharply with life at a large law firm. Try as they might to make the work experience

more enjoyable (or at least less unpleasant), large law firms remain con-
strained by the fact that they are businesses run for profit in which the
product of value is billable time. There will always be intense pressure to
work long hours. Going the extra mile to keep a firm's paying clients
happy will always be the top priority. Of course, firms pay salaries that
are a good deal higher than the government pays. Law firms also offer
other perks, such as top-notch secretarial support and fancy lunchtime
meals at top restaurants. And, if you do beat the odds and make partner,
there can be an astounding difference in pay between senior government
employees (capped at about $190,000) and law firm partners (averaging
about $500,000).

The lawyers who are best able to appreciate what the government has
to offer are those who have worked for at least a few years in private practice. It is difficult to appreciate how unpleasant billing in six-minute incre-
ments or dealing with the office politics associated with trying to make
partner can be unless one has experienced it. Attorneys who join the SEC
directly out of law school tend to romanticize what it is like to work in a
private law firm (the lunches, the big pay packages), whereas those who
have already experienced it feel as though they have found way to regain
some balance in their lives. This is particularly true for lawyers who are
in their mid-thirties and have young children. From the perspective of
the law firm refugee, it is a luxury to be able to take long weekends every
two weeks and spend time with one's family.

HOW COMPETITIVE IS IT TO GET A JOB WITH A FEDERAL GOVERNMENT AGENCY LIKE THE SECURITIES AND EXCHANGE COMMISSION?

IT IS ALWAYS hard to go where the rest of the crowd is going, particularly when there is room for only a few people. The variability one
finds in how difficult it is to get a job at a place like the SEC or like
the Department of Justice depends on two factors: how many people
are seeking those jobs and how many positions are open. Both of
these factors fluctuated widely between 1995 and 2005, the period
with which I am most familiar. During 1995, the SEC was hiring new
attorneys and there were relatively few applicants. I was heavily recruited
by the SEC out of my clerkship for a federal judge in mid-1996,

receiving offers from Enforcement, Investment Management, and the Office of the General Counsel.

From the late 1990s until about 2002, the SEC did less hiring and it was harder to get a job there. I tried to get a job at the SEC's Division of Enforcement during 2002 but was told that they were only hiring attorneys with substantial litigation experience.[2] When the SEC's budget was vastly increased in 2003 after the Enron and other major corporate scandals broke, there was a great demand for new attorney hires and I was offered a job. However, by 2004, while there were many positions to be filled, there were also a large number of qualified applicants. During 2004, my group at the Division of Enforcement hired three new attorneys, each of whom had been at least a junior partner concentrating in civil litigation.

The numbers are instructive. There was a steady increase of applicants for jobs at the SEC between 2000 and 2004. Applications for entry-level attorney positions in 2003 rose 50 percent over applications in 2002. More than 800 graduating law students applied for about twenty positions starting in 2003, meaning that forty people were competing for each slot. This compares with ten people competing for each slot in 1999.[3] By the end of 2005, there were a large number of applicants seeking jobs at the SEC but the agency had largely frozen hiring in most of its divisions.[4]

Another trend has been the SEC's increased interest in hiring experienced attorneys. The SEC recruited fewer than twenty-five law school graduates in 2003, compared with more than fifty in 2000.[5] However, during the same time period and into 2005, the SEC increased its hiring of more experienced attorneys. In my group at the Division of Enforcement during 2004 and 2005, the last five attorneys hired from outside the commission had at least five years of experience practicing law in the litigation field.

WHAT CAN I DO TO INCREASE MY CHANCES OF GETTING A JOB WITH THE SEC?

THE BEST WAY to increase your chances of getting any job in is to find out what skills are particularly valued by the employer. The SEC Division of Enforcement values litigation skills and knowledge of the federal securities laws, and an attorney with strong litigation experience would almost always be more attractive to the hiring committee than one with a strong academic knowledge of the securities regulations. Most of the job is gathering information through depositions called *estimony*, and document production and review. The rest of the job involves drafting memoranda describing the facts and analyzing whether the conduct constituted a violation of securities law. However, where sections of the federal securities laws might have been violated in a new way, the Enforcement attorneys rely on the advice of specialists from the other divisions to help determine whether the law had been violated. As a result, it is litigation-type skills that would most be put to use.

In other divisions, litigation skills are of little value. The Office of the General Counsel has little to do with fact gathering; no one there would ever take a deposition or draft a document production request. Academic knowledge of the law is much more appropriate in a context where interpretation of law and regulation would be the most common role. Therefore, in applying to one division or the other, it is important to know your audience and accentuate the aspects of your experience that most fit that position. I had a former colleague who was a partner in the corporate practice at Hale & Dorr and who wanted to join the SEC as an Enforcement attorney. The firm was not doing well developing corporate work and it wanted him to leave. So, he was a little bit desperate to find a job that would help him support his three children. The problem was that although he had over ten years of experience serving as a lawyer on corporate deals, he had no litigation experience. In order to make him at least competitive, another former Hale & Dorr attorney working at the Enforcement Division and I advised this partner to redraft his résumé to emphasize the work he had done negotiating with adversaries and advising clients, as well as time spent teaching junior associates. We figured that these activities—in contrast to the contract drafting skills that he had emphasized in the first draft of his résumé—were closer to the skill set that would be used interrogating witnesses and negotiating settlements.

HOW IMPORTANT IS WHICH LAW SCHOOL I WENT TO IF I WANT TO WORK FOR THE SEC?

HAVING GONE TO a good law school will help you get a job at the SEC if you are a very recent graduate, but it will not have a significant impact if you are an experienced attorney. This is so for several reasons. First, consider that very few recent graduates of Harvard and Columbia seek jobs at the SEC or other government agencies, with the possible exception of the Honors Program at the Department of Justice. Law firms still pay much more for first-year attorneys than government can pay, and leading law schools work very hard to channel their graduates to Wall Street and other leading firms. The relationship between top firms and top law schools is a symbiotic one that goes back decades. As a result, if you are the rare Harvard Law School third-year who wants to work for the SEC (perhaps after a federal clerkship), you are likely to have an advantage over other candidates. Students from second- and especially third-tier schools will only get jobs at big firms if they were on the law review and had really top grades. Most will be more than happy to get a good job at the SEC, and therefore it is not surprising that most of the lawyers who join the SEC while they are in the early stages of their careers did not go to top schools. This helps to explain some important aspects of the SEC's culture. Specifically, the institution is dominated at all levels except perhaps the very highest level, by attorneys who went to schools other than first-tier schools. These lawyers came directly out of law school, probably did not clerk, and are less likely than others to move on to private firms. In contrast, many lawyers who did go to top schools join the SEC after being in a firm for three to seven years. They come in with the same seniority (but higher pay) as a first-year right out of law school.

The resulting hierarchy is interesting, to say the least. What you end up with are younger lawyers who went to lower-tier law schools but who have been with the commission from the start of their careers being promoted to the mid-level management positions of branch chief and assistant director, while the Harvard and Columbia graduates who worked at top law firms for five years or so after graduation are in subordinate positions. The graduates of top schools are generally smarter and more sophisticated. Admission to top schools requires exceptional intelligence, and top firms train their people exceedingly well, but government work is not particularly difficult and often it is more important to have learned the procedure than to be able to apply deep thought to the project at hand. I don't think it will hurt you to have gone to Yale, but it also won't hurt you to have gone to a third-tier school. In fact, the culture at the SEC frowns on talking about either the law school you went to or the law firm you worked at.

CAN GOING TO A TOP LAW SCHOOL EVER HURT YOUR EMPLOYMENT CHANCES?

YOU PROBABLY THINK that going to a top law school is always going to be to your advantage in seeking jobs. In particular, you likely have bought into the doctrine that if you go to a top law school you will always beat out a candidate from a mid-tier one, all else (experience, grades) being equal. Normally, you would be right, but there are some significant exceptions. Most law firms, for example, prize graduates of top law schools because having someone with top credentials on the roster will help bring in business, and having been accepted into and graduating from a top school is highly predictive of intelligence and drive. However, in certain government jobs it can be a disadvantage, particularly where the people doing the hiring did not go to top schools.

I went to a top law school, but many senior officers at the SEC did not. A good number of these lawyers went directly to the commission from law school and joined at a time (decades ago) when working for the SEC was both underpaid and not particularly competitive. Now, pay and prestige are high, and many Ivy-caliber lawyers clamor to work at the agency. As a result, it is common for senior SEC staffers who went to lower-ranked schools to be making hiring decisions involving a choice between graduates of their alma maters and those of top schools. Human nature being what it is, and given the total lack of a profit motive in hiring, it is common for the selection to go in favor of the person who went to the lesser school.

I have experienced the phenomenon of government lawyers selecting graduates of lower-ranked law schools over graduates of better schools. A number of years ago I applied for a position as chief of one of the branches in the SEC's Corporation Finance division. My credentials were very strong: honors graduate of Columbia Law, adjunct law professor, several articles published in leading journals concerning relevant M&A transactions, and experience with the top law firms. However, the two senior SEC attorneys making the selection had not gone to top-ranked schools. The person they chose had gone to St. John's—a law school ranked 77th in the *U.S. News & World Report*'s 2006 list of American law schools. He had worked at a second-tier law firm and was about the same age.

WHAT ARE THE DISADVANTAGES TO PRACTICING LAW IN A GOVERNMENT AGENCY?

THERE ARE SOME significant disadvantages to working for a government agency. One obvious issue is that government pay is a good deal lower than are private sector salaries. Setting that aside, however, there are additional concerns, such as that government agencies can be highly bureaucratic and are generally not as well managed as private firms, primarily because government does not need to generate a profit. Some types of people are more comfortable working in the generally less pressured government environment, whereas others find the lack of focus on quality and efficiency frustrating.

In describing some negative aspects of government service I will stick with what I know—the SEC. However, based on conversations I have had with attorneys working in other federal agencies, including at the Department of Justice, my observations about the SEC apply equally to other government agencies. In fact, working for other federal agencies likely has more disadvantages than working for the SEC does. In 2005, the SEC was ranked among the top five places to work in the federal government in a study conducted by the Partnership for Public Service and *U.S. News & World Report*. Nevertheless, attorneys who work at the SEC have a number of complaints: the agency is bureaucratic, it rejects efforts at innovation, work is performed inefficiently, promotions are highly political, the worst workers remain while the best return to private practice, and the incentive structure is misguided.

The SEC is a large bureaucracy headed by individuals appointed by the president and staffed by career civil servants. The objectives of the presidential appointees and the civil servants do not always coincide. Given their generally short tenure, appointees are not in place long enough to effect lasting institutional change. Those changes they do introduce are often reversed when the new administration takes office. Career civil servants, on the other hand, are concerned mainly with achieving their own promotions. Promotions come from adhering to the established rules of the bureaucracy. There is little or no focus on increasing the efficiency of the organization. In this environment, it is difficult to introduce innovation. Lawyers content to have a very stable career that pays reasonably well and allows for large amounts of free time will be happy in this environment. Those who are frustrated by having to go through complex steps to obtain approval to take action, or who are innovative by nature, or who seek to improve inefficient operating systems may find government work stifling.

SHOULD I WORK FOR CONGRESS, THE PRESIDENT, OR EITHER THE DEMO-CRATIC OR REPUBLICAN PARTY?

I HAVE KNOWN a number of young lawyers in government who have become frustrated when they suddenly find that one of their peers from law school has been appointed to become their boss's boss's boss. This has happened to people who did all the right things in their legal careers, who graduated from a top law school, clerked for a federal judge, and then went to work for a government agency. They put in all of this hard work only to find that political patronage got people who were arguably less qualified into a more senior government post much faster. You need to ask yourself what happened and how you can end up benefiting from the forces at work.

Within government service there is a dark line between "appointed" positions and "career" or "staff" positions that can seem difficult to cross.[6] At the SEC, for example, there are hundreds of staff attorneys for each politically appointed position. The staff jobs range from entry-level counsel posts to the directors who head the individual divisions of the agency. But the five commissioners are the ones appointed by the president to run the agency from above. While they are empowered to set the agenda for the agency, in reality their tenure will be far shorter than the time many of the staff are employed at the agency. As a result, there is a perpetual struggle between the political agenda of the few appointees and the longer-term interests of the many career staff.

Appointed positions are of limited duration, often lasting only two to four years. Most of these are presidential appointments. When that president leaves office, those jobs go, too. However, appointees to senior government posts have a soft landing in the private sector. When they leave public service, they will be in a position to head other major private sector organizations and take jobs with the title of president or chairman. In contrast, when even very senior staffers leave government employment they will likely become partners at law firms. These are two very different tracks: one of building specific expertise and the other of building relationships and leadership reputations. Neither is without its rewards, but it will benefit you to recognize the distinction early in the process of setting down your legal career plan.

Examples of what joining the right political team at the right time can do for your career are simply mind-blowing. Take, for example, the case of Laura Unger, whom I use as an example because her husband, Peter, and I clerked for the same federal judge, U.S. District Judge Norman C. Roettger—albeit years apart. Laura received her degree from New York Law School in 1987. It is important to keep in mind that New York Law School and New York University (NYU) Law School are two different institutions. In *U.S. News & World Report*'s 2004 "Top 100 Law Schools," NYU Law School is ranked fifth, but New York Law School doesn't even appear on the list. Instead, *U.S. News* simply calls New York Law School a "tier 3" school, while other ranking services, such as www.lawschool 100.com, list it at 97th overall. It is reasonable to assert, then, that New York Law School is far from being considered an academically prestigious school. Nevertheless, what Laura was able to accomplish with her degree (through, possibly, the use of her political connections) is nothing short of miraculous.

After graduating in 1987, Laura went to work for the SEC's Division of Enforcement as an entry-level staff attorney. During the brief time she was on the commission's staff she met her future husband, Peter Unger. Peter's family was deeply involved in Republican politics, and Laura soon secured a job as counsel to the U.S. Senate Committee on Banking, Housing and Urban Affairs, where she was an adviser to Chairman Alfonse D'Amato. On November 5, 1997, Laura was sworn in as the youngest commissioner of SEC, where not long before she had been a junior employee. On February 12, 2001, President George W. Bush designated Laura acting chairman of the SEC, in which capacity she served until August 3, 2001.

To understand what it means for Laura to have become one of the five commissioners of the SEC just a little over ten years after graduating from law school, you need to put her accomplishment in perspective. The SEC's Division of Enforcement, where Laura first worked, is filled with securities attorneys holding degrees from top law schools like Yale and Columbia. These bright people spend decades working in the SEC. After rising slowing through the ranks, they might eventually hold the position of branch chief or assistant director. A commissioner is a branch chief's boss's boss's boss's boss. The most brilliant staff attorneys will be very unlikely ever to get appointed commissioners no matter how many big cases they win or how well they do their jobs.[7] The most reliable way to get a political appointment is by joining the political machine in some way. This could mean getting a job on Capitol Hill working for the right senate or congressional committee, working for or contributing to the campaign of the president[8], or working under the chairman of the Republican or Democratic National Committee.

The question, strategically speaking, is what does the lesson of Laura Unger mean to you? Instances of Washington insiders gaining senior positions through political appointment are not unique to the SEC. Rather, this pattern is more the norm in Washington than the exception. I have a number of friends in other government agencies—including the DOJ—who bemoan the fact that they have put in nearly a decade of dedicated public service and still are only slightly above entry-level attorneys in terms of both title and pay grade. At the same time, they see classmates who went the political route— almost in all cases because they had family members involved in either politics or political fundraising—who are then handed jobs such as Under Secretary of Commerce or Assistant Counsel to the President. These career-changing appointments come about not because of what you know but because of who you know and how trustworthy you have proven yourself to be. Therefore, if you have any family political connections, it pays to exploit them as much as possible. If you do not have such connections, it may be better to abandon the route of getting a staff position with a federal agency in favor of getting in the door of a party's national headquarters, from where you may be able to build relationships and eventually land a job as an attorney with a powerful congressional committee. If you do so, be careful to research what the particular committee you are joining regulates to make sure that there is a good appointment in your future.

HOW CAN I POSITION MYSELF FOR AN EASY TRANSITION FROM GOVERNMENT BACK INTO THE PRIVATE SECTOR?

GOING INTO GOVERNMENT can be a great strategy, particularly for senior associates who have been told (or who otherwise suspect) that they will not be made partners. The truth is that law firm economics support promoting only very few associates to the rank of equity partner. And those associates who are made partner are not always the most effective attorneys. Government can be a great place for these good lawyers to get some truly unique experience and greatly expand their skill sets.

Now, let's get to the specifics. There are two kinds of government: local/state and federal. My experience extends only to working for the federal government, which I have done twice since becoming an attorney. So let me start by talking about what I know less about, which is state government. I know some good attorneys who have gone to work in state government and who have had some success. My cousin, for example, who is a graduate of Columbia Law School and also has an MBA, has been very involved in state politics in New Jersey. While he has remained something of a kingmaker himself, raising money for political parties and elections, several of his friends have left private practice to become state employees. Several have become judges, initially in the family or traffic courts. These positions are either political appointments or elected posts.

Taking this route is not for everyone. It takes a great deal of grassroots networking to do well in the local law/political environment. Nevertheless, with a little luck, the rewards can be substantial. While it is unlikely an attorney who goes into local or state government will be attractive to a major urban law firm again, barring climbing the ladder to a congressional seat, the local experience can make you valuable to local law practices, or set you up to open your own community-based firm. For example, if you decide on the local route and get to know the local zoning boards, you could be a valuable addition to a local real estate practice, and local practices can generate a good living. While hourly billing rates for local lawyers are generally lower than in major urban firms, the infrastructure and other fixed costs are also lower. My father's attorney, who practices general commercial law in New Jersey, easily clears half a million dollars a year in a good year.

Despite the practical benefits to going into local or state government, where it leads—a local practice—is usually not what most Ivy League-caliber attorneys desire. That is, few of us want to be that big fish in the small pond that is community-based law. Instead, we all want to pursue becoming big fish in the big pond that is a national or international legal practice, if we want to stay in law at all. For this, government can still be a good choice but it really needs to be the federal government and usually this means one of the federal agencies based in Washington.

Working for the federal government can be prestigious and career enhancing, or it can simply be a guaranteed decent paycheck until retirement. My work at the SEC illustrated for me what different people can take from the same job. Some enforcement attorneys stuck around for years doing the minimum level of work, arriving each day at 9:00 and leaving at 5:00. They never advanced; they had low-pressure jobs that they knew how to do efficiently. They weren't slackers, but they were not challenged by their jobs either, and they liked it that way. Other, generally younger attorneys came in with a mission to make a difference. They were there for a few years before returning to private practice and wanted to make every day count. Without years of practice they were not as efficient, but they were also more willing to try new things, applying innovative approaches to get better results.

If you want to leave the commission and go back to the private sector, there are a couple of ways to do it. From Enforcement, the main employers are large law firms looking to hire attorneys for their securities litigation practices. The problem is that these are the same types of jobs Enforcement attorneys had originally fled before coming to the commission. As an alternative, if you are willing to spend a couple of years in the Division of Investment Management, which regulates mutual funds, you might land a job with a hedge fund or large mutual fund family as an in-house counsel. These jobs may pay a little less than firm positions, but also come with less stress. In fact, more than a few attorneys in the Division of Enforcement have transferred to Investment Management before leaving for the private sector.

15. CHANGING JOBS

WHAT IS A LATERAL?

THE TERM "LATERAL" means any attorneys who leave one law firm and join another but who generally retain their class year rank for purposes of pay and partnership consideration. The term applies to both associates and partners who make such a move. There is something of a pejorative connotation to the term, even today when increasing numbers of attorneys will work for several firms throughout their careers. If you move from one firm to another, often the assumption is that you were not a good fit at the first firm. The possibility that you are a troublemaker or inept lurks just below the surface. In truth, however, there are many good reasons for changing law firms. As a law student, you have limited and imperfect information about your first firm before joining it. You may find that the culture there is not to your liking or that the firm does not have expertise in the area in which you want to specialize. As a more senior associate, you may find that the firm is not dedicated to developing the practice area you want to pursue, or that there are more senior lawyers in the firm already filling that niche. For these reasons, and others, there can often be sound reasons for changing firms.

SHOULD I CHANGE LAW FIRMS?

LET'S SAY YOU are a junior associate who has just been cold-called by a headhunter. The headhunter has read your profile on Martindale-Hubble legal directory and knows of a great opportunity with a firm across town. They are looking for an attorney with just your credentials. You are urged to at least talk with them. What do you do?

You need to understand two things before deciding whether you should consider changing law firms: the economics of running a law firm and the psychology of the partners at any law firm that may eventually offer you a new job. Only then can you consider your own interests (how much you like your current firm, how much more the new firm will pay you) and make a decision.

There is a definite "window of opportunity" during which you, as a law firm associate, will be considered a good prospect by other firms. During this period you will be highly sought after as a potential lateral associate.

This window of opportunity during which you are an attractive prospect is a product of certain economic and psychological considerations. Economically, associates are most valuable to law firms when they are between two and five years out of law school. This is because it takes a year or two for lawyers—who learned very little of practical value during law school—to gain sufficient experience to be of value to a firm's clients. Therefore, if a law firm can hire a well-trained second- or third-year associate away from another firm, the first law firm absorbs the full cost of training the young lawyer and the hiring firm reaps the financial benefits of that training.

After about five years, however, an associate's salary, which by industry tradition increases each year at a market-set pace, will increase to the point that he will be very expensive to hire. Law firms are reluctant to hire associates for less than they are making at their current firm. This is because firms believe associates will be unhappy in their new, lower-paid position. They are also concerned the associate may not work as hard if he is getting paid less. In addition, hiring firms assume that if attorney were going to make partner at his current firm, he would have a good idea about his status after five years. If a lawyer were going to make partner he would probably not leave. This means, after five years, if a firm succeeds in attracting a lateral, he is probably a reject from the potential partnership pool. Law firms, understandably, do not want to get another law firm's rejects. Therefore, considering that most firms have a seven- to ten-year partnership track, associates become increasingly less attractive as lateral hires.

The fact that the more senior an associate gets the less attractive he is to other law firms is not a good formula. The longer you stay at a firm, the more information you have regarding whether it is the kind of place you are likely to want—and be able—to work at for the long term. The fact that there will be fewer opportunities to make a lateral move later in their careers often comes as a surprise to senior associates who were used to receiving several calls a month from headhunters. The situation is also not good one for law firms that have senior associates who are not going to make partner. This creates a disposal problem for the firms, who may be placed in the uncomfortable position of firing associates rather than having them choose the happier alternative of finding other employment. For that reason, among others, some law firms have instituted the practice of promoting most senior associates, at least those who have served the firm reasonably well but who are not going to be made partner, to the position of counsel. As counsel, a lawyer with eight or so years of experience can move to another law firm, particularly one that is smaller or not as well-regarded, as a partner-track junior partner, or as a non-partner track counsel.

Understanding this dynamic will allow you to evaluate your options when the headhunters call. First, consider your immediate work situation. Are you happy? Are you working for partners who show an interest in developing you as a lawyer? Do you get lots of contact with clients, or are you stuck in your office doing research? Second, consider what the future holds for you at the firm. Does your firm give good feedback to senior associates who are partnership prospects? Does it have a policy of promoting senior associates to counsel positions that will enable them to negotiate better, more senior, jobs when making a lateral move? Remember that eight years out of law school you may be looking for yet another job. It is never too early to plan for that eventual exit, just in case.

Ideally, you will make a lateral move only once. If you move too often, future employees will think you have either an attention problem or a personality conflict. This means that when making a lateral move, you need to make absolutely sure that you are moving into a situation that is markedly better than the situation you are currently in and one from which you will not want to move for at least three years. You need to do your research. Look at why you are unhappy with your current firm. Can you ask to work in another practice area within the same firm? Can you start working with other partners? Remember, every law firm has part-ners who are jerks. Every law firm has practice areas that are not going to be interesting to you. Try to work from within before taking the more drastic step of changing firms. If you stick it out in any law firm for more than four years, it is a sign that you were able to get along with difficult colleagues and do hard work reasonably well. Don't give that up by making a lateral move prematurely.

On the other hand, there are times when a lateral move is the right one. Don't listen to the headhunters for advice on when this is; they are paid solely on the basis of their ability to increase the turnover of associ-ates at law firms. Use your own judgment. For example, it may be a good idea to make a move if, after law school graduation, you were only able to land a job at a second-tier firm. I had a friend from Columbia who spent two years working at Thacher, Proffitt & Wood and then made a lateral move to the more prestigious Simpson, Thacher & Bartlett. Despite the similar sounding names, this was a big jump up for his career. The move was made possible because of two things; first, the market demand for legal talent strengthened markedly between when he gradu-ated from law school and two years later, and, second, Simpson, Thacher was buying an associate already trained by Thacher, Proffitt, as we dis-cussed. Opportunities like this can make the lateral move worthwhile.

I have personally experienced the downside of lateral moves. I began my career at probably the top law firm in Washington: Wilmer, Cutler & Pickering. After two years I began to be called by headhunters on a regular basis. One call was from a headhunter promoting a position at a top law firm in New York. The offer was for a position in their Washington office. The firm paid the same salaries to associates in Washington and New York. Since New York associate salaries were—and remain—a good deal higher than those in Washington, this amounted to quite a windfall for the DC-based lawyers. In all, the pay package would have been about 60 percent more than I was currently making.

I liked my first law firm, but at that time a young former Supreme Court clerk joined the firm and began working with the small practice group in which I worked. He was favored by the senior partner and began taking away some of the best projects. Therefore, coupling my immediate job dissatisfaction with the fantastic pay raise, I decided to interview for the job. I did very little research on the new firm. When I interviewed with the partners, they were extremely welcoming. They told me that I would be working for their best clients. I would officially be in the "structured finance" practice, which was extremely important work. The deals I would be doing would be billion-dollar securities offerings, not the little million-dollar deals I was doing at my old firm. A few associates asked me why I was considering moving from my old firm, which had a relaxed lifestyle, to the New York firm, which was by all accounts a pressure cooker. I told them I was not afraid of a little hard work.

I ended up getting and accepting the offer. My colleagues at my old firm were sad to see me go and asked whether there was anything they could do to get me to stay on. The securities law practice—an area in which I had done a little work well and the strongest practice area for the firm—seemed particularly to want me to stay. But I was committed. Immediately upon joining the new firm, however, I learned that things were not as they had been presented. I had been led to believe that I would have an opportunity to do corporate M&A deals, which I knew and liked, as well as structured finance work, in which I did not have a background. This was not the case. Associates informed me that I had been hired to work on the complex and tedious structured finance offerings that most associates avoided like the plague. While the deals were big, they were cookie-cutter. Each one was like the last and mainly involved editing massive offering memoranda numbering in the hundreds of pages. Travel to New York was frequent but unpleasant, regularly involving staying up all night to ensure that the changes ordered by the investment bankers were reflected in the various deal documents. It was mind numbing, and some of the partners involved were insufferable.

I hope that you will take my experience to heart when considering your own lateral move offers.. Do yourself the favor of learning the economics of why the hiring firm is making you an offer. Is there any intention to put you on the partnership track, or are you being hired, as I was, solely as a tool to be used up as quickly as possible before burning out, to do work no one else would do?

IS IT POSSIBLE TO BYPASS THE HEADHUNTERS?

IT IS DIFFICULT to make lateral moves by approaching prospective law firms directly. Even if you are well qualified, as often as not a résumé sent unsolicited to a law firm will go unread. Instead, law firms much prefer to pay headhunters large sums of money in exchange for acting as intermediaries. Close examination shows the practical reasons they prefer to operate this way.

Headhunters can do things that the recruiting persons working in law firms cannot. For one thing, headhunters can call associates at other firms directly and entice them to apply for lateral jobs. One law firm can not easily call the associates at another law firm. The response from the associate's current firm would be angry and immediate. Partners at the firm would call those at the acquiring firm (it would be kind of like a hostile acquisition, with good associates being the crown jewel assets). This could be quite uncomfortable, particularly if the two firms were already engaged in transactions and lawsuits, either as opponents or as cocounsel. Also, headhunters help to screen associates. Many headhunters are former attorneys and usually know what their client firm is looking for. They can save the firm's own recruiters a good deal of time winnowing out the prospects not worth pursuing.

Getting in touch with headhunters is usually not difficult. When you are a junior to mid-level associate, they will likely call you with regularity. Some headhunters will also post job openings online, including on

Monster.com. You can contact them anonymously to find out what positions they are hawking. While I am not a great fan of headhunters, some have earned my grudging respect. Find out who are the best headhunters in your town. Return their calls and maintain a cordial relationship. Avoid the ones who will give you bad advice and who will try to get you to take dead-end jobs. One way to tell bad headhunters is to ask your fellow associates if they got a call from the same headhunter. A headhunter who is calling every associate in the firm rather than reviewing the profiles and picking associates that are a natural fit for the opportunity are probably to be avoided.

WHAT DO SENIOR ATTORNEYS LOOK FOR WHEN CHOOSING A NEW LAW FIRM?

LAWYERS WHO HAVE spent a number of years practicing law are better prepared to make a good choice of which law firm to join in the future. Take, for example, the case of a senior lawyer who has practiced law, gone into government, and is not considering moving back to private practice. Chances are the lawyer was not completely happy with his former firm; lawyers commonly use government as a way to escape an unpleasant working environment as well as a way to gain specific legal skills. Now the lawyer knows why he was unhappy with his old firm— too much pressure to attract new clients or perhaps too much infighting over division of firm profits—and knows what to look for and what to avoid in a new firm's practice profile and culture.

Experienced lawyers will be more sophisticated about choosing a law firm. They will not be as blinded by a large pay package and will instead look at considerations such as the quality of clients and the reputations of other partners. High-quality clients will be more likely to pay bills on time, and partners with good reputations will be more likely to bring in work whether or not the overall economy is strong. Experienced lawyers will also take the time to talk with individual attorneys at a firm that has given them an offer. They will try to find out how partnership profits are distributed and whether the attorneys at the firm get along with each other.

WHAT SHOULD I ASK FOR WHEN NEGOTIATING A LATERAL MOVE?

MAKING A LATERAL move gives you the opportunity to negotiate a number of different aspects of your compensation package and career track. The degree to which you have negotiating room depends on your experience and relative bargaining position. If you are a recognized expert in a hot area of the law and were recruited by the firm, you are going to have relatively more negotiating power than if you simply applied for a lateral position advertised on the firm's Web site. Several points can be negotiated. One is salary. Many law firms peg salary to the year in which you graduated from law school. Some law firms attempt to drop lateral hires back a year, so that if you graduated from law school in 2003 they may pay you as though you graduated in 2004. You might take issue with this, and it is certainly fair for you to request that you be paid with your class.

Another point of negotiation is what year you will be assigned for partnership-track purposes. Because of the up-or-out system, you generally have only about eight years after graduation from law school to make partner. Otherwise, you may be forced to find other employment. If you came to the firm laterally, you can make the argument that you would like the partners to have more years to get to know you. Thus, for partnership purposes, you might want to be considered in the class of 2004 rather than the class of 2003.

There is other money on the table as well. Some firms offer a signing bonus to lateral hires. This is probably only the case when a particular attorney is very highly qualified in a specific area of law, such as a Supreme Court law clerk or a patent attorney with a PhD in physics. It would be unusual for most law firms to offer such bonuses because if it became industry practice, it would increase lateral moves and cost law firms more money.

Headhunters get a healthy percentage of a lateral attorney's first year's pay. This can be as much as six months' pay and is often contingent on the lateral attorney remaining with the firm for at least one year. Laterals are therefore sometimes asked by their headhunter to sign such an agreement. In exchange, it may be possible to extract an additional payment from your headhunter. You may need to negotiate this, or the headhunter may unilaterally make an offer to pay you if you seem to be wavering on whether to accept the firm's offer.

HOW ARE LATERALS VIEWED AT THE LAW FIRMS THEY JOIN?

LATERAL ASSOCIATES FACE a certain degree of distrust when they join a new firm. This stems from the perception that they left their old firm either because they have a defective personality or were unable to perform in the rigorous law firm environment. There is also the stigma that they are outsiders and have not made the same contribution to the firm as other associates with their seniority. Loyalty to one's firm is still respected. Being a lateral associate means you were not loyal to your former firm.

This initial stigma can be overcome with either time or a very good explanation of why one made the lateral move. In addition, associates who transfer from the very best firms—such as Davis, Polk & Wardwell or Cravath, Swain & Moore—can carry with them some of the positive aura of those firms. This is particularly true if the hiring firm is not as well regarded. In fact, one reason second-tier firms lure associates away from a leading firm is to benefit from the rigorous and excellent training programs employed by top firms. On this basis, top associates may be brought in and groomed for potential partnership. Another advantage laterals may have over longtime associates is that they will not have shown their warts. Associates who join firms out of law school inevitably make mistakes during their training period. Mistakes are often long remembered by the partnership. Therefore, if an associate can get all of his mistakes out of the way at firm X and then transfer to firm Y, he can potentially build a new, unblemished reputation for excellence at the new firm.

However, the negative characteristics associated with being a lateral associate are difficult to overcome. Some law firms do not even seriously consider lateral associates for partnership, particularly when the lateral associates were hired to fill narrow practice areas such as compliance with blue sky laws (which are designed to protect investors against fraudulent sales practices) and even for some structured finance practice groups. In the past, several leading firms did not take lateral associates at all, preferring to train and promote from their more junior associate ranks on an exclusive basis. You should enter into any lateral move with your eyes wide open regarding what future roles at the firm will be open to you.

Lateral partnership is a different animal altogether. The principal reason firms bring in lateral partners is to bolster a particular practice area, or more generally to increase firm revenues. As such, lateral partners must have a "book of business" in order to be attractive to a firm. Compensation is then usually based on how much money the partner will likely deliver in annual billings. For most of you, it will be many years before you are in a position to negotiate a lateral move as a partner. By that time, you should have a good feeling for the economic value of your practice. When the time comes to make a move, you will need to negotiate with more than one firm to determine the best fit and the greatest value you can extract. You may be negotiating to bring over not only yourself, but also a group of other attorneys—associates and perhaps other partners—whom you deem critical to your practice.

In fact, in the nearer term, you are more likely to be considering a lateral move that is tied to a move by a partner for whom you work. If you do much of your work for a particular partner and that partner is switching firms, then you would be well advised to consider moving with him if you are asked. The circumstances and attractions of such a move will very considerably based on the particular circumstances. Discussions with that partner and with other partners in your firm should reveal whether your better course is to move with your team or remain at the firm in an attempt to take over the mantle (and practice) of the exiting partner.

WHAT ABOUT "GOING IN-HOUSE"?

"GOING IN-HOUSE" means that you stop working for a law firm and go to work as a lawyer for a single company, becoming their in-house counsel. . What this means can vary a great deal. Some companies have a single in-house lawyer while others have hundreds. Some industries (like insurance) hire only attorneys with litigation experience, while other industries hire lawyers with primarily corporate expertise. Public firms require a different set of skills than privately held businesses.

In general, the lifestyle of attorneys practicing law in-house is much better than for those working for a law firm. You no longer have to juggle multiple clients because you have only one. You no longer have to count your hours because you are no longer billing for your services. Your pay package will be different and could include stock or options to purchase stock in the company for which you work. If you are hired as a senior in-house attorney, you may find that much of your time is spent supervising and reviewing the work done by outside attorneys (perhaps from your old law firm) who are hired to do it. You may find that a major function of your role is to make sure that your old firm does not bill your new employer too much.

It is rare to go in-house early in your career. Usually, the best in-house opportunities are presented to attorneys who have four or five years of experience working for a major firm. In fact, there may come a time in your career when you are particularly open to the idea of joining a company as an in-house attorney. Imagine you are an eighth-year associate at a well-respected firm. You have developed some expertise. But you have been advised by the partnership that they are not going to make you a partner. Your options are limited. You are past the prime years when you would have been attractive to other law firms as a lateral associate. Your best option, aside from working for a government agency, may be to go in-house.

The easiest transition is from your firm to a client of your firm for which you have provided services in the past. They are comfortable with your work and you are knowledgeable about their business and legal services needs. It is also an ideal way for a law firm to leverage the remaining value in its senior associates. The law firm will support you in such a move if they believe (as they certainly will) that you will be likely to funnel more work their way once you are in-house. They will be very nice to you and will give you good references to try to get you into the spot.

Many lawyers get in-house jobs through channels other than former client relations. When you become a fifth-year associate, the calls from headhunters trying to entice you to leave for another firm slow to a stop. But in the next year, the calls about interesting positions as an in-house attorney increase. A good headhunter can come to you with valuable information about potential company jobs that you might not otherwise learn about. Some of these jobs are posted on the company's Web site. However, sometimes a headhunter is tapped to be the exclusive finder for an attorney to fill the spot. It's impossible to list the reputable headhunters because there are so many and the list changes so rapidly. The best rule is not to send your résumé to a headhunter without a thorough reference check and comparison of notes with your peers.

Both associates and partners take jobs with private companies. Partners at leading firms are occasionally tapped to become the general counsel of large public companies and investment banks. Sometimes they are also given executive titles, like vice chairman, when the business is in a particularly regulated industry or is subject to major litigation and the partner has established a strong reputation in that area. One example is the investment banking industry, which in recent years was subject to significant regulatory scrutiny.[1]

Associates generally obtain more junior positions, like assistant general counsel or even just counsel. The job description depends on the size of the company and the business it is in. At an investment bank, for example, associates with securities experience are commonly hired as compliance officers. It is a very narrow function and one unlikely to result in much expanded authority. In contrast, joining a small but quickly growing startup firm can result in tremendous responsibility and a job with a very broad scope. Joining a company pre-IPO can mean taking on a great deal of risk but also a great deal of upside potential in the form of stock options and seniority. When new attorneys are hired, there is a good chance that they will report to you. Associates who joined the right young company can find themselves with a much more interesting and lucrative career than that of the associates and partners who remained at the law firm.

You may want to figure out how to position yourself for a top-quality in-house position. Some of the best positions will be filled by attorneys who were in the right place at the right time.

Firms value certain types of legal experience over others. Large public companies need to hire attorneys who have experience in preparing the types of legal documents that are filed with the SEC as part of their required disclosure process under the Securities Acts. To get this experience, you will need to work at a law firm whose clients are public companies. You are likely to get the best experience working for a large corporate practice in New York. You are not likely to work with many large public clients in Washington, even at the top corporate law firms there. Few large public companies rely on Washington firms as their primary corporate counsel, and those that do generally turn to the more experienced New York forms for major public transactions.

If you want to position yourself to join a promising startup company, you need to devise a strategy early on. First, you need to be in a geographical position to have contact with such firms. If you are interested in technology, you may want to join a law firm in Palo Alto or San Francisco to be in or near Silicon Valley. This remains a hot spot for software and other tech start-ups. If you are interested in biotechnology, you might want a position with a firm in San Diego—a difficult prospect—or in Boston, though the area is in some decline as a technology hub. In addition, if you have a good idea of what sector you want to be in, you want to select your practice area carefully. Biotech firms are obviously going to demand a large number of lawyers knowledgeable about intellectual property—particularly patent—law, with a background in the biological and chemical sciences. If you want to join an investment bank as an attorney, you want to get experience in a leading securities law practice, and even more specifically in one involving the Investment Company Act. These practices will help you develop the specific knowledge base that will make you a viable candidate for the specific jobs these companies need done.

One frustrating thing you may find is that certain companies want to hire attorneys who already have in-house experience. This may seem strange to you, since most good lawyers start out by practicing in top law firms. I experienced it a few years ago when a headhunter called me and described a couple of positions, one with a software firm in San Francisco and one with a biotechnology firm in San Diego. I applied for both jobs; they seemed interesting and I thought I might want to leave Washington to live in California. The headhunter warned me in advance that the software firm ideally wanted someone who had been an in-house lawyer with a company that had more than a dozen in-house attorneys. She said their reasoning was that such a person would know how to operate in an environment such as theirs. She also said that the biotechnology firm, though hiring for a general corporate position, preferred someone with some knowledge of the biotechnology industry. I did not have much of that. I was not asked to interview for either position, even though my paper credentials are about as good as you can get. That illustrates the value of developing an area of expertise and a professional background that will specifically meet the criteria of the in-house position. Of course, that requires knowing in advance what kind of job you will want five to eight years after starting your legal practice, which can be quite near impossible.

SHOULD I DO SOMETHING CRAZY LIKE ACCEPT THAT OFFER TO BECOME THE ATTORNEY GENERAL OF YAP?

WHILE MOST GRADUATES of top law schools work at large law firms immediately after their graduation or clerkship, it remains truly amazing the variety of jobs young people can get with a law degree. Some of these jobs are quite unusual. I was not aware of these opportunities until several years after graduation, and I don't think I would have been in a position to take one of them even if I had know about them. When I was an associate in Washington, one of the other young associates, who I recall had spent some time in the Peace Corps, left to live for a year in the South Pacific as the assistant attorney general of one of the small island nations there. He told me that he actually read about the position in an advertisement in the back of *The American Lawyer* and had applied on a lark. I don't think the position paid very well, but it offered the benefits of year-round sun and scuba diving, as well as doing something really different for a year of your career (who knows when you will have the chance again).

Apparently, other lawyers have forgone the existence of a law firm associate to take positions like this. If you go on the Internet, you will find references to positions such as the one for Assistant Attorney General of Yap[2]. Normally, I would think this kind of thing was a fantasy, but I know someone who took such a job. In any event, if you are interested enough to find positions like this, you can probably succeed. I understand they are contractual positions that last for maybe one or two years.

You would not want to stay longer in any case. After two years or less, you can return to the states and probably pick up where you left off as a law firm associate. In fact, the stories you will have will probably make interviewing a cinch. But if you remain in such an nonconforming job too, long it could be difficult to convince stateside employers that you are serious about practicing as an attorney.

16. ESCAPING FROM YOUR LEGAL CAREER

WHAT TYPE OF JOB CAN A LAWYER HAVE OTHER THAN PRACTICING LAW?

ONE OF THE things young students about to embark on a legal education hear is, "Oh, it's so useful, you can do anything with a law degree!" The legal field is remarkably varied, but law school is only the most efficient way of becoming a lawyer, not a banker, a real estate investor, a Hollywood agent, or the president of the United States. Sure, you can become any of those things with a law degree, but it is probably not the law degree that will get you there.

Lawyers can have any job they want. They fill many roles: lots of U.S. senators, a decent percentage of investment bankers, and the CEOs of a few of the largest public companies have law degrees, But that is because a lot of smart people went to law school, not because a legal education particularly prepared them to fill these roles. Let's face it—going to law school barely prepares you to practice law. When you graduate, you know some academic stuff about the Constitution and civil procedure but nothing about drafting an offering memorandum or selecting a jury.

You learn that practical stuff on the job. Law school performs more of a screening function than serving as a practical training ground. So it is just too much of a stretch to say that law school gives you the skills to be any of those other things. If you have intelligence, ambition, and luck, you will find yourself advancing in your chosen field.

A lot of lawyers say they want to stop practicing law and do something else. There are plenty of opportunities to do so, but you have to be practical about it. Lawyers have useful skills for practicing law: they can reason well, give great attention to detail, and are willing to work very long hours. These are transferable skills. But they do not have some things that are required for success in particular fields. They do not have the financial modeling and mathematics background needed to be a successful banker. They do not know the entertainment industry unless they have practiced in that area. They do not have the experience managing a diverse workforce they would if they had been corporate managers.

Thus, while there is no limit to what you can do after you get your law degree, you need to find your own opportunities. I personally had to work very hard to reinvent myself as an investment banker. I went to Georgetown University and took a calculus class. I went to Wharton and earned an MBA in finance. Then I accepted a junior associate position at an investment bank so that I could build my valuation skills from scratch. All of these steps entailed significant sacrifices, but the result is that I got "over the wall." The wall is hard to get over because everyone on the other side views you as a lawyer and wants to keep you in that category. They think you do not know the numbers, or that you are too risk averse to come to the other side. However, you can make the transition to a principal role and, if it is what you really want and are willing to make the sacrifices, you will find a way over.

CAN I LEAVE THE LAW FOR A CAREER IN INVESTMENT BANKING?

MANY CORPORATE ATTORNEYS dream of leaving their law practice and joining an investment bank. I have had many conversations with my corporate law colleagues about the desirability of shifting to an investment-banking career.[1] I made this move the hard way, by going back to business school and starting out at the bottom as an associate in an investment bank. If you are a senior lawyer, you will probably not want to do this and instead will want to look into more senior banking positions.

The high level of interest in changing roles from lawyer to banker is not surprising. Corporate lawyers doing deals alongside investment bankers see how much more money young I-bankers are making.[2] They recognize that they, the attorneys, are essentially providing the service of documenting the deals that the bankers and their corporate clients think up and negotiate. This is not the situation most corporate attorneys expected to be in when they started down the path of a corporate law career. In fact, most corporate attorneys envisioned themselves as the ones negotiating the economic terms of deals. But this is rarely the case, and it is never the case where more junior attorneys are concerned. More likely, the attorney will find himself serving as a very expensive scribe who occasionally has the opportunity to point out potential legal pitfalls and recommend technical terminology for long and complex agreements that are often afterthoughts for the deal makers.

It is understandable that a good number of attorneys want to move over to the banking side. Why then, one might ask, didn't they go to business school in the first place and go directly into investment banking? There are probably many answers to this question, chief among them being that when applying for law school, they did not think ahead to whether they wanted to be on the giving or the receiving end of the attorney-client relationship. More important, however, is the fact that the senior investment bankers doing the hiring are going to ask this very question. They will ask why you, a lawyer, want to change careers. They will also be incredulous that the person who has been offering them variations on a liquidated damages clause has the perspective to advise a client why to make a strategic business acquisition. Regardless of the circumstances, changing roles from counselor to deal maker is difficult.

Certain factors will influence exactly how hard it is to make the switch from lawyer to banker. First, it matters for what law firm you work. If you want to make the switch from law to a bulge-bracket investment bank, you had better be practicing law at one of the very top New York corporate firms. There are enough lawyers seeking to become bankers that the banks do not need to look beyond the cream of the crop, and they will hire from the firms they know and have confidence in. Second, you had better be a corporate attorney working on deals; the skills of a litigator (trial lawyer) will be even less valued than those of a draftsman. Third, your age matters a great deal. Investment banks want to bring law firm associates in at the associate level. Investment banking associates are at the level of employees who are most often hired directly out of business school. Their ages range from roughly twenty-three to twenty-seven. If you are older than that, an investment bank viewing you as too old. It will be a tough sell to get them to take a chance with you. Investment banks simply do not want experienced attorneys when they are hiring for banking positions. In fact, too much experience can be a negative thing. Banking partners want smart young people whom they can teach the business. They can hire experienced lawyers as needed.

It is possible to get non-law firm jobs directly out of law school, but it takes an extra level of effort.

The best thing you can do is to identify your interest in areas other than the law early on. I have several friends who went into banking, and one who joined McKinsey & Co. as a consultant, directly out of law school. It is possible to get non-law firm jobs directly out of law school, but it takes an extra level of effort, and cooperation from the economy. If the economy is weak, investment banks will have plenty of young geniuses to choose from among the graduates of the Harvard and Wharton business schools. Even in the best of times, it will be hard to land that banking associate position. My friends who were trained as lawyers who joined investment banks both graduated from Harvard Law School and used personal connections to land their banking offers. My roommate from Columbia joined McKinsey after graduation, and I believe he was the only graduate of his class to join a leading strategy consulting firm.

That sounds pretty discouraging for those of you who think you might be interested in I-banking. So let's focus for a moment on the rare but encouraging success stories. Take, for example, the case of Peter A. Thiel. Peter received his BA in philosophy from Stanford, graduating Phi Beta Kappa. He then went on to graduate from Stanford Law School in 1992 at the age of twenty-five. He served as a speechwriter for former

Secretary of Education William J. Bennett and was a law clerk for Judge J. L. Edmondson of the 11th U. S. Circuit Court of Appeals. He then began practice with Sullivan & Cromwell, one of New York's most prominent corporate law firms. After just a couple of years of practice as a corporate-securities lawyer, Thiel was able to get a job in investment banking as a derivatives trader with Credit Suisse Financial Products, for which he worked first in New York and then in London. He left investment banking in 1996 and set up a small fund in Silicon Valley called Theil Capital International, starting with just $1 million in investment capital, primarily from his friends and family. That fund invested in a company that evolved into PayPal, Inc., which made Theil its CEO in 1998. Theil took PayPal public in February 2002 and then, just five months later, sold the company to eBay for approximately $1.5 billion. Theil's 4 percent stake in PayPal netted him personally around $60 million. By early 2004, he was running Clarium Capital Management, a hedge fund based in San Francisco that had more than $250 million under management. This illustrates what a young lawyer can accomplish who is willing to take big risks and follow a nontraditional path.

CAN I BECOME A BUSINESS CONSULTANT?

A COUPLE OF months after I began practicing as a lawyer in Washington, I saw an advertisement in the Washington Bar Association's monthly publication that the business consulting firm Boston Consulting Group (BCG) was interviewing lawyers for possible employment as entry-level business consultants in its Bethesda office. The firm was holding interviews on an upcoming Saturday afternoon, and attorneys were encouraged to bring their résumés and go through a round of interviews. BCG would hire three to five attorneys as associates.

BCG is one of the better-respected business consulting firms, not quite at the level of McKinsey & Co. or Monitor, but a cut above other strategy consulting firms such Booz Allen Hamilton and Deloitte Consulting. I was not sure what they did in Washington. There was some telecommunications business and defense contracting in the area, but Washington was not a center of commerce. Nevertheless, being a corporate associate and therefore almost necessarily disillusioned by the nature of my corporate legal work, I decided to update my résumé and appear at the local BCG office on the afternoon. I was not alone. Dozens of other young attorneys were there, too.

SHOULD I GET AN MBA?

I HAVE KNOWN quite a few lawyers who have decided to get an MBA after having practiced law for a few years. They enrolled in some fairly high-profile business programs. Specifically, of my law school friends, one went back to Stanford Business School after practicing law with Simpson, Thacher & Bartlett in New York as a corporate attorney. He played it very smart, transferring over to the strategy consulting firm Booz Allen Hamilton before applying to schools and getting that firm to pick up the tuition tab. Another law school friend went to the Anderson Graduate School of Management at UCLA after practicing corporate law at Brown & Wood in New York for three years. A third went to Stanford Business School after practicing for less than two years as a lawyer in the tax department of the leading accounting firm Deloitte & Touche. Of my law firm associates, one got an MBA from Harvard after practicing for about four years and the other went to Stanford after practicing for about five years.[3]

The reasons that lawyers went to business school in the past might not be the same ones in the future. The number of attorneys going to business schools seems to have peaked between 1999 and 2000. At that time, the tech bubble was at its height, and young attorneys were jealously eyeing the bonus packages and stock gains of investment bankers and Internet entrepreneurs. There was also a general feeling that the world was changing and that lawyers were not, with the exception of some deal lawyers and patent counsel participating in the revolution. However, since the bubble burst and with several years of flat Wall Street earnings and few IPOs, the steady pay of a large firm attorney has seemed pretty attractive. Investment banking compensation has risen in the last year or so, but conditions have not replicated the kind of career dissatisfaction many young attorneys felt at the height of the bubble.

Today, the reasons that some attorneys go to business school seem more complex than simply envying the great riches being amassed by

Internet entrepreneurs. Many young people go into law thinking that they are going to lead major deals. The reality is that, even as senior lawyers, they will be merely documenting deals and generally following the lead of the business principals and the investment bankers who advise them. Therefore, going to business school today may be a means of rising in the deal hierarchy. Lawyers also may be motivated by the fact that, unlike in law, as investment bankers and business people gain seniority, their hours spent in the office actually decrease.

Despite the end of the Internet bubble, some of the motivation for lawyers wanting to go to business school seems intact and likely to continue. For one thing, working as a corporate lawyer continues to mean that your personal potential for advancement is limited to providing legal advisory services. Individuals who have an unquenchable desire to be the ultimate decision maker will be disappointed in this role. The client will always remain the ultimate boss, with the investment bankers serving as a kind of intermediate supervisor. Drawing simply from my own experience as a lawyer, it seems some people are inherently unsuited to a law firm existence. The law firm environment—in which young attorneys are expected to sit in their offices and execute the research and drafting assignments given to them by partners, who in turn get their marching orders from clients—is repugnant to them. These individuals will naturally look for more hands-on work opportunities where they can have greater interaction with people and make more fundamental business decisions. Going to business school seems, to some, a low-risk gateway to embarking on a more business-oriented career.

It is not clear, however, that going to business school is the most direct path to exchanging a legal for a business career. Rather, there is evidence that some young lawyers choose to pursue an MBA because it is relatively easy. That is, lawyers are accustomed to using education to achieve their goals. Law school brought them a legal career, after all. Going to business school is an established path to a fairly certain outcome: employment by an investment bank or strategy consulting firm. But going back to school also has its costs. For one thing,

A lawyer leaving an $180,000-a-year law firm job for business school may find that, upon graduation two years later, he is offered an entry-level associate position with an investment bank offering a $95,000 base salary plus a projected $30,000 performance bonus.

enrolling in a full-time business school program generally entails a two-year time commitment and perhaps $100,000 or more in tuition and support bills. Moreover, gaining a suitable business position for a lawyer out of an MBA program is not certain. For example, a lawyer leaving an $180,000-a-year law firm job for business school may find that, upon graduation two years later, he is offered an entry-level associate position with an investment bank offering a $95,000 base salary plus a projected $30,000 performance bonus. At the same time, he could go back to the law and make a guaranteed $200,000 salary. I have known lawyers who have completed business school only to rejoin a law firm when faced with this choice.

In fact, it may be better to pursue specific career objectives without going back to school at all. Ask yourself what you could accomplish in two years with the $100,000 you would have spent on business school tuition. The answer may guide you to your dream career. For example, imagine that your goal is to become a movie producer in Hollywood. This is a pretty attractive and yet seemingly unattainable objective for many people. You could plan to go to business school—perhaps the Anderson School at UCLA—and study entertainment industry finance with the purpose of obtaining a job in the industry after graduation. You would find, however, that obtaining a mid-level job in entertainment is fiercely competitive and that employers generally want candidates who have some background in the field, which many of your classmates will have if they started out in low-level positions after college before getting their business degree. Instead, what if you went out to Hollywood and got yourself a job in the mailroom at one of the big talent agencies, or as a low-paid assistant to an established producer? These are the ways many successful producers and agents have entered the entertainment field. Of course, you are taking a big risk and a big pay cut for at least a year or two. But at the end of two years, while you will not have an additional degree for your résumé, you will have industry-specific experience and, if you network as you should, a decent file of contacts. You will be farther down the path to the specific goal you set for yourself than had you gone the low-risk route of getting an MBA.

WHAT ABOUT AN EXECUTIVE MBA?

IT IS VERY easy to bring yourself to believe that getting an MBA is the cure for all that ails your legal career. The scenario has been played out many times: you have spent several years as a corporate attorney only to find that you are working at an investment bank documenting deals and taking orders from some twenty-eight-year-old business school graduate who is making twice your salary. Many corporate attorneys, both associates and partners, consider at some point in their careers that they wish they had gone to business school instead of law school. In this environment it can be very tempting to make the jump and go back to get that MBA, particularly if you are still relatively young and have a long career ahead of you.

However, going to business school involves a considerable investment. The opportunity cost—two years of lost salary—plus the tuition can be quite high. An executive MBA program (known as EMBA or Weekend Executive MBA program) may be an attractive choice. These programs are, by and large, a recent phenomenon. Although some programs, like The Wharton School's at the University of Pennsylvania, have been around for over thirty years, most other executive MBA programs have been introduced since 2000. Most universities started up their EMBA programs in the last five years or so because these programs have only recently demonstrated their significant revenue-generating potential. Business schools across the country have begun to offer the EMBA as a result of growing demand for MBA degrees among young professionals (a considerably broader market than just disaffected attorneys) who view the degree as a way to increase their salaries and career advancement potential. In some ways, the MBA is increasingly viewed as the new bachelor's degree. Since lawyers make a lot of money and often have families to support by the time they consider going for a master's degree, the EMBA seems ideally suited to lawyers who are dissatisfied with their careers.

As an initial matter, you need to be clear on what, exactly, the EMBA degree actually is and what it is not. Executive MBA degrees are master's degrees in business administration that can be earned, often from leading business schools, at night or, more commonly, over long weekends, and usually over a period of about two years. This is the same amount of time that it would take to earn an MBA in a full-time program, but it allows you the option of working full time while you are earning your degree. As part of the marketing for their EMBA programs, business schools usually stress that the degree confers the same academic achievement as a full-time MBA program. However, whether this is actually true depends a great deal on the institution where you are getting the degree. Remember that the MBA is different from a JD. There is no professional standard by which the MBA degree is measured comparable to the American Bar Association's accreditation of selected law schools and the state bar associations' regulation of legal education through bar examinations and by establishing standards for legal education.

You also need to be realistic about what an executive MBA can actually accomplish for your career. Business, law, and medical schools all grant professional degrees, but business school is fundamentally different from the other two. Law and medical schools lead to degrees that qualify a person to join a licensed profession. After law or medical school you become a lawyer or doctor. Business schools, on the other hand, do not lead one to become anything directly. For that, you need to get a job in finance, marketing, business strategy, or any of the other arenas that business school can prepare you for. The fact that business schools do not direct you into one particular field but rather position you to seek employment in a broad range of careers means that your MBA is only as good as the university that awarded it. One of the things you are paying for by going to a good business school is the opportunity to interview with firms seeking bright young businesspeople. Such firms rely on business schools to do the initial screening for them. If you graduated from a top MBA program, employers are going to assume that you can do their work. For this reason, an MBA from Harvard is an entirely different degree from the one you would receive from a bottom-ranked school.

Executive MBA degrees are no exception. Unlike full-time MBA programs, however, the reputation of the EMBA program can differ from the reputation of the school more generally. The most important consideration is the reputation of the school. An EMBA program from one of the top ten business schools is going to benefit from the reputation of the school regardless of the actual quality of the EMBA program. However, the reputation of the EMBA program can also be critical. The reputation of the program among employers (the most important constituency) will depend largely on how competitive the admissions requirements for the program are and how effective the program is at actually teaching you something practical that you can parlay into a job. EMBA programs that are as competitive as full-time programs will be better received by employers. Graduates of programs that demand the same rigorous academic study as full-time programs will be given greater consideration by prospective employers.

Not all EMBA programs are created equal. In fact, the disparity in the quality of different EMBA programs—even at various top ten business schools—can be startling. The current number of EMBA programs is increasing exponentially, and lawyers interested in pursuing a degree can certainly find a good match to their schedules and academic abilities.

It is difficult to determine whether even the most well regarded and rigorous executive MBA program is worth the time, effort, and expense. Thus, while an EMBA may be a practical choice for working lawyers, it is far from ideal. When I went to Wharton, I was working for the Securities and Exchange Commission. That job allowed me to take off every other Friday as part of my "flex" schedule in return for coming in early on the other days. However, private law firms may not be as enthusiastic about their lawyers taking off a day every other week. Private firms expect every waking hour to be spent billing time to clients. They may view your desire to go to business school as an expression of your wanting to leave the practice of law. Your best bet may be to convince your supervising partners that enrolling in the program will put you in touch with potential clients likely to be in need of legal counsel. In this you would be telling the truth. There are many cases in which, had I been in private practice, I would have had an opportunity to bring my classmates in as paying clients.

Another alternative is to earn a certificate at a business school. Harvard offers such a program but does not offer an executive MBA. However, these programs do not confer a degree. They last a few weeks and admission is not competitive. There are some networking opportunities, but they do not result in the credentials of an MBA or the intense academic experience that is needed to really understand quantitative methods and modern management theory. I have known some senior lawyers, including managing partners, who have registered for certificate programs. They are much more practical, given their short time duration, than full-time MBA programs. However, they are no substitute, and I do not recommend them for attorneys who are looking to embark on a business career.

WHAT ABOUT LAW FIRM SABBATICALS?

A SABBATICAL ALLOWS an attorney to take a paid leave after having completed a certain period of service to the firm, not unlike academic sabbaticals, but not necessarily after seven years. Not all firms offer sabbaticals. If you are picking a firm for the long haul, you should at least consider whether the firm offers a sabbatical program.

Sabbaticals are usually offered only to partners and, in some cases, counsels. As a practical matter, even if sabbaticals were offered to associates it is rare that any individual associate would be in a position to take advantage of the program. Consider that sabbaticals usually require an attorney to have worked about six years prior to taking time off. That means an associate would need to take off time in his seventh year, precisely when he or she is being considered for partnership. It would be career suicide to take time off during the year of your final assessment.

In the longer term, however, sabbaticals can be valuable perks. The business of law is extremely competitive and demanding. It is easy for attorneys to burn out. At the same time, it can be very risky for an attorney to take even a short break from the law. There is a significant risk that in his absence his clients will find alternative counsel. A sabbatical program in which the firm is obligated to temporarily support the absent partner's practice and guarantee that his slot will remain open is a great solution.

Sabbaticals can be used for various purposes. On one hand, they can serve as an opportunity to teach as a full-time adjunct professor at a law school—perhaps one in another geographical area. On the other hand, you might want to do nothing but sit on a beach and recharge your batteries, or volunteer to help with relief efforts in some drought-stricken region. A sabbatical can also be a time to try out an alternative career, with the knowledge that if it does not work out, your old job is waiting for you.

Sabbaticals can range in length from three months to a year. Extending beyond a year would not be wise, because clients would forget you and your expertise would grow stale. Pay during that year may also differ, from half pay in some cases to full pay with partnership participation in others. Although I would not recommend asking about sabbatical programs before you have an offer from a firm—you don't want to give the impression that you are just looking forward to taking time off, after all— you might try to learn the details of any such program after you have an offer in hand. At that point, the firm will be glad that you are considering being around that long.

WHEN CAN I WRITE MY OWN TICKET?

PRETTY MUCH NEVER. The reality is that there are dozens of lawyers out there with backgrounds such as yours. I have a solid résumé, but there is no job for which I can write my own ticket. The myth exists that certain criteria will set you up for an easy life. If you didn't go to the best law school (Yale), you can always say, "If only I had gone to Yale, I would be offered this job." Only the guys who went to Yale don't have that excuse, and they don't get all of the jobs they want either. Every position you apply for, if it is a job worth having, will be one you will need to compete for, unless you can take advantage of nepotism or networking.

OTHER CAREERS

ALTHOUGH THIS IS a book about your legal career, you should think more broadly about what you want to do for the rest of your professional life. Do you really want to be a lawyer, particularly now, after some of the mystique the profession has been imbued with by the entertainment industry has been rubbed off?

There is a conversation you are likely to have several years down the road, particularly if you become a corporate attorney. I had this conversation when I was doing my MBA at Wharton. I was sitting with a couple of investment bankers at lunch and the talk turned to what it was like to be a lawyer. They said they always felt bad about the plight of the lawyers they used on deals. For one thing, the bankers said the lawyers never got to see the real deal. They never got to know about the business of the company they were doing an underwriting on and never got to spend time thinking about the economics of the deal. The lawyers were desperate for any information that would provide a context for the rote work they were doing. Lawyers who had worked hundreds of hours on offerings really had no knowledge about the nature of the firm. The banker, on the other hand, knew all about the finances of the company, its growth prospects, and other really interesting parts of the transaction. The bankers also felt bad about giving the lawyers last-minute work on Fridays that had to be completed by Monday morning.

You may also want to consider a career that is even more far a field. For example, at least consider a medical career. When I worked at the SEC, I was sitting at my desk at my office in the SEC building, I heard someone yell "does anyone know the Heimlich maneuver?" I ran to my door, looked down the hall, and saw ten of my colleagues standing around another colleague who was clearly choking. She could not speak or cough and was holding her throat. I had been a lifeguard—fifteen years earlier. Nevertheless, my first aid training kicked in and I ran over and quickly straddled her from behind and initiated Heimlich compressions on her diaphragm. A piece of bagel dislodged from her windpipe and, though frightened and gasping for breath, she was out of danger. As we waited for paramedics to arrive, I thought how good it felt to have helped someone in danger. Later on I overheard a conversation between colleagues about how everyone else just stood around while I was the only one to take action. I could not help but think to myself that, had I become a doctor instead of a lawyer, I could feel the sense of incomparable accomplishment of saving life on a regular basis. My chance for making such a career change has long since passed—I would be well over 40 if I were to go back to medical school now. But those of you who are younger, in college, or even in law school, might want to think more broadly about what you want out of your career-and life—while all the options remain open to you. My advice: Go spend a day in a hospital emergency room. Visit the trading floor of an investment bank. Spend a day with a partner at a large accounting firm. Tour a top restaurant's kitchen and talk to the chefs. Just do whatever you need to do to get as educated as possible about the very many career opportunities out there.

CONCLUSION

ON THE VALUE OF RELATIONSHIPS

MY ANECDOTAL STORIES, experiences, and observations are meant to give you insight into the repercussions of the important decisions you will need to make, starting with whether you want to go to law school and continuing through the complex framework of options available to you as a lawyer. Even late in your career, as the possessor of a highly versatile and useful education, you have many options. I hope this book has given you the knowledge and insight to take advantage of the many doors open to you and to help you to open some doors that would otherwise be closed and even locked.

The thought I want to leave you with is that relationships matter, sometimes even more than intellect or experience. The old saying is that it's not what you know but who you know. One of the most important things you can do in developing your career in a way that will get you job security is to build a specialty in an area of law that is in high demand, but it is also true that the relationships you build along your career route can be of immense value.

I wish you luck in your career, whatever form it takes.

APPENDIX A

A Unaccredited Law School Bar Exam Pass Rate

Unaccredited Law School	Number who passed bar in last 9 years	% of first time test takers who passed	% of repeaters who passed
American	60	5%	5%
California Southern	112	21%	11%
Irvine	2	0%	1%
Larry H. Layton	5	25%	17%
Pacific Coast	72	28%	22%
Pacific West	12	11%	5%
People's	4	5%	.8%
Ridgecrest	25	24%	19%
Northern California Lorenzo Patino	45	8%	8%
Western Sierra	30	25%	9%

Source: Nancy McCarthy, "Bar pass rates under scrutiny: Unaccredited law schools targeted in Sacramento," *California Bar Journal*, official publication of the State Bar of California, April 2006.

APPENDIX B

NALP LAW FIRM Questionnaire 2003-2004 Academic Year

This form reflects information for:
- ☐ one office only
- ☐ multiple offices

Date completed _____

NALP member   Y ☐   N ☐

Office size (attys):   ☐ 2-10   ☐ 11-25   ☐ 26-50   ☐ 51-100   ☐ 101-250   ☐ 251-500   ☐ 501+

Total firm size (attys):   ☐ 2-10   ☐ 11-25   ☐ 26-50   ☐ 51-100   ☐ 101-250   ☐ 251-500   ☐ 501+

CONTACT INFORMATION
Firm: _____
Street Address: _____
City: _____ State/Province: _____ Zip: _____ Country: _____
Tel: (_____) _____ Fax: (_____) _____

Hiring Attorney: _____
ADDRESS INQUIRIES TO: ☐ Ms.   ☐ Mr.
Name: _____
Title: _____
Firm: _____
Address: _____

Phone: (_____) _____
E-mail: _____
Web site: _____

DEMOGRAPHICS (as of 2-1-2003)
Size of Office Completing Form

Ptrs/Mems	_____	Paralegals	_____
Of Counsel	_____	Other Prof.	_____
Associates	_____	Support	_____
Senior Attys.	_____	School-Term	_____
Staff Attys.	_____	Law Clerks	_____
Total Attys.	_____		

Other Offices

City	No. Attys
_____	_____
_____	_____
_____	_____
_____	_____
_____	_____

as of 2-1-2003	Ptrs/Mems	Of Counsel	Assocs.	Senior Attys	Staff Attys	Summer 03
Men						
Women						
Totals						
Black						
Hispanic						
Am. Ind./Alsk.						
As. & Pac. Isl.						
Multi-Racial						
Disabled						
Openly Gay						

as of 2-1-2002	Ptrs/Mems	Of Counsel	Assocs.	Senior Attys	Staff Attys	Summer 02
Men						
Women						
Totals						
Black						
Hispanic						
Am. Ind./Alsk.						
As. & Pac. Isl.						
Multi-Racial						
Disabled						
Openly Gay						

PRIMARY PRACTICE AREAS	No. Ptrs/Mems & Of Counsel	No. Other Lawyers

EMPLOYMENT DATA
Number in parens ( ) represents former summer associates

		Hired 2002	Expected Hires 2003	2004
Attorneys	Laterals	( )		
	Post-clerkship	( )		
	Entry-level	( )		
	LLMs	( )		
	Foreign LLMs	( )		
Summer	Post-3Ls	( )		
	2Ls	( )		
	1Ls			

No. 2002 summer 2Ls considered for associate offers _____
No. offers made _____

Split summers allowed?   Y ☐   N ☐   Min. weeks: _____
1Ls hired?   Y ☐   N ☐   Other _____
When after 12/1 should 1Ls apply? _____
Accept applications for 2004 summer program from:
 Joint degree applicants graduating in 2006 or later?
  Y ☐   N ☐   Considered as 1L ☐   2L ☐
 Judicial clerks?   Y ☐   N ☐
 Students at foreign law schools?   Y ☐   N ☐
Hiring criteria _____

	2002	2003
Avg. annual assoc. hrs. worked		
Avg. annual assoc. billable hrs		
Min. assoc. billable hrs.		
1L summer $/week	$_____	$_____
2L summer $/week	$_____	$_____
Post-3L summer $/week	$_____	$_____
Entry-level base $/year	$_____	$_____

Notes: _____
_____
_____

APPENDIX C

One Possible Format for a Law Student Resumé

First Name Last Name
[Address]
[Address]
[Email Address]
[Phone Number]

EDUCATION

University School of Law   City, State
Juris Doctor expected May 2009; LSAT   May 2009
Academic Honors (e.g., Harlan Fiske Stone Scholar)
Articles Editor, XXX Law Review XXX
Club President Best Brief,
Moot Court Competition

University Bachelor of Arts, Summa cum laude;   City, State
Major in XXX   May 2009
Academic Honors (e.g., Phi Eta Sigma, Phi Beta Kappa)
Dean's List; Dean's List with Distinction
Captain, XXX Team

EXPERIENCE

Law Firm Name Here   City, State
                                                           Summer

- Summer Associate / Summer
- Researched and drafted memorandum concerning
  [a specific legal issue] for [a specific legal issue]
- Assisted in preparation for and attended depositions
  of witnesses in [a particular type of litigation].

SUMMER EMPLOYMENT HERE

Summer Intern

City, State
Summer 2007

- Researched and drafted memorandum concerning [a specific legal issue] for [a specific legal application].
- Researched and drafted memorandum concerning [a specific legal issue] for [a specific legal issue]
- Assisted in preparation for and attended depositions of witnesses in [a particular type of litigation].

PREVIOUS EMPLOYER NAME HERE

Title

City, State
2004–2006

- Any promotions received during time period of employment.
- Activity relevant to research, writing, critical thinking, or leadership skills
- Activity relevant to research, writing, critical thinking, or leadership skills

ADDITIONAL INFORMATION

University, summer calculus class, 2004.
Oxford University, XXX College, study abroad, English legal system, 2003.

PUBLICATIONS

Law review note titled
Published in the *Law Review*.

INTERESTS

APPENDIX D

Associate Bonus Eligibility 1996–2001

	Number of Attorneys / Percent of Offices							
Based on meeting goals or targets	2–10	11–25	26–50	51–100	101–250	Over 250	251–500	Over 500
1996	17.5	20.2	36.7	30.6	36.5	52.6	N/A	N/A
1997	10.7	21.6	32.3	33.7	29.4	49.4	N/A	N/A
1998	30.3	38.3	34.2	39.6	48.5	53.7	N/A	N/A
1999	32.9*		32.7	41.7	53.2	57.9	N/A	N/A
2000	24.1*		46.4	45.9	59.5	N/A	76.3	77.6
2001	39.7*		55.4	58.8	56.5	N/A	70.7	84.2
Based on discretion	2–10	11–25	26–50	51–100	101–250	Over 250	251–500	Over 500
1996	72.5	72.3	43.3	59.7	61.5	42.3	N/A	N/A
1997	75.0	64.7	63.1	55.8	54.6	55.6	N/A	N/A
1998	66.7	55.0	53.0	53.2	48.5	45.8	N/A	N/A
1999	68.4*		57.3	60.2	56.7	47.7	N/A	N/A
2000	65.5*		46.4	70.3	54.3	N/A	43.4	55.3
2001	69.2*		58.7	80.4	61.1	N/A	78.0	73.4

* Figures are for the 2–25 category.
Note: Firms could report using both bases to determine eligibility.
Source: Reprinted with permission from "Finding from NALP's Associate Salary Survey—A Historical Perspective 1996–2001" from the Web site of NALP—The Association for Legal Career Professionals. For more current summary information on associate salaries, see the research section of www.nalp.org.

APPENDIX E

Median Starting Salaries for First-Year Associates
by Firm Size, 1996–2001

	Firm Size—Number of Attorneys					
	2–10	11–25	26–50	51–100	101–250	Over 251
1996*	$35,000	$41,000	$52,000	$58,500	$60,000	$70,000
1997*	$40,000	$52,000	$50,000	$60,000	$65,000	$71,502
1998*	$39,500	$52,000	53,000	$61,000	$60,000	$75,000
1999	51,000**		$57,500	$67,000	$70,000	$85,000
2000	60,000**		$63,000	$70,000	$75,000	$110,500
2001	60,000**		$70,500	$75,900	$90,000	$110,174
% Change 1996–2001	NC		35.6%	29.7%	50.0%	57.4%

* Figures for 1996 are as of July 1; figures for 1997 are as of August1; figures for 1998 are as of January 1; figures for all other years are as of April 1.
** Figures are for the 2–25 firm size range.
Note: Medians for each size range are calculated based on firms in that size range responding to the survey for the year specified. Some medians appear to decline; this is a result of a different pool of respondents in each year rather than a decrease in salaries on the part of any one firm.

Source: Reprinted with permission from "Finding from NALP's Associate Salary Survey—A Historical Perspective 1996–2001" from the Web site of NALP—The Association for Legal Career Professionals. For more current summary information on associate salaries, see the research section of www.nalp.org.

APPENDIX F

Median Starting Salaries for First-Year Associates in Firms of 251 or More—Chicago, Los Angeles, New York, and Washington, D.C.

	Chicago	Los Angeles	New York	Washington D.C.
1996*	N/A	$75,000	$85,000	$72,500
1997*	$73,000	$80,002	$87,000	$74,000
1998*	$80,000	$82,500	$87,500	$80,000
1999	$90,000	$92,004	$96,000	$91,000
2000	$117,500	$125,000	$125,000	$114,000
2001	$125,000	$125,000	$125,000	$125,000
% Change 1996–2001	N/C	66.7%	47.1%	72.4%

* Figures for 1996 are as of July 1; figures for 1997 are as of August 1; figures for 1998 are as of January 1; figures for all other years are as of April 1.

Note: Although the figures shown are technically medians (the middle value in a series of salaries ranked from low to high), for these specific cities and this firm size, the figures shown are more usefully thought of as simply the prevailing salary in that city at that time.

Source: Reprinted with permission from "Finding from NALP's Associate Salary Survey—A Historical Perspective 1996–2001" from the Web site of NALP—The Association for Legal Career Professionals. For more current summary information on associate salaries, see the research section of www.nalp.org.

APPENDIX G

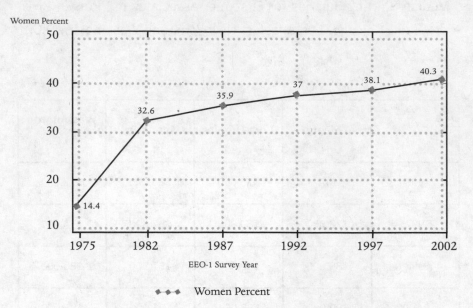

Source: *Diversity in Law Firms,* study by the U.S. Equal Employment Opportunity Commission, 2003

YEAR	1997	1982	1987	1992	1997	2002
Women Percent	14.4	32.6	35.9	37	38.1	40.3

In 1975, women represented just 14.4 percent of all professionals in the legal services industry based on their filing of EEO-1 reports. By 2002, this figure had risen to 40.3 percent.

Source: *Diversity in Law Firms,* study by the U.S. Equal Employment Opportunity Commission, 2003

APPENDIX H

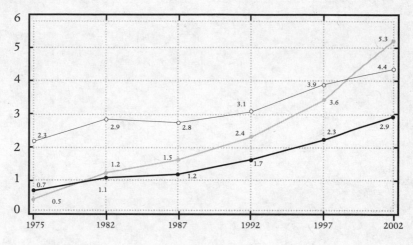

Minority Percent

EEO-1 Survey Year

○—○—○ African-American Percent   ●—●—● Hispanic Percent   ● ● ● Asian Percent

YEAR	1975	1982	1987	1992	1997	2002
Percent Asian	0.5	1.2	1.5	2.4	3.6	5.3
Percent African American	2.3	2.9	2.8	3.1	3.9	4.4
Percent Hispanic	0.7	1.1	1.2	1.7	2.3	2.9
Percent Native American	0	0	0.2	0.1	0.1	0.2

Source: *Diversity in Law Firms,* study by the U.S. Equal Employment Opportunity Commission, 2003

NOTES

Introduction

1. I should also note that this book is quite a bargain. Consider, for example, that as an attorney I would bill at about $650 an hour. Just 1,000 hours of work—much less than I spent on this book—would cost $650,000 in time alone.

2. Peter Lattman, "Law School by Default," *Wall Street Journal*, June 23, 2006, W11.

3. Ibid.

4. Diana Nelson Jonas, "Legally unhappy: Experts worry about growing tide of lawyers abandoning careers," *Pittsburgh Post-Gazette*, May 4, 2005 (citing authority that as many as 70 percent of practicing lawyers are disaffected).

5. Lattman.

6. Scott Turow received his JD from Harvard in 1978 and is now a partner with Sonnenschein, Nath & Rosenthal in Chicago.

7. However, you should consider that by taking a bunch of English classes you will have reduced your chance of getting a finance job on Wall Street or ever getting into medical school!

8. Of course, in adopting this "SEC First" strategy you are accepting certain risks. You are taking the risk that the practice of securities law would be "hot" in eight years and that you would be able to find a firm willing to pay you a lot of money for your securities law experience. While this was a relatively safe bet, as securities law is a perennially strong practice area, it is still difficult to predict the market eight years down the line. Also, you are accepting a risk by earning a lower

initial salary. The present value of a dollar in year one is much greater than the present value of a dollar in year nine. You need to, at least roughly, calculate your present-value break-even point. After how many years of private practice as a partner will you make up for having lost salary in the early years of your career? In all likelihood, given the extent to which partner salaries are higher than associate salaries, this should not take more than a couple of years. Thus, based on this deliberate and somewhat quantitative analysis, you may well conclude that adopting a strategy like the "SEC First" approach is well advised.

CHAPTER 1:   DECIDING ON A LEGAL CAREER

1. That is, there were more than a million lawyers listed in the *West Legal* Directory as of January 2005. I've read a number of tertiary sources claiming that, as of early 2005, there were 1.05 million lawyers practicing in the United States.

2. There is some interesting literature on the topic of depression among highly driven professionals generally. For example, one article discussing the practice of clinical psychologist Alden Cass describes how "an unforgiving drive to succeed breeds an unhealthy fear of not succeeding." While the article focuses on Wall Street traders and other professionals, the lesson seems applicable to young lawyers as well, particularly those who have gone to the best schools and have an expectation of becoming partners in highly competitive law firms. See Jeanne Sahadi, *How Wall Street Can Wreck Your Life,* CNNMoney.com, October 26, 2006.

3. The envy experienced by members of the professional class, which includes lawyers, for the "super rich" class, including Internet entrepreneurs and, sometimes, investment bankers and hedge fund managers is discussed in an interesting article titled "Revolt of the Fairly Rich." In this article, author Matt Miller chronicles the ironic plight of American professionals doing better than "99 percent of the humans who have ever walked the planet" who can't help but notice that people with their same academic backgrounds (or less) are making "ten or 50 or 100 million dollars in a single year while [they are] working [themselves] ragged to earn a million or two—or, God forbid, $400,000. . . ." Certainly, there was some of this envy evidenced among lawyers during the Internet boom for young company founders and again today for highly compensated hedge fund managers. It is even harder for young corporate lawyers who have to work hand-in-hand with the offending businessmen and financial specialists. See Matt Miller, "Revolt of the Fairly Rich," *Fortune,* October 25, 2006.

4. In an *American Lawyer* article titled "Misery," a successful Covington & Burling partner and past Harvard Law School alumni association president stated, "If any of my children ends up going into practice of law, I will consider myself to have been defeated."

5. Colin Pope and Ann Hatchitt, "Brobeck Law Firm to Dissolve," *Austin Business Journal/San Francisco Business Times,* January 31, 2003.

CHAPTER 2: BEFORE YOU GO TO LAW SCHOOL

1. "Dustin Drives Down Memory Lane," *60 Minutes,* broadcast November 25, 2004.

2. Some advisers state flatly that, unless you want to spend the rest of your life practicing law, you should not go to law school but rather directly pursue your career of choice. See, e.g., http://www.legalcareer.com/faq.html (This Web site has some thoughtful and pointed answers to a number of FAQs commonly posed by students considering going to law school.) I do not disagree with the advice that it is better to pursue your goals as directly as possible as a general matter. However, as a practical matter you are unlikely to know exactly what it is you want to do—or what you will have the realistic opportunity to pursue—as a long-term career. Therefore, it is good to know that a legal education can and has formed the basis for many types of careers other than the actual practice of law. For example, in my experience working as a Wall Street investment banker, I found that about one in ten bankers had a law degree, including managing directors, one of whom was the global head of one of the bank's main business practices.

3. "Real" options are options to do or not engage in a business transaction or investment. This term is contrasted with "financial" options, which are exchange-traded securities granting an option to buy or sell an underlying security.

4. Think of it this way: The admissions officer knows that there were other students in the C student's class who obtained better grades than he did. For all the admissions counselor knows, the student who received the A average in a less rigorous class was the smartest student in that entire school. Coupled with a high LSAT score, the English student easily appears to be a more attractive candidate than the physics student. Moreover, since the law school is ranked at least in part on the basis of its average GPA for admitted students (regardless of their undergraduate majors), there is an added incentive for the counselor to let in the applicant with the higher GPA without weighting for the difficulty of the underlying classes.

5. This language dated from between 800 and about 1200 C.E. and read something like this:

Ne weað wæl mare
on þis eiglandeæfer gieta
folces gefylledbeforan þissum
sweordes ecgum, þæs þe us secgað bec,
ealde uðwitan,siþþan eastan hider
Engle & Seaxeup becoman,
ofer brad brimuBrytene sohtan,
wlance wigsmiþas,Weealas ofercoman,
eorlas arhwateeard begeatan

From *The Battle of Brunanburh,* written in 937.

6. Sometimes fraternities do even more, of course. Legend has it that some fraternities, maintain records of past exams and other study aids that may give their members an edge over classmates (though the partying that often accompanies fraternity membership can serve to relevel the academic playing field!).

7. http://careers.state.gov/officer/.

8. Some observers have commented that people pursuing a second career in the law can face obstacles, including, for example, that they face the perceptions that they "could not hack it" in their former careers, that they "may lack the vigor of a younger colleague," or that they "will not be able to take direction well from younger supervisors." See Steven C. Bennett, "The Issues Facing Second-Career Lawyers," *New York Law Journal,* January 2, 2003. Bennett's article is a good one, but in my experience working in both business finance and the law, I can report that the bias against older career entrants is much greater in finance—particularly in investment banking—than it is in the law. While you will certainly need to be prepared to explain your decision to embark on a new career, and why you left your old one, most interviewers will be persuaded that your having had real-world experience has tempered your expectations to the extent that that you will be more likely to have a realistic outlook and as a result be more likely to find satisfaction in a legal practice.

9. The admissions process at English universities is very different from those at American universities. Interviews are required, as are tests in the subject matter in which you intend to major. You also will need to select an individual college—Oxford and Cambridge each comprise dozens of individual colleges—and address your application directly to that school. Moreover, you will need to plan your application process at least before September of the year prior to that in which you hope to matriculate. For more information, take a look at Oxford's Web site for American applicants, www.admissions.ox.ac.uk/int/usa/apply.shtml.

10. Note that I am a bit biased, having attended Emmanuel College at Cambridge University for a semester.

11. If you went to the University of London instead, you would receive an LL.B. degree.

12. Note, however, that just your undergraduate degree in law from an English university would be enough to allow you to practice in some American jurisdictions. New York permits holders of Oxford and Cambridge B.A. degrees and University of London LL.B. degrees to take the bar, and both New York and Massachusetts permit holders of a Canadian LL.B. to sit for the bar.

CHAPTER 3: DECIDING ON A LAW SCHOOL

1. When I last looked, the information was at www.abanet.org/legaled/approvedlawschools/approved.html.

2. Graduates of any of these schools can sit for the California bar examination.

See Nancy McCarthy, "Bar pass rates under scrutiny, Unaccredited law schools targeted in Sacramento," *California Bar Journal,* official publication of the State Bar of California, April 2006, p. 1.

3. Ibid.

4. Interestingly, as of late 2005, there were only nineteen ABA-accredited law schools in California, which is less than the number of unaccredited and CBA-accredited law schools combined.

5. McCarthy, op. cit.6. Since the bar exam is given twice a year, this means the school has had two passes out of eighteen bar exams given.

7. See Rebecca Carroll, "For some lawyers, legal training means skipping law classes," *Associated Press,* September 22, 2005.

8. Ibid.9. See Section 520.5 of the Rules of the Court of Appeals for the Admission of Attorneys and Counselors at Law.

10. Ibid.

11. Ibid.

CHAPTER 4: SOME SOCIAL ISSUES TO CONSIDER

1. See Seth Stern, "Fifty Years After Admitting Women, Law School Hires Woman Dean," *Christian Science Monitor,* April 15, 2003, p. 12.

2. Pamela Thomas-Graham, President and CEO, CNBC, JD, MBA Harvard University 1989, *What I Learned at Harvard Law School,* speech presented at Celebration 50 at Harvard Law School on May 3, 2003.

3. *Diversity in Law Firms,* published by the U.S. Equal Employment Opportunity Commission, 2003 The full text can be found at at www.eeoc.gov.

4. See Joan Williams, "What Stymies Women's Academic Careers? It's Personal," *Chronicle of Higher Education,* December 12, 2000, http://plsc.uark.edu.

5. Ibid.

6. Why the EEOC study focused on "white women" and not "women" generally is something I do not clearly understand. Nevertheless, this is how the study data is presented in the EEOC report.

7. *Diversity in Law Firms,* op cit., p. 2.

8. *Diversity in Law Firms,* op cit., p. 1.

9. *Diversity in Law Firms,* op cit., p. 3.

10. In general, the larger firms or companies tend to be more gay friendly. See Fortune 500 Firms Seen as More Gay Friendly, CNNMoney.com, June 19, 2006. This trend is reflected in the law as well. There are certainly a number of reasons for this, including the fact that any individual partner's biases will have less of an impact on a large firm's corporate policies, as well as the reality that most larger firms are located in urban centers, where people are more open-minded.

11. NALP was founded in 1971 as the National Association for Law Placement, (now called the Association for Legal Career Professionals. Its Web site states that its formation was "in response to a perceived need by many law schools and legal employers for a common forum to discuss issues involving placement and recruitment." www.nalp.org.

12. Of course, it is also possible to finish American college programs in three years. My roommate at Columbia graduated from Yale with a degree in economics in three years. But, of course, a four-year course of study remains the standard in the United States.

CHAPTER 6: WHAT TO DO IN LAW SCHOOL

1. Harlan Fiske Stone attended Columbia Law School from 1895 to 1898, was dean of Columbia Law School from 1910 to 1923, and was appointed to the Supreme Court in 1925.

2. James Kent was, among other things, the first professor of law at Columbia College, in 1793–98.

3. The SEC runs a paid internship program. I worked with the committee that selected our interns for the summer of 2006. I personally interviewed one candidate, whom I later hired for the office I was working in. The process was quite competitive. About a hundred students applied. The best cover letters were brief and specific. The worst were long diatribes describing the student's career objectives and philosophies. The best résumés were not longer than one page in length. (See Appendix C for suggestions about the form a résumé could take.) My advice is to show both your cover letter and your résumé to at least three other people who actually care whether you get the job. One of them should be a lawyer working in the field in which you are applying. They will be able to advise you on whether the experience you are describing is relevant to the position.(For example, good performance in a law school moot court competition would be highly relevant to getting an internship or a job with the Division of Enforcement at the SEC or with any branch of the Department of Justice.) If it is not relevant, you should consider scaling your down descriptions or, in some cases, omitting them.

CHAPTER 7: JUDICIAL CLERKSHIPS

1. In 2005, federal clerkship salaries were around $51,000.

2. There are other federal courts, some of which are quite prestigious to clerk for, that I do not discuss in detail in this book. These include the Court of Appeals for Veterans' Claims (not too prestigious), the U.S. Court of Appeals for the Armed Forces (good if you are thinking of pursuing a military career), the U.S. Court of International Trade (great, obviously, if you know you are interested in a legal career in the trade field), the U.S. Tax Court, and the U.S. Court of Federal Claims (a fairly prestigious court that has original jurisdiction over certain

specialized matters, including tax refunds, federal application of eminent domain [appropriating private property for public use], and constitutional and statutory rights of military personnel and their dependents). See www.uscourts.gov/courtlinks/. If you are interested in bankruptcy law, you might want to also investigate clerking for one of the U.S. Bankruptcy Courts, or, if you have an interest in intellectual property law, the U.S. Court of Appeals for the Federal Circuit. See www.fedcir.gov.

3. Historically, the D.C. Circuit, Second Circuit, and Ninth Circuit have been the most competitive appellate courts on which to get a clerkship.

4. For a map of the United States showing the geographic coverage of the various courts, go to www.uscourts.gov/courtlinks/.

5. These rules were set in place by agreement because judges are also competing for the top law school graduates, and some judges had been making offers to top candidates very early on, even to second-year students.

CHAPTER 9: PURSUING OTHER DEGREES

1. This stigma is not entirely fair. Business people know lawyers in the context of the services lawyers provide to businesses. That is, lawyers are tasked with thinking about what could go wrong with a business deal, which then needs to be addressed in the agreements. Even unlikely negative scenarios need to be addressed. This makes business people think lawyers are more risk-averse than they may actually be in their personal lives. Lawyers are just doing their jobs in anticipating the negative in their professional capacity.

CHAPTER 10: BUILDING A LEGAL CAREER

1. Most major U.S. corporations are incorporated in the State of Delaware. Skadden, Arps maintained an office in Wilmington, Delaware, because of the great importance of Delaware corporate law and the Delaware Chancery Court in corporate litigation. Rather than rely on the handful of local Wilmington law firms for assistance in matters involving Delaware law, Skadden found it cost-effective to build their own presence there. If you worked in this office, you would be addressing matters relating to Delaware corporate law.

2. See NALP press release of April 1, 2005, "Entry-Level Lawyer Salaries Remarkably Stable: NALP Survey Details Private Practice Compensation Ranges," at www.nalp.org.

3. Posting by Abe2, April 8, 2002, 1:27 p.m., at www.styleforum.net/archive/index.php/t-1115.html.

CHAPTER 11: WORKING FOR LAW FIRMS

1. This is the model that requires all firms to bill out a constantly replenishing stream of new associates at hourly rates that will, it is hoped, result in a return

that is higher than the fixed costs (salary and administration) of employing the associates.

2.   You will notice that I use the terms up-or-out system and pyramid structure interchangeably.   This is because the up-or-out system, which requires a large number of junior-level employees supervised by a small number of senior partners above them, is widely considered to be the most successful when new junior people—recent law firm graduates—are continually brought in to replenish their ranks. Contrast this with a system in which there is no up-or-out requirement but there remains only a small number of partners. Fewer junior people would be brought in each year because the middle group had not moved on to other jobs. The resulting structure would be better characterized as an egg, with a large middle tier, and few senior partners and entry-level attorneys.

3.   Note that while it is not always the case, high billable hours often translate into partners liking an associate's work well enough to assign more work to him or her. As a result, there is usually a high correlation between hours billed and partner feedback.

4.   From my experience working at the SEC, it is an environment where there exists only minimal use of discretionary bonuses, yet dedicated employees consistently perform at a high level. In such an environment, the key to getting lawyers to produce their best work is to create a sense of mission and to a give individual direct positive feedback.

5.   See "Young Lawyers, Big Salaries", *New York Times,* http://dealbook.blogs. nytimes.com/comments, March 31, 2006 (discussing that in early 2006, several Chicago firms raised entry level associate salaries to $135,000).

6.   You can see this stagnation in 2000 and 2001 illustrated at Appendix E, showing median law firm salaries from 1996 to 2001.

7.   The two exceptions I have in mind are the law firms of Wachtel, Lipton, Rosen & Katz and Cravath, Swain & Moore, each of which have one office, in Manhattan.

CHAPTER 12: THE POLITICS AND PITFALLS OF LAW FIRM LIFE

1.   "Does it pay to be a flirt? Report says women in the workplace who use sexual behavior may not get that next promotion or raise," http://money.cnn.com/2005/08/05/news/economy/women_raises/index.htm, August 5, 2005.

2.   Here are the citations:

"Augmenting the Duties of Directors to Protect Minority Shareholders in the Context of Going Private Transactions—The Case for Obligating Directors to Express a Valuation Opinion in Unilateral Tender Offers After Siliconix, Aquila, and Pure Resources," *Columbia Business Law Review,* Vol. 2003, Number 3, Winter 2003.

"The National Securities Markets Improvement Act of 1996: Summary and Discussion," with Robert G. Bagnall, *Securities Regulation Law Journal,* Vol. 25, Number 1, Spring 1997.

"Protecting Minority Shareholder Rights Under Delaware Law: Reinforcing Shareholders as Residual Claimants and Maximizing Long-Term Share Value by Restricting Directorial Discretion," with Patrick Tangney, *Columbia Business Law Review,* Vol. 1995, Number 3, Autumn 1995.

3.   Here are some selected citations to my published works: 53 Duke L.J. 1337 n. 120 (February 2004); 152 U. Pa. L. Rev. 785 n. 211 (December 2003); 113 Yale L.J. 119 n. 99 (October 2003); 50 Stan. L. Rev. 273 n. 10 (January 1998).

CHAPTER 13: MAKING PARTNER

1.   Roger Parloff, "Scandal Rocks Silicon Valley's Top Legal Ace," *Fortune,* November 17, 2006.

CHAPTER 14: ALTERNATIVES TO LAW FIRM LIFE

1.   "Recruiting and Retaining Qualified Personnel," by Daniel J. McNamara (paper at http://som.csudh.edu/dkarber/sep01pub501/mcnamarad/res.htm).

2.   At the time, most of my legal experience was in corporate transactional work.

3.   "Law grads turn to corporate crime fighters," *CNN.com,* December 10, 2002.

4.   This freezing of hiring at the SEC was mainly instituted as a result of budgetary considerations.

5.   "Law grads turn to corporate crime fighters," op. cit.

6.   The top twenty-five students of this summer honors program were apparently offered places on the SEC's new two-year training program starting in June 2005 in which trainees will be paid around $60,000 annually. See Sarah Butcher, "Regulators Go After Grads," efinancialcareers.com, March 3, 2005.

7.   One of the more recent SEC Commissioners, Annette Nazareth, was head of the Division of Market Regulation for six years, and is an example of a member of the staff becomng a commissioner. She is unusual in that she also was formerly a managing director at Smith Barney and has held an impressive array of other senior positions in the securities industry. Nevertheless, even though she has impeccable credentials, including having been a Harlan Fiske Stone Scholar at Columbia and a Phi Beta Kappa from Brown, I doubt she would have garnered the presidential attention needed to be appointed a commissioner if she had not been married to Roger Ferguson, the former vice chairman of the Federal Reserve Bank.

8.   Working for the president can mean working on an election campaign, but the risk is that your candidate might not win, and then you are totally out of a job!

CHAPTER 15: CHANGING JOBS

1. One example is Gary Lynch, a former Davis, Polk partner who once served as director of the SEC's Division of Enforcement. I met Gary for the first time when I interviewed at Davis, Polk in 1995 during my judicial clerkship. He was later appointed vice chairman of Credit Suisse First Boston, at the height of the equity analyst scandal on Wall Street. The scandal had a significant economic impact on investment banking firms and resulted in the leading brokerages agreeing in December 2002 to pay almost $1 billion to settle conflict-of-interest allegations. The ten firms involved in the settlement included Citigroup, Goldman Sachs, and Credit Suisse First Boston. 2. "Devoted readers of the Yap Chronicles, lend me your eyes and perhaps your assistance. Whether I move on to Washington DC or to Pohnpei, I will be leaving my job as the Yap State Assistant Attorney General when my contract expires at the end of June. Yap has treated me well and both out of appreciation and courtesy I would like to help my employers find a suitable replacement for me. I am appealing to all of you to put me in contact with anyone you know of who may be interested in replacing me. There are a few basic parameters:

- Must be willing to stay for the two-year contract duration
- Must be a graduate from an accredited law school
- Must be admitted to practice law in some U. S. state

"I would prefer the person has 3-5 years' legal experience, but a minimum of two would suffice in a pinch. Someone just out of law school could not handle the imitative and responsibilities required by this job.

"The pay isn't great but the experience is unparalleled. Vacation time is extremely generous (20 days a year, but no one really counts). Yap will pay for transportation from anywhere in the world and will ship 2,000 pounds of household goods. If the hire is married, they will pay for the spouse's airfare and grant 4,000 pounds of goods. The hire will be exposed to a wide variety of law (criminal, maritime, environmental, contract, regulatory, legislative, historical preservation, and US agency compliance) and given tremendous autonomy. The hire can make the situation as challenging or as stress free as they like.

"If anyone is interested in this most worthwhile opportunity, please have them contact me via email. The position is available July 1, 2004. I look forward to seeing the referrals from this most interesting group of people." Found at www.jdedman.com.

CHAPTER 16: ESCAPING FROM YOUR LEGAL CAREER

1. It may surprise you to learn how many senior attorneys say they wish they had switched to investment banking early in their careers. I know that one reason for

this is the perception that investment bankers are farther up the food chain than lawyers. That is, they have more contact with the real business decision makers— the ultimate clients—and can make the transition to being deal makers themselves far more easily than lawyers can. This is because bankers know the numbers. Also, investment bankers earn higher salaries, and as they gain seniority, they work fewer hours, unlike many partners. Lawyers who have told me personally that they should have joined an investment bank when they were younger include the managing partner of the top securities law firm in the United States and one of the commissioners of the SEC. These are lawyers who have achieved enormous success in their chosen fields—rising up to the very top. The fact that they even express yearning for the banking field may give some young attorneys pause in considering their career paths.

2. A first-year banking associate just out of business school can take home as much as $250,000 the first year. My brother, who went to a top business school and worked for a small San Francisco investment bank during the summer of 2005, reported that associates at his firm took home at least $250,000 during the previous year, with bonuses easily eclipsing basc salaries.

3. Each of these five lawyers-turned-businessmen graduated from business school between 1998 and 2001. This corresponds to the great tech-bubble. It is therefore possible that the sample is not representative of post-bubble behavior. That is, since the tech bubble burst, it is possible that the allure of business school for lawyers has worn thin.

INDEX

ABA. *See* American Bar Association (ABA),
adjunct law professor, 189–90
African-Americans, 77–78, 269
American Bar Association (ABA), 1–2
accreditation, 49, 59–67
American Lawyer, The, 158, 162, 240, 272
American University, 70
Anderson Graduate School of Management,
  132, 248, 250
Andover, 178
appellate judges, 114
Asian-Americans, 77–78, 269
associates, 5–7, 11–14
  salaries, 145–46, 266–67
Associates Committees, 187–89
Association for Legal Career Professionals
  (NALP), 79–80, 158, 265–67, 276
  questionnaire, 262

Bagnall, Robert C., 279
banking jobs. *See* investment banking
Bankruptcy Court, 277
Bannister, Roger, 204
BarBri, 127
bar examination, 125–27
  California, 65–66, 126, 136–37

Maine, 67
New York, 67, 136
unaccredited schools, 261, 265
Vermont, 66
Virginia, 66
Washington State, 66
Wyoming, 67
BCG (Boston Consulting Group), 247
Bennett, Steven C., 274
Bennett, William J., 247
big lie, 139–41
billable hours, 8, 173, 175–76, 182–84, 202,
  271, 278
biotechnology firms, 239
Boalt Hall Law School, 207
bonuses, 168–71, 174–76
  discretionary, 170–71
  See also salaries
Booz Allen Hamilton, 132, 247–48
Boston law firms, 239
Boston Consulting Group (BCG), 247
Brobeck, Phleger & Harrison, 6, 19
Brown, 29
Brown & Wood, 248
Bush, George W., 58, 222
business careers, 130–32

consultants, 247–48
Business Law Review, 97–98, 190–91
business school, 129–32, 248–54
    See also MBA
Buthcer, Sarah, 279

California Bar Association (CBA), 60, 63–64,
    261
California Bar Examination, 65–66
California Bar Journal, 64
California law schools, 62–66, 275
California Lawyer, 1
Cambridge, 50–51, 91, 274
Caproni, Valerie, 56
cascading principle, 122
Cass, Alden, 272
CBA (California Bar Association), 60, 63–64,
    261
(CBLR Columbia Business Law Review), 97–98,
    190–91
certificate programs, 253–54
Chancery Court case law, 105
changing jobs, 227–41, 274
        going-in-house, 236–40
        headhunters, 228–34, 237–39
        lateral moves, 227–36
        unique opportunities, 240–41
Cheney, Dick, 58
Chicago law firms, 62, 79, 160, 162, 267, 278
Circuit Courts of Appeal, 117
cities to work in, 176
Clarium Capital Management, 247
class year, 169
CLE (continuing legal education), 127
Cleary, Gottlieb, Steen & Hamilton, 6, 162,
    174, 178
clerkships. *See* internships; judicial clerk-
    ships
Clifford, Chance, 175–76
clinics, 98–99
Clinton, Bill, 58
college, 29–30
        career counselors, 14–15
        classes, 32–34, 271
        foreign schools, 91–92
        GPA, 35–39, 81–86
        internships, 82–83

majors, 34–36
prelaw, 33
seminars, 37–38
small classes, 37–38
Columbia, 51–52, 55, 57–59, 65, 81, 85–86,
    92, 94, 158, 162
        business school, 129
        foreign students, 136
        law journals, 97–98, 192
        law review, 175
Columbia Business Law Review (CBLR), 97–98,
    190–91
Columbia Journal of Law and the Arts, 97–98
Columbia Law Review, 192
Congress, 43
continuing legal education (CLE), 127
copyright law, 134
Cornell, 29, 52, 137
corporate associates. *See* associates
corporate paralegals, 42
corporate transactional work, 165
counsel, 164, 229
Counsel Connect web site, 13–14
Court of Appeals, 115–17
Court of Appeals for the Armed Forces, 276
Court of Appeals for the Federal Circuit, 277
Court of Appeals for Veterans' Claims, 276
Court of Federal Claims, 276
Court of International Trade, 276
Covington & Burling, 272
Cox, Christopher, 43–44
Cravath, Swain & Moore, 56, 162, 166, 174,
    179, 235
Credit Suisse Financial Products, 247

D'Amato, Alfonse, 222
Dartmouth, 29
Davis, Polk & Wardwell, 56, 132, 148, 162,
    175, 179, 235
Dean, Howard, 58
Delaware law firms, 277
Delaware Corporate Code, 105–6, 148, 192
Deloitte & Touche, 248
Deloitte Consulting, 247
Denver law firms, 183
Department of Justice (DOJ), 143, 159
        internships, 101–2

depression, 272
discretionary bonuses, 170–71, 278
District Court, 115–17
Diversity in Law Firms, 70,
    268–69, 275
DOJ. *See* Department of Justice (DOJ)
due diligence, 11
Duke, 29, 143–44

eBay, 247
Ebbers, Bernie, 212
economy, 16–20
    counter-cyclical nature of law,
        17–19
Edmondson, J. L., 247
Educational Testing Service, 89
EEOC (Equal Employment Opportunity
    Commission), 71–72, 77–78, 268–69, 275
EMBA, 251–54
Emmanuel College, 91, 274
England, 92, 274
    educational system, 50–51
    entrepreneurs, 165
    Equal Employment Opportunity Com-
        mission (EEOC), 71–72, 77–78,
        268–69, 275
    ethnic diversity, 75–78, 268
    Executive MBA, 251–54
    Exeter, 178

    family money, 179–80
    Federal Communications Commission,
        211
    federal judges, 117, 121
    federal prosecutor, 7
    Federal Trade Commission (FTC), 101
    female attorneys, 69–75, 169, 185–86,
        268, 275
    Ferguson, Roger, 279
    financial options, 273
    flirting, 185–86
    Ford, Gerald, 58
    Fordham, 56, 144
    foreign offices, 177–78
    foreign schools, 91–92
    Foreign Service, 45–46
    foreign students, 134–38

four-legged, two-headed partners,
    184–85
fraternities, 274
FTC (Federal Trade Commission), 101

general litigation, 165
Georgetown, 91, 133–34, 137, 244
Ginsberg, Ruth Bader, 58, 69
going-in-house, 236–40
government jobs, 209–25
    advantages, 108, 202–3, 209, 213–14
    appointed positions, 220–21
    career positions, 220–21
    disadvantages, 219–20
    local government, 223–24
    salaries, 214, 217
    top law schools, 218–19
    transition to private sector, 223–25
    and women, 72
    See also political careers
GPA, 35–39, 81–86, 91, 273
graduate degrees, 39–40
Greenberg, Traurig, 56

Hale & Dorr, 216
Harlan Fiske Stone Scholar, 86, 94, 276
Harvard, 29, 55, 57–59, 65, 69–70, 85–86,
    121, 142–44, 158, 178
    business school, 246, 252–53
    foreign students, 136
    law review, 175
Hatchitt, Ann, 272
headhunters, 228–34, 237–39
Hispanics, 77–78, 269
Hoffman, Dustin, 27, 273
homosexuality, 79–80, 275
Hong Kong law firms, 162
Howard Law School, 144

internet entrepreneurs, 5–7, 248–49, 272
internships
    college, 82–83
    law school, 100–102, 107–9, 276
interviewing, 146–55
    attire, 148–49, 153–55
    honesty, 149–50
    resumé, 151–53

investment banking, 17, 110–12, 165,
   244–48, 272
      salaries, 21–22, 281
Ivy League schools, 137

James Kent Scholar, 94, 276
JD/Master en Droit, 52
JD/Master of Public Health, 52
JD/MBA, 53, 131
JD/MPA, 52
Johns Hopkins University, 1–2
joint degrees, 129–31
Jonas, Diana Nelson, 271
Journal of Law and the Arts, 97–98
Journal of Transnational Law, 97–98
judicial clerkships, 113–23
      appellate clerkship, 116–17
      district court clerkship, 116–17
      salaries, 119, 276
      seeking a clerkship, 120–23
      state court judges, 119–20
      when to clerk, 118–19
junior partner, 164

Kaplan test preparation, 89–90
Kent, James, 276
Kerry, John, 58
Kirkland & Ellis, 162

lateral moves, 227–36
Latham & Watkins, 162
Lattman, Peter, 271
law firms
      Associates Committees, 187–89
      bonuses, 168–71, 174–76
      career stability, 17
      changing, 227–41
      ethnic diversity, 75–78, 268–69
      firing associates, 22–25
      foreign offices, 177–78
      going-in-house, 236–40
      interviewing, 146–55
      lateral moves, 227–36
      mentors, 201–2
      partnership, 195–207
      pitfalls, 181–94
      practice area, 159–61, 166–68

pyramid structure, 165, 172, 184–85,
   278
ranking, 158, 161–63, 175
sabbaticals, 254–55
salaries, 144–46, 168–69, 171–74, 214
satellite offices, 176–77
small firms, 151, 173
up-or-out system, 10, 165, 278
white shoe law firm, 178–79
working for, 140–42, 157–94
See also associates; partnership
law journals, 97–98
law readers, 66
law review, 94, 96–98, 120, 175
law school, 93–112
      accreditation, 49, 59–63, 66–67, 275
      admission to, 35–36, 81–92
      after graduation, 14–15, 141–45
      age of student, 46–49
      alternative degrees, 52
      California schools, 62–66
      career advisors, 140–41
      clerkships, 100–101
      clinics, 98–99
      cost, 31–32
      double-degree programs, 51
      foreign schools, 50–52
      foreign students, 134–38
      grades, 93–95
      internships, 100–103
      joint degrees, 52–53
      law review, 94, 96–98
      LSAT (Law School Admissions Test),
         81–91
      outline writing, 95–96
      ranking of schools, 55–62, 221
      reasons to attend, 30–32, 273
      study groups, 95
      summer, 1st year, 99–103
      summer, 2nd year, 102–9
      time commitment, 49–51
      when to attend, 40–45
Law School Admissions Counsel (LSAC),
   61, 86–87, 90
Law School Admissions Test (LSAT), 81–91
      preparatory courses, 90–91
legal careers

changing, 243–57, 274
dissatisfaction, 1–16, 272
number of lawyers in U.S.A., 3, 272
paths, 139–55
personal characteristics of lawyers, 7
practice area, 159–61
planning, 27–28
satisfaction, 1–16, 272
Legally Blonde, 7, 39
Lesbian and Gay Law Association of New
York, 79
Lincoln, Abraham, 68
litigation paralegals, 42
LL.B degree, 51, 274
LL.M degree, 133–38
lockstep, 196
London law firms, 162
London School of Economics (LSE), 51
Los Angeles law firms, 160, 162
LSAC (Law School Admissions Council), 61,
86–87, 90
LSAT (Law School Admissions Test), 81–91
preparatory courses, 90–91
luck, 59
Lynch, Gary, 280

M&A transactions, 71, 166, 192, 198, 219, 231
Martindale Hubbell lawyer directory, 105
Masback, Craig, 204
Massachusetts Institute of Technology, 132
masters degrees, 39–40
MBA, 111–12, 129–32, 248–50
certificate programs, 253–54
executive MBA, 251–54
McCarthy, Nancy, 261
McGill University, 91
MCI-WorldCom, 212
McKinsey & Company, 132, 246–47
McNamara, Daniel J., 279
memo writing, 109–10
mentors, 201–2
Microsoft, 140
Miller, Matt, 272
minorities, 75–78, 268–69
Monitor, 247
Monmouth College/University,
85–86

Montana Supreme Court, 64
Morgan Lewis & Bockius, 19, 176–77
Munich, law firms, 162

NALP (Association for Legal Career Profes-
sionals), 79–80, 158, 265–67, 276
questionnaire, 262
NASDAQ (New York Stock Exchange), 212
National Institutes of Health (NIH), 101
Native Americans, 269
Nazareth, Annette, 279
New York City law firms, 160–62, 178, 239
salaries, 174–76, 231
New York Law School, 221
New York Stock Exchange (NASDAQ), 212
New York University (NYU), 51, 93–94,
133–34, 136, 221
NIH (National Institutes of Health), 101
Nixon, Richard, 58
nonequity partner, 164
nonscienter, 153

O'Connor, Sandra Day, 58
option valuation technique, 34–35
outline writing, 95–96
Oxford, 50–51, 91–92, 274

Palo Alto law firms, 118, 206–7, 239
Paper Chase, 29
paralegals, 42, 150–51
Parloff, Roger, 279
partnership, 11–14, 164–65, 195–207
lateral moves, 234–35
personality types, 199–201
Partnership for Public Service, 219
Pataki, George, 58
patent law, 134, 239
PayPal, Inc., 247
Pennsylvania Bar Admission Rule 204, 60
Piper, Rudnick, 175
political careers, 58, 204, 220–23, 279
Pope, Colin, 272
practice areas, 159–61, 166–68
corporate law, 161, 167–68
litigation, 161, 167
Princeton, 29, 52, 85, 178
Princeton Review, 89–90

pro bono, 182–83
professional articles, 190–94
publishing, 190–94
pyramid structure, 165, 172, 184–85, 278

Quattrone, Frank, 6

real options, 273
Rehnquist, William, 58
relationships, 30, 259
resumé, 151–53, 263–64
Roberts, John, 58
Roettger, Norman C., 221
Rutgers, 56

sabbaticals, 254–55
Sahadi, Jeanne, 272
salaries
    associates, 145–46, 266–67
    Federal Communications Commission,
        211
    government jobs, 142–43, 214
    investment banking, 21–22, 272
    judicial clerks, 119, 276
    lateral moves, 234
    law firms, 22, 144–45, 168–69, 171–74,
        214, 272
    lawyers with MBA, 250
    lockstep method, 196
    SEC (Securities and Exchange Com-
        mission), 142–43
    See also bonuses
San Diego law firms, 239
San Francisco law firms, 162, 239
SAT, 86
satellite offices, 176–77
scienter, 153
Seattle law firms, 183
SEC (Securities and Exchange Commission)
    chairmen, 43–44, 222
    Division of Corporate Finance, 212,
        219
    Division of Enforcement, 134, 143,
        212–13, 215–16, 222, 225
    Division of Investment Management,
        212, 225
    Division of Market Regulation, 212

hierarchy, 217–18
hiring, 214–15, 218–19
internships, 82–83, 101–2, 276
Office of Compliance, Inspections and
    Examinations (OCIE), 212
Office of the General Counsel, 212,
    216
salaries, 142–43, 211, 271–72
working for, 159, 211–13, 219–21,
    271–72, 279
secondary law journals, 97–98
securities law, 133, 159, 271
Securities Regulation Law Journal (SRLJ), 190–91
sexual behavior, 185–86
Silicon Valley, 6, 206, 239, 247
Simpson, Thacher & Bartlett, 132, 162, 173,
    230, 248
Skadden, Arps, Slate, Meagher & Flom,
    23–24, 145, 151, 160–62, 277
Socratic method, 88
soft offer, 108
Sonnenschein, Nath & Rosenthal, 271
Sonsini, Larry, 206–7
Southern California Institute of Law, 64
special counsel, 164
SRLJ (Securities Regulation Law Journal),
    190–91
St. John's, 219
Stanford, 29, 51, 55, 57–58, 65, 132, 158, 246,
    248
state bars, 126–27
Stern, Seth, 275
Stewart, Martha, 212
Stone, Harlan Fiske, 276
student loans, 8, 174
study groups, 95
Sullivan & Cromwell, 79, 92, 162, 175, 247
summer associates, 99–107
    memo writing, 109–10
Supreme Court, 69, 96–97, 117

Tangney, Patrick, 279
taxation law, 133
teaching, 189–90
technology companies, 6, 19, 206–7, 239,
    248–49, 272
Thacher, Profitt & Wood, 230

Theil Capital International, 247
Thiel, Peter A., 246–47
Thomas-Graham, Pamela, 275
Tulane University, 185
Turow, Scott, 271

U.S. Army Judge Advocate General's school, 60
U.S. Department of State, 45–46
U.S. News & World Report, 81, 219, 221
UC Irvine College of Law, 64
undergraduate studies. *See* college
Unger, Laura, 221–22
Unger, Peter, 221
Université Paris I Panthéon Sorbonne, 52
University of California at Berkeley, 29, 138, 207
University of California at Los Angeles (UCLA), 29, 53, 136, 138, 248
University of Chicago, 6, 33, 65, 136–37, 158
University of Dayton, 49–50
University of Georgia, 56
University of London, 51, 274
University of Maryland, 56
University of Miami, 56
University of Pennsylvania, 29, 91, 112, 136, 152, 251
University of Southern California (USC), 29
University of Virginia, 29
University of West Los Angeles School of Law (UWLA), 64–65
University of Wisconsin, 85
up-or-out system, 10, 165, 278

Vault, 161–62
VLA (Volunteer Lawyers for the Arts), 98

Wachtel, Lipton, Rosen & Katz, 132, 160–62, 175, 179, 183, 278
waive into, 60
Washington law firms, 160–63, 239
    salaries, 231
Washington College of Law, 70
Weekend Executive MBA programs, 251–54
Weil, Gotshal & Manges, 162
Wells Notice, 152–53
Wells Submission, 152

Western Association of Schools and Colleges (WASC), 64–65
Wharton, 111, 151–52, 244, 246, 251
white shoe law firm, 178–79
Williams, Joan, 70–71, 275
Williams & Connolly, 161
Wilmer, Cutler & Pickering, 163, 204, 230
Wilson, Sonsini, Goodrich & Rosati, 117–18, 206
Wisconsin State Bar, 1
Witherspoon, Reese, 7
women, 69–75, 169, 185–86, 268, 275
Woodrow Wilson School of Public and International Affairs, 52

Yale, 29, 55, 65, 85, 91, 158, 178, 255
    business school, 112
    foreign students, 136
    ranking, 57–58